Solutions Manual

Object-Oriented Modeling and Design

James Rumbaugh
Michael Blaha
William Premerlani
Frederick Eddy
William Lorensen

General Electric Research and Development Center
Schenectady, New York

PRENTICE HALL
Englewood Cliffs, New Jersey 07632

Editorial/Production Supervision: **Naomi J. Nishi**
Cover Design: **Karen Marsilio**
Acquisitions Editor: **Alice Dworkin**
Manufacturing Buyers: **Linda Behrens** and **Patrice Fraccio**

Printed in the United States of America

10 9 8 7 6 5

ISBN 0-13-629858-3

Prentice-Hall International (UK) Limited, *London*
Prentice Hall of Australia Pty. Limited, *Sydney*
Prentice-Hall Canada Inc., *Toronto*
Prentice-Hall Hispanoamericana, S.A., *Mexico*
Prentice-Hall of India Private Limited, *New Delhi*
Prentice-Hall of Japan, Inc., *Tokyo*
Simon & Schuster Asia Pte. Ltd., *Singapore*
Editora Prentice-Hall do Brasil, Ltda., *Rio de Janeiro*

Contents

Preface

We have prepared these answers to the exercises in *Object-Oriented Modeling and Design* as an aid to instructors in grading students' answers. Others may find these answers useful in reinforcing their understanding of the concepts presented in the book. We have put forth our best efforts, but it is possible that we have made a few mistakes. If a majority of your students produce answers which contradict one of ours, you should scrutinize the exercise carefully.

We suggest that you look at the answers before assigning exercises as homework. In answering the exercises, we found a few that were longer or more difficult than we had anticipated. Also we found that a few exercises had errors or could be stated more precisely. We have used square brackets to denote meta comments, that is comments about the exercise for the benefit of the instructor.

The exercises are intended to be learning tools. The process of answering them is more important than the answer. In grading students' work, we suggest that you look at the thought process that went into the answer rather than the answer itself. Most of the exercises have more than one answer. In particular, the answer to many questions depends on the assumed purpose of the exercise: For what specific application is the model intended? Some questions ask for personal experience. Several exercises ask for opinions or discussion. Do not be too harsh in grading. In a design course, you can argue with any answer, including many of ours. There are often different approaches to a problem. Even we argue among ourselves about the "best" answer to many questions. There is usually no "best" answer, only many "good" answers. Also, there is considerable latitude in the length of an answer.

We have included considerable explanation of the reasoning behind many answers. Do not ask for or expect such explanations from students when it is not called for in the question. We have provided it to help the instructor understand the answers, particularly in subtle or confusing cases.

Because of sheer volume, at times we have been somewhat casual in our answers to exercises. This is particularly evident for threaded exercises, where you may find slight discrepancies between answers on a related theme.

With a few exceptions, we have answered all parts of all exercises. Exceptions include projects, which are too long to present here, and a few flawed exercises. Our answers indicate which exercises are too vague, too difficult, or beyond the scope of the book. In some cases we have suggested a rewording of the question.

Exercises for Chapters 15 and 16 call for executable code. In the interest of space, we have condensed some of our answers by cross referencing code that is common to several answers or by omitting incidental code.

We ask for explanations of how to carry out certain operations in some exercises and ask for pseudocode for the same operations in other exercises. Our intent was that the explanation should be a concise, natural language summary of the operation and that the pseudocode should be a more detailed, formal description of the operation. In several cases we found that answers in the form of an explanation were vague and we provided pseudocode instead, particularly in Chapter 8. In those cases, do not expect pseudocode from the students, unless you ask for it. Also, we have intentionally used a variety of styles in preparing pseudocode.

We assume that you are using this answer key together with a copy of the book *Object-Oriented Modeling and Design*. Answers refer to diagrams in the book as well as to diagrams in the answer key. Any diagram number from the answer key is preceded by the letter 'A.' Any diagram number from an exercise in the book is preceded by the letter 'E.' A diagram number from a chapter in the book is not preceded by any letter. A reference to a section refers to the section from a chapter in the book. Diagrams in the answer key that are not referenced in other answers do not necessarily have numbers.

1

Introduction

[There are no right or wrong answers to the first 4 exercises, which are intended to give you some feedback on the background of the students and to get them thinking about the value of using a formal software design methodology. We give specific examples of our experience in Chapters 18-20.]

1.1   The amount of time spent on analysis, design, coding, and testing/debugging/fixing depends on the methodology used. Using an object-oriented approach, we find that our effort is split approximately 20% on analysis, 30% on design, 40% on coding, and 10% on testing/debugging/fixing problems. The exact split depends on factors such as the type of system and the amount of experience with similar systems. We have found that paying extra attention to analysis and design cuts the total development time. It is a lot easier to avoid a problem during analysis and design than it is to find and fix it later on.

One of the most difficult areas of project management is estimating how much effort a project will require. One method that we use is to break the total effort down into several tasks. We think about each task separately and estimate how much effort is required, based on our experience with similar tasks.

One major problem that we have encountered is underestimating the time and effort required to complete a project. Most software projects are finished late and over budget. A problem that we face in a research environment is one of overselling. We may be pressured into preparing a partially complete prototype. 90% of the functionality is demonstrated with 10% of the effort. Later it becomes difficult to justify an additional, large effort to complete the project.

Premature implementation is another problem. Because of an anxiety to complete a project, implementation is sometimes substituted for design, resulting in systems that are very hard to debug. Unwarranted assumptions are made or fuzzy thinking goes into the design. Later on it is easy to get bogged down in details and difficult to see flaws. In one of our projects a trivial master-slave communications system was rapidly proto-typed. Initial coding was done in a week without benefit of thoughtful design. Occasion-al data communications errors due to noise crashed the system. We applied many patch-es to the system over a period of three months. Each time we thought we understood the problem only to find that we really did not. The problem seduced us into investigating many dead ends. We finally scrapped our initial design for the communications system and started over again. We put more thinking into our second design and successfully completed the system.

Another problem we often face is uncertain or changing requirements. For example, another one of our projects changed its hardware platform several times during the course of the project, from a PC to an Apollo workstation, to a VAX workstation, finally back to the PC. Each time, we ported an uncompleted system, wasting a great deal of time and effort. This was a contributing factor to the failure of the project. What we should have done was complete the system on one platform first and port it to other plat-forms later on.

1.2   [Expect a wide range of answers to this question. The following answer, based on the system described in Chapter 20, is one example.]

We created an editor for the preparation of power system circuit diagrams that could be used as a graphical front end for the capture of parameters needed to simulate the per-formance of power systems. The main obstacle we encountered was integrating several subsystems that we had no control over. We used structured analysis and design tech-niques, including formal system requirements. The methodology was selected for us by someone else over our objections. We would have preferred to take a rapid prototyping approach. The focal point of the system was a database, which we designed using object oriented techniques. Although the project failed, several good ideas were salvaged for other projects.

1.3   [Expect a variety of answers.] Most software systems suffer from one or more of these problems, including the system described in the previous answer, which was behind schedule and over budget. Contributing factors were pressures to underestimate the ef-fort and the decision to build the system on top of several subsystems that were being developed separately. Development of one of the subsystems, a graphical interface, ran into problems of its own, and did not become available until after the target completion date of our system.

1.4   [The point of this exercise is for the students to realize that it is easy to create systems that annoy users, and to motivate them to consider the user's position.]

Software systems which truncate names is the pet peeve of one of the authors. This has resulted in many unexpected problems. One check issuing system in particular trun-cates first names to 5 letters and last names to 7 letters, resulting in checks that some banks refuse to cash. This could have been avoided by more thoughtful design.

Another annoying situation is the handling of foreign currency by vending machines. Change dispensed by bill changing machines may contain foreign currency which is refused by adjacent food vending machines.

1.5 a. Addresses can be used to identify mail recipients. The format of an address, which varies with country, often includes name, street, city, state, and country. An address both identifies the recipient of mail and encodes instructions for its delivery.

b. Criminal investigations can use combinations of photographs, fingerprinting, blood-typing, DNA analysis, and dental records to identify people, living and/or deceased, who are involved in, or the subject of, a criminal investigation.

c. Banks can use a variety of schemes to identify safe deposit customers. Usually name plus some other piece of information such as an account number or address is used. In the United States, social security number is often used, since the bank usually needs it anyway for tax purposes. Other answers are possible.

d. Telephone numbers are adequate for identifying almost any telephone in the world. In general a telephone number consists of a country code plus a province, city, or area code, plus a local number plus an optional extension number. Businesses may have their own telephone systems with other conventions. Depending on the relative location of the telephone that you are calling, parts of the number may be implied and can be left out, but extra access digits may be required to call outside the local region. In North America local calls require 7 digits. Long distance calls in North America use an access digit (0 or 1) + area code (3 digits) + local number (7 digits). Dialing Paris requires an access code (011) + country code (33) + city code (1) + local number (8 digits). The access code is not part of the identifier.

e. Accounts can be used by telephone companies for billing purposes. A single account may be for one or for several telephone numbers. Account information includes account ID, name, and address. The account ID identifies the account. One of the telephone numbers in the account could be used in the construction of the ID. A bill for the service provided to all of the telephone numbers in an account can be sent to the address of the account.

f. There are logical as well as physical electronic mail addresses used in electronic networks. The formats depend on the particular network. A physical address is a sequence of bytes assigned to a hardware device such as a workstation or a computer at the time of its manufacture, and uniquely identifies the device. A logical address identifies a user on a system. On the BITnet, the format of an address is *userid@node*.bitnet, where *node* is the name of node on the net and *userid* is the name of a user at that node.

g. One way that employees are given restricted, after-hours access to a company is through the use of a special, electronically-readable card. Of course, if an employee loses a card and does not report it, someone who finds it could use it for unauthorized entry. Other approaches include a picture ID which requires inspection by a guard, fingerprint readers, and voice recognition.

1.6   [The question really should have asked for lists of object classes instead of lists of objects. Expect a wide variety of answers. The point of the exercise is for the student to begin to think in terms of object classes.]

  a. Object classes that you would expect in a program for laying out a newspaper include *Page*, *Column*, *Line*, *Headline*, and *Paragraph*.

  b. Object classes that you would expect in a program to compute and store bowling scores include *Bowler*, *Frame*, *Pin*, *Score*, and *Ball*.

  c. [Do not expect many classes for a simple telephone answering machine, since it is dominated by dynamics. You might suggest the students consider a sophisticated digital, multiple user system with delivery options, message forwarding, and group lists.] Some object classes for sophisticated systems include *Telephone*, *Greeting*, *Message*, and *Distribution List*.

  d. Object classes for a controller for a video cassette recorder include *Timer*, *Channel*, *Tapedeck*, and *TV*.

  e. For a catalog store order entry system, object classes include *Customer*, *Order*, *Store*, and *Item*.

1.7   For a variable length array the operations behave as follows:

  - *Append* adds an object to the end of an array. Duplicates are allowed.

  - *Copy* makes a copy of an array. All values in the array elements are copied but the objects referenced are not copied recursively.

  - *Count* returns the number of elements in an array.

  - *Delete* removes an element from an array. The position of the element to be deleted must be specified. All higher numbered elements are shifted down by one position. If the position is out of range, the operation is ignored. The operation returns the change in size of the array, -1 if deletion occurs, otherwise 0.

  - *Index* retrieves an object from an array at a given position. A NIL is returned if the index is out of range.

  - *Intersect* is not defined for arrays.

  - *Insert* places an object into an array at a given position. All elements at the given index or higher are shifted up by one position. An error message is printed if the position is out of range.

  - *Update* places an object into an array at a given position, overwriting whatever is there. If the position is out of range, the array is extended with NILs. The operation returns the change in the size of the array.

  For a symbol table (also known as a dictionary) the operations behave as follows:

- *Append* makes sense only for sorted tables, in which case an entry goes at the end unless the table already contains the keyword. In that case the new entry replaces the old entry. Duplicates are not allowed. The operation returns the change in the size of the table.
- *Copy* makes a copy of a table.
- *Count* returns the number of entries in a table.
- *Delete* removes an entry from a table. The entry to be deleted is specified by key word. If the entry does not exist the operation is ignored. The operation returns the change in the size of the table.
- *Index* retrieves an entry from a table that matches a given keyword.
- *Intersect* is not defined for symbol tables.
- *Insert* is not defined for symbol tables. Use *update* instead.
- *Update* adds an entry to a table. If the keyword is not yet in the table, a new entry is made. If the keyword is already in the table, the entry in the table is updated. The operation returns the change in the size of the table.

Operations on sets behave as follows:

- *Append* is not defined for a set, since elements of a set are not ordered.
- *Copy* makes a copy of a set.
- *Count* returns the number of elements in a set.
- *Delete* removes a given element of a set. If the element does not exist the operation is ignored. The operation returns the change in the size of the set.
- *Index* is not defined for a set.
- *Intersect* performs set intersection of two given sets, creating a new set.
- *Insert* is not defined for sets. Use *update* instead.
- *Update* adds an element to a set. If the element is not yet in the set, it is added to the set. If it is already in the set, the operation is ignored. The operation returns the change in the size of the set.

1.8 [Adding more classes to each list is optional. We have given a few classes to get the student to think in terms of abstraction. We made no attempt to give exhaustive lists in the exercise.]

a. Electron microscopes, eyeglasses, telescopes, bomb sights, and binoculars are all devices that enhance vision in some way. With the exception of the scanning electron microscope, all these devices work by reflecting or refracting light. Eyeglasses and binoculars are designed for use with two eyes; the rest of the objects on the list are designed for use with one eye. Telescopes, bomb sights, and binoculars are used to view things far away. A microscope is used to magnify something that is very small. Eyeglasses may enlarge or reduce, depending on whether the prescription is for a near-sighted or a farsighted person. Some other classes that could be included in this list are optical micro-scopes, cameras, and magnifying glasses.

b. Pipes, check valves, faucets, filters, and pressure gauges are all plumbing supplies with certain temperature and pressure ratings. Compatibility with various types of fluids is also a consideration. Check valves and faucets may be used to control flow. With the exception of the pressure gauge, all of the items listed have two ends and have a pres-sure-flow characteristic for a given fluid. All of the items are passive. Some other classes include pumps, tanks, and connectors.

c. These objects are all means for transportation. Bicycles, cars, trucks, motorcycles, and horses are used on land. Sailboats are used on water. Airplanes and gliders are used in the air. Students may discover other common traits.

d. These are all fasteners. The terms screw and bolt have similar meanings. The term screw is used to refer to wood screws, self-tapping sheet metal screws, and bolts. The term bolt refers to a straight threaded screw. Nails, screws, and bolts are used for carpentry. Bolts and rivets are used in the assembly of machinery.

e. These are all forms of shelter. Any of them afford protection from the rain. People nor-mally live in houses or skyscrapers, although the rest would do in an emergency. Tents, sheds, garages, barns, houses, and skyscrapers are man made. Caves are natural. All ex-cept tents are more or less permanent structures. Garages, barns, sheds, and houses are typically made out of wood, brick, or sheet metal. Skyscrapers require special construc-tion techniques. Sheds, garages, and barns are used to store things.

f. Square root, exponential, sine, and cosine are all functions of a single variable. Both real and complex definitions are commonly used. As real functions, each maps a real input to a real output. As a real function, square root is defined only for nonnegative numbers. As complex functions, each maps a complex input to a complex output.

2

Modeling as a Design Technique

[The point of the first four exercises is that aspects of the real world that are covered by a model are driven by their relevance to the problem to be solved. The first three exercises are hardware oriented. Exercise 2.4 is software oriented.]

2.1 In purchasing a tire for a car, size is generally constrained to fit the car. In selecting tires, many consumers pay close attention to cost and expected life. Tread design and internal construction are broadly matched to the expected service. For example snow tires provide extra traction in snow. Material and weight are generally not considered.

Size, material, internal construction, tread design, and weight are important physical parameters that would be taken into account in simulating the performance of a computerized anti-skid system for cars. Other physical parameters of the car itself would have to be considered. Cost and expected life would be irrelevant.

In building a tire swing for a child, cost would probably be the main consideration. A discarded tire would be a good candidate. Weight and size would also be a consideration. You would probably not use a giant truck tire for a swing, although you might use it in constructing a playground

2.2 Cost, stiffness, availability, and strength would be considered in selecting a wire to unclog a drain. Depending on the urgency of the situation, you might prefer something immediately available. If you went out to buy something you would not want to pay more for the wire than what it would cost to hire a plumber. The wire would have to be stiff enough to push through the clog but would have to be flexible enough to follow the bends of the drain pipe.

We have not had much luck unclogging drains with most common wire such as coat hanger wire or electrical wire. We have had some modest success with a special coiled spring sold in some hardware stores and with chemical caustics. For really tough jobs you should hire a plumber.

2.3 **a.** For a transatlantic cable, resistance to saltwater is the main consideration. The cable must lie unmaintained at the bottom of the ocean for a long time. Interaction of ocean life with the cable and the effect of pressure and salinity on cable life must be considered. The ratio of strength/weight is important to avoid breakage while the cable is being installed. Cost is an important economic factor. Electrical parameters are important for power consumption and signal distortion.

b. Color, cost, stiffness, and availability are the main considerations. An assortment of colors will probably be needed to make the artwork interesting. The wire should be stiff enough to hold its shape after being bent, but flexible enough to be shaped.

c. Weight is very important for wire that is to be used in the electrical system of an airplane, because it affects the total weight of the plane. Toughness of the insulation is important to resist chafing due to vibration. Resistance of the insulation to fire is also important to avoid starting or feeding electrical fires in flight.

d. Cost, stiffness, availability, and strength should be considered in selecting wire to hang a bird feeder. The wire should be flexible enough to work with and strong enough to hold up the bird feeder. Another consideration not mentioned in the exercise that is important if bare wire is selected is resistance to corrosion.

e. Cost, stiffness, availability, strength, and resistance to stretching are important considerations in selecting wire for use as piano strings. Because the strings are under a great deal of tension, strength and resistance to stretching are important. Stiffness is important because it affects the way the strings vibrate.

f. Because the filament of a light bulb operates at a high temperature, resistance to high temperatures is important. Tungsten is generally used because of its high melting point, even though tungsten filaments are brittle.

2.4 Electrical noise, buffering and flow control, and character interpretation are relevant in designing a protocol for transferring computer files from one computer to another over telephone lines. Data transmission rate is a secondary factor since it limits the overall speed of the protocol.

Electrical noise determines how much error detection and correction is needed.

Buffering and flow control are techniques that are used in some protocols if the receiving computer cannot keep up with the incoming stream of data.

Control characters in the transmitted data could cause problems if the protocol is not designed with them in mind since they could be interpreted as part of the protocol or the receiving computer could interpret them as commands instead of as data.

2.5 [This exercise points out the importance of having multiple models or views of a problem.]

a. (Students who are familiar with electrical machines may be quick to point out that power rather than energy is required to run a motor.) The electrical model is the most important model to determine how much electrical power is required to run a motor. It is used to relate voltage, current, and perhaps frequency to the speed and torque requirements of the load. Mechanical and fluid models play secondary roles. A mechanical model is used to compute friction and a fluid model is used to compute the energy needed to drive any fans used in the motor to keep it cool. Waste heat is equal to the difference between the electrical input power and the mechanical output power.

b. The mechanical model is the only one needed to determine motor weight. The weight of each part can be determined from its mechanical dimensions and its density. The total motor weight is equal to the sum of the weights of all of its parts.

c. Electrical, mechanical, thermal, and fluid models must be considered to determine how hot a motor gets. Electrical, mechanical, and fluid models are used to compute waste heat. The amount of cooling air is determined from a fluid model. The temperature rise of the motor is determined from the waste heat, the thermal model, and the cooling air flow rate.

d. Vibration is computed from electrical and mechanical models. An electrical model is used to determine time variations in electrical torque and motor speed. A mechanical model is used to determine the dynamic mechanical behavior of parts of the motor driven by electrical torques, mechanical loads, and unbalance.

e. Bearing wear is computed from electrical, mechanical, thermal, and fluid models. The mechanical model is used to compute the forces on the bearing. Electrical, mechanical, thermal, and fluid models are used to determine bearing temperature. Fluid and mechanical models are used to analyze the lubrication of the bearing.

2.6 a. Object and dynamic models are relevant to the user interface. An object model can be used to represent the pieces being moved. A dynamic model is used to define the protocol of the user interaction.

b. An object model is used to show a board configuration.

c. All three models are used to consider a sequence of moves. An object model is used to represent the relationships among the pieces. A functional model is relevant to the algorithm for exploring the space of possible moves. The dynamic model plays a minor role if a time limit is imposed.

d. Move validation involves object and functional models. The object model represents the pieces and a functional model is relevant to the process of validating the move.

3

Object Modeling

3.1 A class diagram for international borders is shown in Figure A3.1.

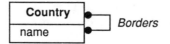

Figure A3.1 Class diagram for international borders

3.2 A class diagram for polygons and points is shown in Figure A3.2. Our choice of data type for x and y are arbitrary. For example, you may choose to model the x-y combination as a coordinate. The smallest number of points required to construct a polygon is three. One way to express the fact that points are in a sequence is to indicate that the association is ordered. The multiplicity of the association depends on how points are identified. If a point is identified by its location, then points are shared and the association is many-to-many. On the other hand, if each point belongs to exactly one polygon, as shown in the diagram, then several points may have the same coordinates. The difference between the two situations is clarified in the next answer.

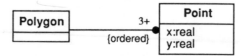

Figure A3.2 Class diagram for polygon and points

3.3 a. An instance diagram for two triangles with a common side in which a point belongs to exactly one polygon is shown in Figure A3.3.

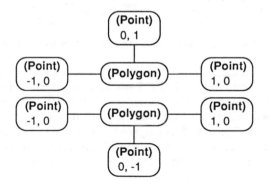

Figure A3.3 Instance diagram where each point belongs to exactly one polygon

b. An instance diagram for two triangles with a common side in which points may be shared is shown in Figure A3.4.

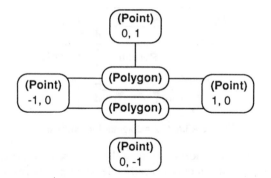

Figure A3.4 Instance diagram where each point can belong to multiple polygons

3.4 Figure A3.5 corresponds to the instance diagram in the exercise. Figure A3.5 has some flaws that Figure A3.2 does not have. Figure A3.5 permits a degenerate polygon which consists of exactly one point. (The same point is first and last. The point is next to itself.) The class diagram also permits a line to be stored as a polygon. Figure A3.5 does not enforce the constraint that the first and last points must be adjacent.

Figure A3.2 and Figure A3.5 share other problems. The sense of ordering is problematical. A polygon that is traversed in left-to-right order is stored differently than one that is traversed in right-to-left order even though both visually appear the same. There is no constraint that a polygon be closed and that a polygon not cross itself. In general it is difficult to fully capture constraints with object models and you must choose between model complexity and model completeness.

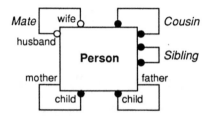

Figure A3.5 Another class diagram for polygon and points

3.5   *Description for Figure A3.2.* A polygon consists of at least three points; each point has an x coordinate and a y coordinate. Each point belongs to exactly one polygon but whether or not this constraint is required was not addressed by the exercise statement. The points in a polygon are stored in an unspecified order.

  Description for Figure A3.5. A polygon has a first and a last point. Each point has an x coordinate and a y coordinate. A point may be first, last, or in the middle of a sequence for a polygon. It is not specified whether a point can be shared for multiple polygons. Each point is linked to its next point.

3.6   Figure A3.6 shows a class diagram for a family tree consistent with the instance diagram in the exercise. Other models are also possible such as those showing divorce and remarriage.

Figure A3.6 Class diagram for family trees

  We used our semantic understanding of the exercise to determine multiplicity in our answer. In general, you can only partially infer multiplicity from an instance diagram. An instance model, by itself, can establish the need for many multiplicity but does not permit you to conclude that exactly 1 or 0,1 multiplicity applies.

3.7   Figure A3.7 is just one of several possible answers for this exercise. You could use fewer generalization relationships and still have a correct answer. The advantage of thorough categorization as we have shown is that it is easier to inherit and reuse code and easier to extend the model to other primitive shapes such as parallelograms, polygons, and 3-dimensional figures.

  The exercise as stated is incomplete. The attributes listed do not fully specify an arc. We have fixed this deficiency by adding *arc angle* to the object model. For an arc, *diameter* is the diameter of the corresponding circle, *arc angle* specifies the fraction of the circumference of the circle, and *orientation* specifies the angle of the line tangent to the start of the arc.

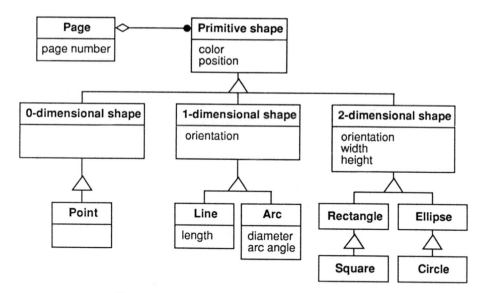

Figure A3.7 Class diagram for geometrical documents

The object model contains width and height for both square and circle, even though they must be equal. Software would be required to enforce this equality constraint. We also show *Circle* inheriting *orientation* even though the symmetry of a circle makes orientation irrelevant

3.8 a. An instance diagram for the expression (X+Y/2)/(X/3+Y) is shown in Figure A3.8. The object diagram in the exercise is actually a metamodel (see Section 4.5.) for binary expressions. Parentheses are required for an infix representation but are not needed in the metamodel. There are other representations, such as postfix, in which parentheses also are not needed. For example, the same expression becomes *X Y 2 / + X 3 / Y + / in a* postfix representation.

The diagram in this exercise contains recursion. Expressions are formed from terms which themselves may be expressions. Very complex expressions may be represented leading to complex instance diagrams.

Figure E3.6 indicates that terms may be shared by expressions. The situation is analogous to sharing of points discussed in Exercise 3.3. If the direction of the links in the corresponding instance diagrams are taken into account, then instance diagrams are directed acyclic graphs.

The instance diagram shown in Figure A3.8 treats *Term* as an abstract class, since only direct instances of the classes *Expression, Variable,* and *Constant* are shown.

The partial expressions in the instance diagram are shown for clarity. To save space, *1st* and *2nd* have been substituted for the role names *first operand* and *second operand.* In reading the instance diagram, remember that the role names are on the *Term* end of the associations.

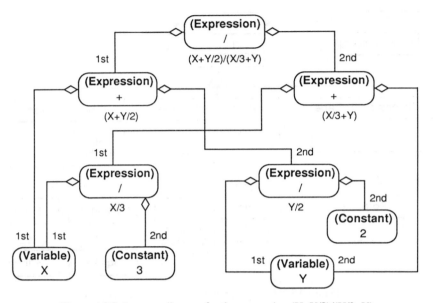

Figure A3.8 Instance diagram for the expression (X+Y/2)/(X/3+Y)

b. The extensions for not sharing terms and handling unary minus are shown in Figure
A3.9. Note that because of the possibility of a unary operator, the multiplicity of the second operand is zero-one. Also the diagram does not express very well the fact that every
term must belong to exactly one expression. The diagram could be further improved by
replacing the two associations between *Term* and *Expression* with a single, qualified association with the qualifier *operand*. This would result in a multiplicity of exactly one
on the *Expression* end of the association. Several other variations are possible.

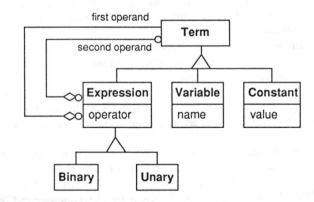

Figure A3.9 Extended class diagram for simple arithmetic expressions

3.9   Figure A3.10 adds multiplicity balls to the model of an air transportation system. Note that we have not specified the multiplicity of the ternary association. This requires the use of candidate keys and is discussed in Section 4.6.

Some associations in Figure E3.7 are unlabeled and require interpretation in order to assign multiplicity. For example *airport located in city* is one-to-many and *airport serves city* is many-to-many. It is important to properly document object models so that this kind of uncertainty does not arise. A possible improvement to the object model would be to partition *Flight* into two classes: *Scheduled flight* and *Flight occurrence*.

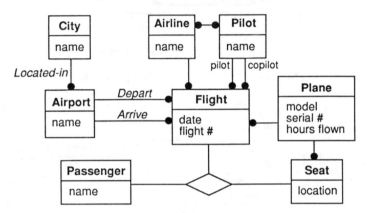

Figure A3.10 Object model of an air transportation system

3.10   Figure A3.11 uses the object class *Seat* as a qualifier. We draw *Seat* twice in the object model in order to distinguish its use as a qualifier in one association and as an ordinary object class in another association. A passenger may take many flights and multiple seats on the same flight.

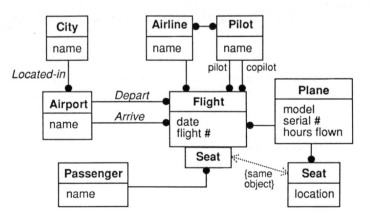

Figure A3.11 Seat as qualifier in object model of an air transportation system

3.11 Figure A3.12 adds operations, association names, and role names to the air transportation system object model. We chose to add the *reserve* operation to the *Seat* class since
Seat is the most direct target of the operation. This is not an obvious assignment since
reserve operates on *Seat*, *Flight*, and *Passenger* objects. Section 10.3.4 discusses heu-
ristics for determining which class should own an operation.

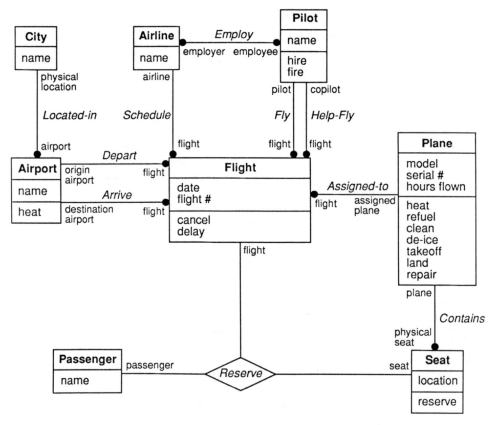

Figure A3.12 Object model of an air transportation system with operations,
association names, and role names

3.12 See answer to Exercise 3.11.

3.13 Figure A3.13 shows an instance diagram that corresponds to the exercise statement. Note that most attribute values are left unspecified by the problem statement, yet the instance model is still unambiguous. All objects are clearly identified by their attribute values and relationships to other objects. The exercise states that "you took a round trip between cities last weekend"; we make the assumption that this is also a round trip between airports. The two seats connected by the dotted line may be the same object.

   [It is also an acceptable answer if students supply values for the "?" values.]

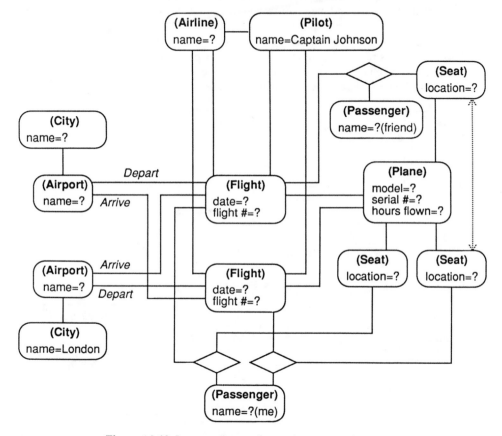

Figure A3.13 Instance diagram for an air transportation system

3.14 See answer to Exercise 3.11.

3.15 [Do not be overly critical of the object models for Exercise 3.15 as most of them are for toy problems. Remember that the precise content of an object model is driven by its relevance to the problem to be solved. For Exercise 3.15, we have not clearly stated the problem to be solved. For example, are we trying to design a database, program an application, or just construct a model to understand a system.]

   a. One possible object diagram for a school is shown in Figure A3.14.

     A school has a principal, many students, and many teachers. Each of these persons has a name, birthdate, and may borrow and return books. Teachers and the principal are both paid a salary; the principal evaluates the teachers. A school board supervises multiple schools and can hire and fire the principal for each school.

     A school has many playgrounds and rooms. A playground has many swings. Each room has many chairs and doors. Rooms include restrooms, classrooms, and the cafeteria. Each classroom has many computers and desks. Each desk has many rulers.

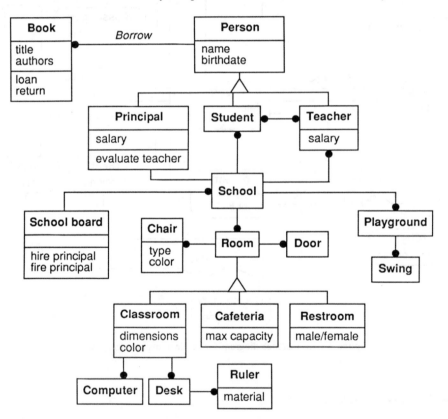

Figure A3.14 Object diagram for a school

b. An object diagram for a castle is shown in Figure A3.15.

A castle has many rooms, corridors, stairs, towers, dungeons, and floors. Each tower and dungeon also have a floor. The castle is built from multiple stones each of which has dimensions, weight, color, and a composition material. The castle may be surrounded by a moat. Each lord lives in a castle; a castle may be without a lord if he has been captured in battle or killed. Each lady lives in a castle with her lord. A castle may be haunted by multiple ghosts, some of which have hostile intentions.

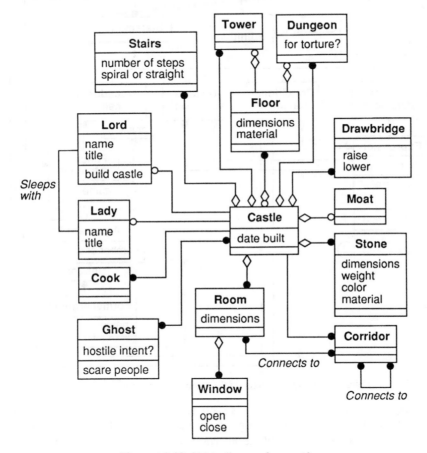

Figure A3.15 Object diagram for a castle

c. An object diagram for a program is shown in Figure A3.16 and Figure A3.17.

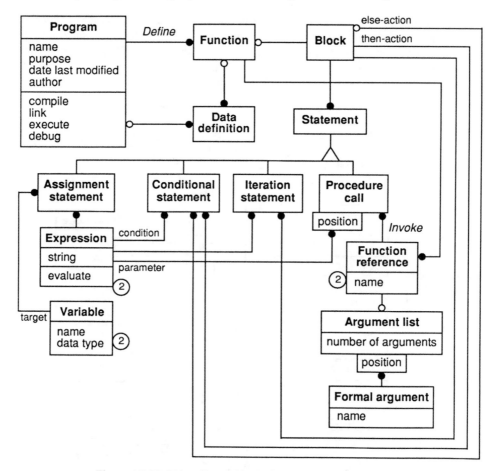

Figure A3.16 Object diagram for a computer program — Sheet 1

A program has descriptive properties such as its name, purpose, date last modified, and author. Important operations on programs include: compile, link, execute, and debug. A program contains global data definitions and many functions. Each function has data definitions and a main block. Each block consists of many statements. Some types of statements are assignment statements, conditional statements, iteration statements, and procedure calls. An assignment statement sets a target variable to the result of an expression. A conditional statement evaluates an expression; a then block is executed if the expression is true and an optional else block is executed if the expression is false. An iteration statement continues to execute a block until a loop expression becomes false. A procedure call invokes a function and may pass the result of one or more expressions in its argument list.

Sheet 2 details the structure of expressions and parallels the structure of the programming code that would be used to implement expressions. An expression may be enclosed by parentheses. If so, the parentheses are removed and the remaining expression recursively defined. Otherwise an expression contains a relational operator such as '>', '=', or '<=' or is defined as a term. Terms subsume binary addition, binary subtraction, or factors. Factors subsume multiplication, division, or unary expressions. Unary expressions can be refined into unary positive or negative expressions or terminals. A terminal may be a constant, variable, or a function. The many multiplicity that appear on *Parenthesized expression* and the other subclasses indicate that expressions may be reused within multiple contexts. (See Exercise 3.3.)

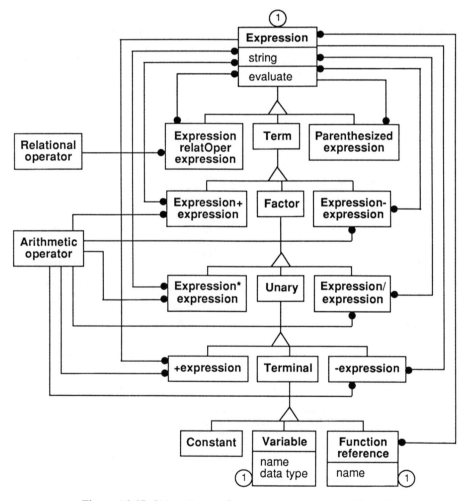

Figure A3.17 Object diagram for a computer program — Sheet 2

d. An object diagram for a file system is shown in Figure A3.18.

A drive has multiple disks; a hard drive contains many disks and a floppy drive contains one disk. (*Platter* may be a better name instead of *Disk.*) A disk is divided into tracks which are in turn subdivided into sectors. A file system may use multiple disks and a disk may be partitioned across file systems. Similarly a disk may contain many files and a file may be partitioned across many disks.

A file system consists of many files. Each file has a filename, owner, permissions for reading and writing, date last modified, size, and checksum. Operations that apply to files include create, copy, delete, rename, compress, uncompress, and compare. Files may be data files or directory files. A directory file is associated with a directory. A directory hierarchically organizes groups of presumably related files; directories may be recursively nested to an arbitrary depth. Each file within a directory can be uniquely identified by its file name. A file may correspond to many directory—file name pairs such as through UNIX links. A data file may be an ASCII file, executable file, or both. The shaded triangle is the OMT notation for an overlapping generalization relationship and is discussed in Section 4.4.

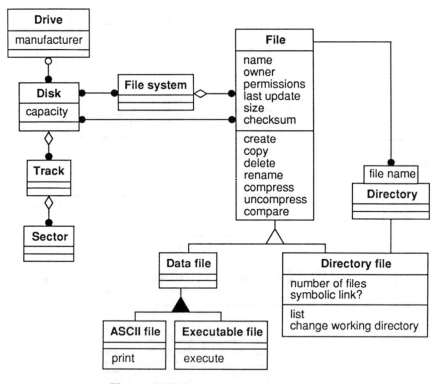

Figure A3.18 Object diagram for a file system

e. An object diagram for an automobile is shown in Figure A3.19.

An automobile is an assembly that is composed of a variety of component parts. An automobile has one engine, one exhaust system, many wheels, many brakes, many brake lights, many doors, and one battery. An automobile may have 3, 4, or 5 wheels depending on whether the frame has 3 or 4 wheels and the optional spare tire. Similarly a car may have 2 or 4 doors. The exhaust system can be further divided into smaller components such as a muffler and tailpipe. A brake is associated with a brake light which indicates when the brake is being applied.

Note that we choose to make manufacturer an attribute of automobile, rather than an object class which is associated with automobile. Either approach is correct, depending on your perspective. If all you need to do is to merely record the manufacturer for an automobile, the manufacturer attribute is adequate and simplest. If on the other hand, you want to record details about the manufacturer, such as address, phone number, and dealership information, then you should treat manufacturer as an object class and associate it with automobile.

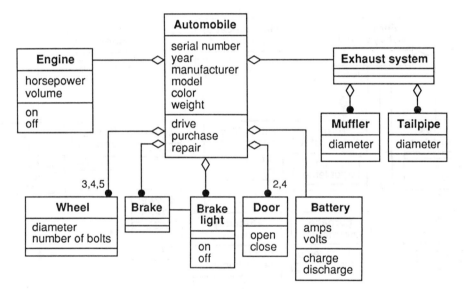

Figure A3.19 Object diagram for an automobile

f. An object diagram for a gas fired, hot air heating system is shown in Figure A3.20. A heating system is composed of furnace, humidification, and ventilation subsystems.

The furnace subsystem can be further decomposed into a gas furnace, gas control, furnace thermostat, and many room thermostats. The room thermostats can be individually identified via the room number qualifier.

The humidification subsystem consists of a humidifier, humidity sensor, and other parts.

The ventilation subsystem has a blower, blower control, and many hot air vents. The blower in turn has a blower motor subcomponent.

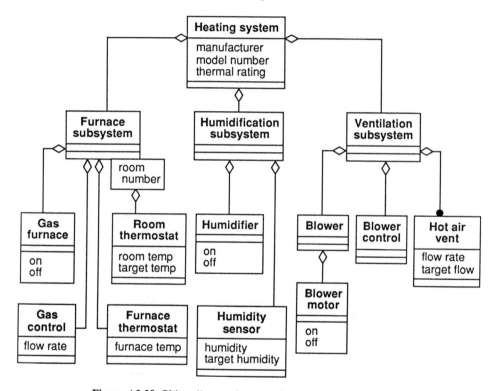

Figure A3.20 Object diagram for a gas fired, hot air heating system

g. An object diagram for a chess game is shown in Figure A3.21. We assume that the purpose of this object model is to serve as a basis for a computerized chess game.

A chess game involves many chess pieces of various types such as rooks, pawns, a king, and a queen. A chess game is also associated with a board and a sequence of moves. *Sequence of moves* is better modeled as a *Tree of moves*. Each time the computer contemplates a move, it computes a tree of possible moves. There are various algorithms which can be used to evaluate potential moves, and restrict the growth of the search tree. The human player can change the difficulty of the computer opponent by adjusting the depth of the strategy lookahead.

Each chess piece is positioned on a square or off the board if captured; some squares on the board are unoccupied. A move takes a chess piece and changes the position from an old position to a new position. A move may result in capture of another piece. The square for a move is optional since the chess piece may start or end off the board. Each square corresponds to a rank and file; the rank is the y-coordinate and the file is the x-coordinate.

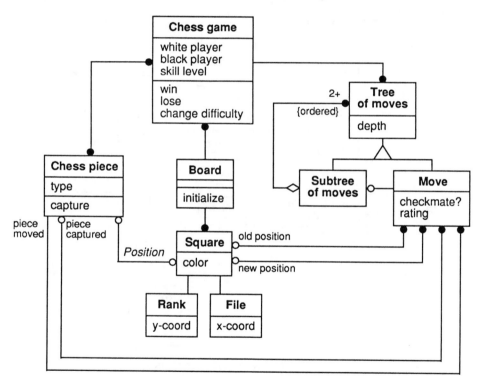

Figure A3.21 Object diagram for a chess game

h. An object diagram for a building is shown in Figure A3.22.

Figure A3.22 is very simple and self-explanatory. An interesting point to make with the object model is the distinction between association and aggregation. A room is *a part of* a building, thus the relationship between building and room is aggregation. In contrast cheese is not part of a refrigerator but is merely stored within a refrigerator. The proper relationship between cheese and refrigerator is association.

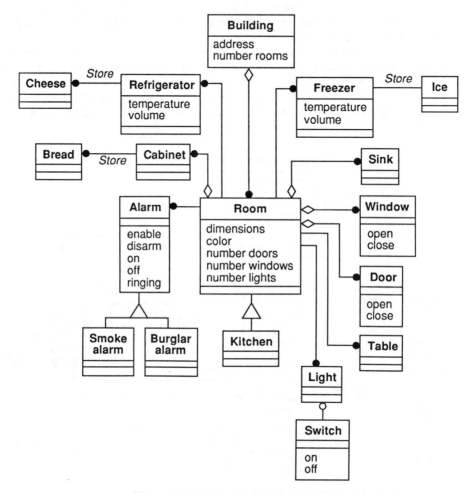

Figure A3.22 Object diagram for a building

3.16 See answers for Exercise 3.15.

3.17 An object diagram for a card playing system with operations added is shown in Figure A3.23. This answer improves upon that given in the book.

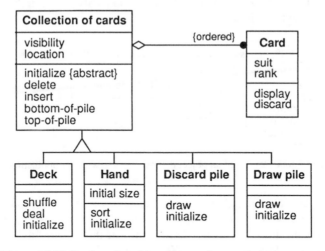

Figure A3.23 Portion of an object diagram for a card playing system

Initialize deletes all cards from a *Hand, Discard pile*, or *Draw pile. Initialize* refreshes a deck to contain all cards.

Delete(Card) deletes a *Card* from a *Collection of cards*.

Insert(Card) inserts a *Card* into a *Collection of cards*. We assume that insertion is done at the top of the pile, but other strategies are possible.

Bottom-of-pile and *top-of-pile* are functions which return the last or first *Card*, respectively, in a *Collection of cards*.

Shuffle randomly shuffles a *Deck*.

Deal(hands) deals cards into *hands,* a set of *Hands*, removing them from the *Deck* and inserting them into each *Hand. Initial size* determines how many cards are dealt into each hand. Since all hands are the same initial size, a better approach would be to convert *initial size* into a class attribute or to pass it to *deal* as an argument.

Sort reorders the cards in a *Hand* into a standard order, such as that used in bridge.

Draw is a function which deletes and returns the top card of a *Discard pile* or a *Draw pile*.

Display(location, face_up?) displays a card at the given location. The *face_up?* argument determines whether the front or the back of the card is shown.

Discard deletes a *Card* from its *Collection of cards* and places it on top of the *Draw pile*.

3.18 Figure A3.24 permits a column to appear on multiple pages with all copies of a column having the same width and length. If it is desirable for copies of a column to vary in their width and length, then the column attributes should also be made link attributes along with x location and y location.

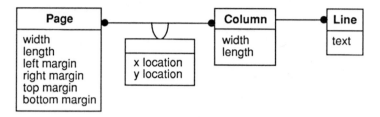

Figure A3.24 Portion of an object diagram for a newspaper publishing system

3.19 Figure A3.25 adds multiplicity balls and attributes to the object model for an athletic event scoring system. All role names are the same as class names, so role names are unnecessary in the diagram. Age is a derived attribute that is computed from birth date and the current date. (See Section 4.7.) We have added an association between *Competitor* and *Event* to make it possible to directly determine what events a competitor intends to try without first traversing class *Trial*.

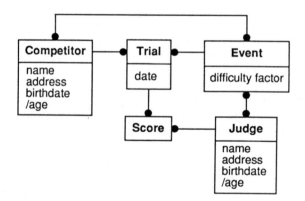

Figure A3.25 Portion of an object diagram for an athletic event scoring system

3.20 See answer for Exercise 3.19.

3.21 See answer for Exercise 3.19.

3.22 An object diagram for the dining philosopher's problem is shown in Figure A3.26. The one-to-one associations describe the relative locations of philosophers and forks. The *In use* association describes who is using forks. Other representations are possible, depending on your viewpoint. An instance diagram may help you better understand this problem.

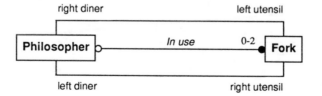

Figure A3.26 Object diagram for the dining philosopher problem

3.23 This is an important exercise, because graphs occur in many applications. Several variations are possible, depending on your viewpoint. Figure A3.27 accurately represents undirected graphs as described in the exercise. Although not quite as accurate, your answer could omit the class *Undirected graph*.

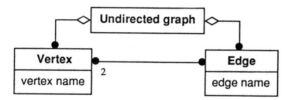

Figure A3.27 Object diagram for undirected graphs

We have found it useful for some graph related queries to elevate the association between vertices and edges to the status of an object class as shown in Figure A3.28.

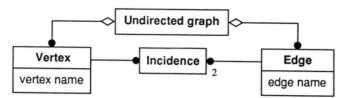

Figure A3.28 Object diagram for undirected graphs in which the incidence between vertices and edges is treated as an object class

3.24 Figure A3.29 is an instance diagram for the object model in Figure A3.27.

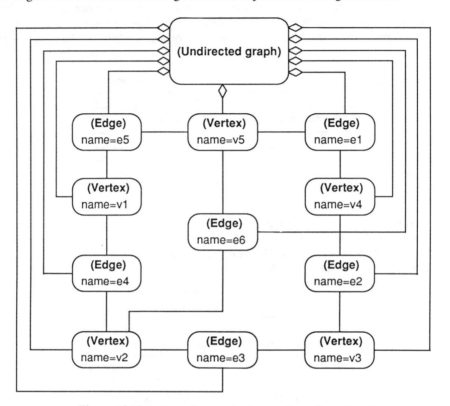

Figure A3.29 Instance diagram for the sample undirected graph

3.25 Figure A3.30 adds geometry details to the object model for an undirected graph. It would also be a correct answer to add geometry details to the *Vertex* and *Edge* classes. For complex models, it is best not to combine logical and geometrical aspects. (See the OMTool example in Section 10.1.3.).

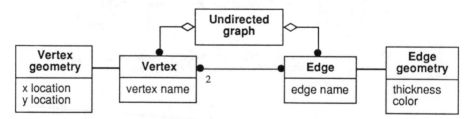

Figure A3.30 Object diagram for undirected graphs that accommodates geometrical details

3.26 An object diagram describing directed graphs is shown in Figure A3.31.The distinction between the two ends of an edge is accomplished with a qualified association. Values of the qualifier *end* are *from* and *to*.

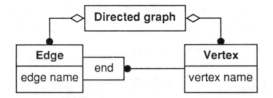

Figure A3.31 Object diagram for directed graphs using a qualified association

Figure A3.32 shows another representation of directed graphs. The distinction between the two ends of an edge is accomplished with separate associations for the two ends of an edge.

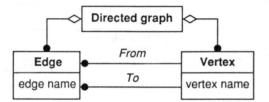

Figure A3.32 Object diagram for directed graphs using two associations

The advantage of the qualified association is that only one association must be queried to find one or both vertices that a given edge is connected to. If the qualifier is not specified, both vertices can be found. By specifying *from* or *to* for the *end* qualifier, the vertex that is connected to an edge at the given *end* can be found.

The advantage of using two separate associations is that the need to manage enumerated values for the qualifier *end* is eliminated.

3.27 Figure A3.33 is an instance diagram corresponding to the object model in Figure A3.32.

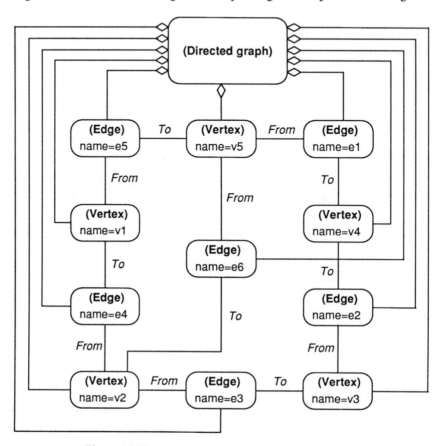

Figure A3.33 Instance diagram for the sample directed graph

3.28   An object diagram for car loans in which pointers are replaced with relationships is shown in Figure A3.34.

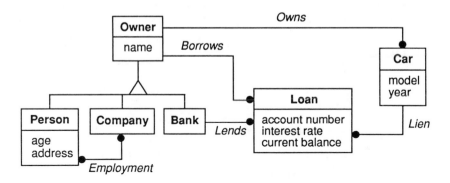

Figure A3.34 Proper object model for car loans

In this form, the arguably artificial restriction that a person have no more than three employers has been eliminated. Note that in this model an owner can own several cars. A car can have several loans against it. Banks loan money to persons, companies, and other banks.

3.29   Method *a* will not work. The owner does not uniquely identify a motor vehicle, because someone may own several cars. Additional information is needed to resolve multiple ownership. In general, it is best to identify an object by some intrinsic property and not by a link to some other thing. For example, what happens when an owner sells a car, a person changes his or her name, or a company that owns a car is acquired by another company?

Method *b* also will not work. The manufacturer, model, and year does not uniquely identify a car, because a given manufacturer makes many copies of a car with the same model and year. The problem here is confusion between a pattern and an instance. (See Section 4.5.)

Method *c* seems to be the best solution. The vehicle identification number (VIN) uniquely identifies each car and is a real-world attribute. Anyone can inspect a car and read the VIN stamped on it.

Method *d* will uniquely identify each car, but is unworkable if agencies need to exchange information. The ID assigned by the department of motor vehicles will not agree with that assigned by the insurance company which will differ from that assigned by the bank and the police. Also the ID generation logic can be a nuisance to program.

3.30 Figure A3.35, Figure A3.36, and Figure A3.37 contain an object model of a 4-cycle lawn mower engine that may be helpful for troubleshooting. A state diagram (discussed in Chapter 5) would also be helpful in capturing the dynamic behavior of the engine. It is debatable whether "air" and "exhaust" are truly objects. (See definition of *object* in Section 3.1.1). Whether they are objects depends on the purpose of the model which is unclear. [Students may find other correct answers for this exercise.]

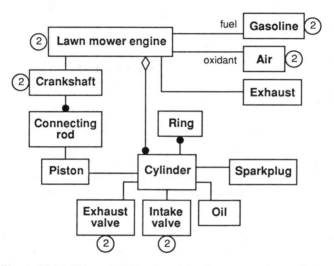

Figure A3.35 Object model for 4-cycle lawn mower engine — Sheet 1

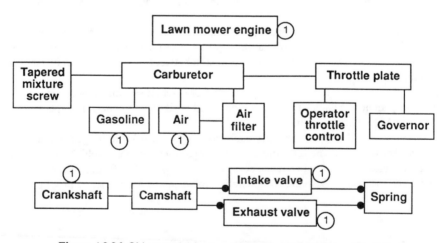

Figure A3.36 Object model for 4-cycle lawn mower engine — Sheet 2

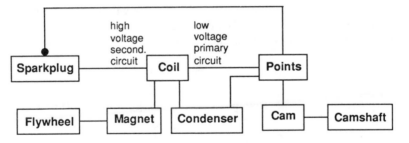

Figure A3.37 Object model for 4-cycle lawn mower engine — Sheet 3

3.31a. The object diagram for the tower of Hanoi problem in which a tower consists of 3 pegs with several disks in a certain order is shown in Figure A3.38.

Figure A3.38 Simple object model for tower of Hanoi problem

b. The object diagram for the tower of Hanoi problem in which disks are organized into stacks is shown in Figure A3.39. Use of an aggregation relationship instead of a simple association between *Stack* and *Disk* is somewhat a matter of viewpoint.

Figure A3.39 Tower of Hanoi object diagram with disks organized into stacks

c. The object diagram for the tower of Hanoi problem in which pegs are organized into recursive subsets of disks is shown in Figure A3.40. The recursive structure of a stack is represented by the self association involving the class *Stack*. Note that the multiplicity of the role of the class *Disk* in the association between *Stack* and *Disk* is exactly one. Use of aggregation in this answer is also subjective.

Figure A3.40 Tower of Hanoi object diagram in which the structure of stacks is recursive

d. The object diagram for the tower of Hanoi problem in which stacks are in a linked list is shown in Figure A3.41. The linked list is represented by the association *Next*. Note the zero-one multiplicity of both of the roles of *Next*.

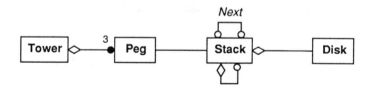

Figure A3.41 Tower of Hanoi object diagram in which stacks are organized into a linked list

3.32 In principle, none of the four object models presented in Figure A3.38 through Figure A3.41 are intrinsically better than the others. All are reasonable models. We will evaluate the models purely on the basis of how well each model supports the algorithm stated in the exercise.

Figure A3.38 is not well suited for the recursive stack movement algorithm, because it does not support the notion of a stack.

Figure A3.39 is better than the previous figure, since it does include the concept of a stack. However Figure A3.39 does not support recursion of a stack within a stack.

Figure A3.40 would be easiest to program if the multiplicity between *Peg* and *Stack* was changed to one-to-one (one stack per peg, the stack may recursively contain other stacks). Figure A3.42 makes this change and adds attributes and operations to the object model. The data structures in Figure A3.42 precisely mirror the needs of the algorithm. The *move(peg-number)* operation moves a stack to the specified peg. *Add-to-stack (peg-number)* adds a disk to the bottom of the stack associated with *peg-number*. *Remove-from-stack (peg-number)* removes the disk at the bottom of the stack associated with *peg-number*.

Figure A3.41 also is a good fit though not as good as Figure A3.40. If a recursive call to the move-stack operation includes as an argument the location in the link list, then descending via recursion is equivalent to moving right through the linked list. The disadvantage of Figure A3.41 is that if software improperly looks to the left of the link list during descent, it could be difficult to debug.

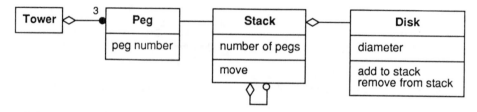

Figure A3.42 Detailed tower of Hanoi object diagram in which the structure of stacks is recursive

4

Advanced Object Modeling

4.1 Figure A4.1 improves the object diagram in the exercise by changing some associations to aggregations. Note that we have added an aggregation to this model between *Automobile* and *Wheel*. For a bill-of-material parts hierarchy, all parts except the root must belong to something. The answer to this exercise is related to that for Exercise 3.15e.

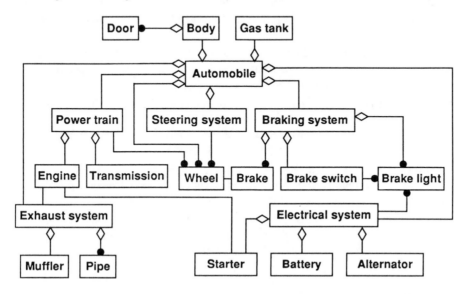

Figure A4.1 Portion of an object diagram of the assembly hierarchy of an automobile

4.2   The object diagram in Figure A4.2 abstracts the classes *Buffer, Selection*, and *Sheet* into the superclass *Collection*. Overall, this revision is recommended. Using the generalization relationship promotes code reuse because many operations apply equally well to the subclasses. Six aggregation relationships in the original diagram, which shared similar characteristics, have been reduced to two. Finally, the constraint that each *Box* and *Link* should belong to exactly one *Buffer, Selection,* or *Sheet* has been captured by the structure of the diagram.

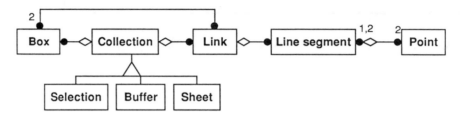

Figure A4.2 Abstraction of the classes *Selection, Buffer,* and *Sheet* into the class *Collection*

4.3 a. *A country has a capital city.* Association. A capital city and a country are distinct entities so generalization certainly does not apply. You could argue that a capital city is a part of a country and thus they are related by aggregation.

   b. *A dining philosopher is using a fork.* Association. Dining philosophers and forks are completely distinct entities and are therefore not in a generalization relationship. Similarly, neither object is a part of the other and the relationship is not aggregation.

   c. *A file is an ordinary file or a directory file.* Generalization. The word "or" often is an indicator of generalization. *File* is the superclass and *Ordinary file* and *Directory file* are subclasses.

   d. *Files contain records.* Aggregation. The word "contain" is a clue that the relationship may be aggregation. A record is a part of a file. Some attributes and operations on files propagate to their component records.

   e. *A polygon is composed of an ordered set of points.* Aggregation. The phrase "is composed of" should immediately make you suspicious that there is an aggregation relationship. An ordered set of points is a part of a polygon. Some attributes and operations on a polygon propagate to the corresponding set of points.

   f. *A drawing object is text, a geometrical object, or a group.* Generalization. Once again, the word "or" should prompt you to think of generalization. *Drawing object* is the superclass. *Text, Geometrical object*, and *Group* are subclasses.

   g. *A person uses a computer language on a project.* Ternary association. *Person, Computer language*, and *Project* are all classes of equal stature. None of these classes are a-kind-of or a-part-of another class. Thus generalization and aggregation do not apply.

h. *Modems and keyboards are input/output devices.* Generalization. The keyword "are" is the obvious clue. *Modem* and *Keyboard* are the subclasses; *Input/output device* is the superclass.

i. *Object classes may have several attributes.* Association or aggregation. It depends on your perspective and the purpose of the model whether aggregation applies.

j. *A person plays for a team in a certain year.* Ternary association. *Person, Team,* and *Year* are distinct classes of equal stature.

k. *A route connects two cities.* Association. Either *Route* is a class associated with the *City* class, or *Route* is the name of the association from *City* to *City*.

l. *A student takes a course from a professor.* Ternary association. *Student, Course,* and *Professor* are distinct classes of equal stature.

4.4 An object diagram for a graphical document editor is shown in Figure A4.3. The requirement that a *Group* contain 2 or more *Drawing object*s is expressed as a multiplicity of 2+ on *Drawing object* in its aggregation relationship with *Group*. The fact that a *Drawing object* need not be in a *Group* is expressed by the zero-one multiplicity.

It is possible to revise this diagram to make a *Circle* a special case of an *Ellipse* and to make a *Square* a special case of a *Rectangle*.

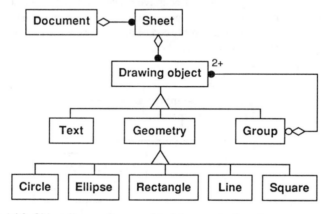

Figure A4.3 Object diagram for a graphical document editor that supports grouping

4.5   Figure A4.4 models directories and files. Also see the answer to Exercise 3.15d.

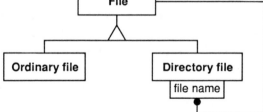

Figure A4.4 Object diagram for a file system

4.6   Recursion in object models is common.

For example a block in a computer program consists of many statements which may reference lower level blocks. The recursion terminates with simple statements. Figure A3.16 shows an object diagram for a computer program.

A mathematical expression may be parsed into smaller portions which are in turn expressions. The recursion terminates with constants and variables. Figure A3.17 shows an object diagram for expressions. Recursive descent similar to that shown in the object diagram is a common technique for programming expression evaluators.

A third example is that an assembly can be decomposed into parts and subassemblies. Ultimately the recursion stops when there is nothing but parts. Figure A4.5 shows the corresponding object diagram.

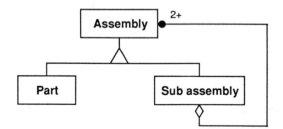

Figure A4.5 Object diagram for a parts explosion

4.7   [This exercise is too advanced and should not be assigned. The one page explanation of propagation in Section 4.1.4 is not adequate for answering this exercise.]

4.8   An object diagram showing the relationships among several classes of electrical machines is shown in Figure A4.6. We have included attributes that were not requested.

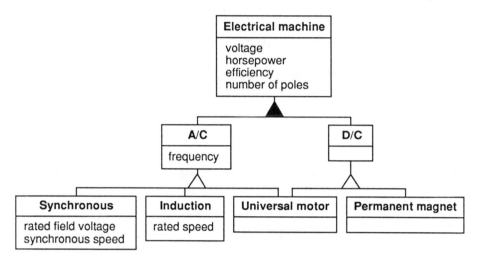

Figure A4.6 Partial taxonomy for electrical machines

4.9   One way to eliminate the multiple inheritance is to convert the overlapping combination of classes into a class of its own as shown in Figure A4.7.

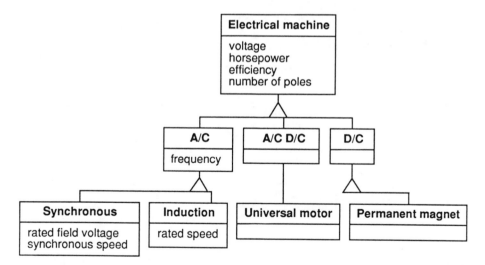

Figure A4.7 Elimination of multiple inheritance

4.10 Figure A4.8 is a metamodel of the following subset of the OMT notation: object classes, attributes, and binary associations. You could have chosen to include link attributes in your answer by adding an *Association — Attribute* association with multiplicity 0,1 to many. You would also have to change the multiplicity of the *Object class — Attribute* association to multiplicity 0,1 to many.

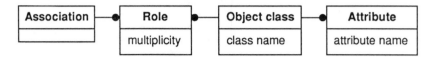

Figure A4.8 Metamodel for a subset of the OMT notation

4.11 Figure A4.9 treats the metamodel as an object diagram that can be described by itself. Thus the metamodel in Figure A4.8 is self-descriptive. (In general some metamodels are self-descriptive and some are not.)

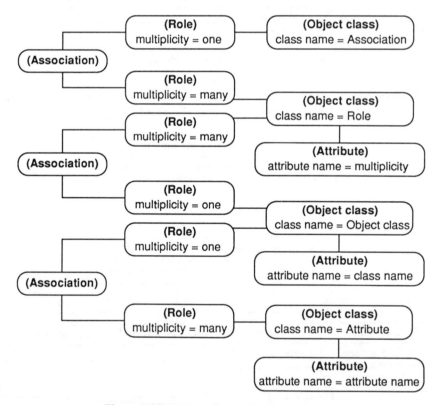

Figure A4.9 Instance diagram for the metamodel

4.12a. See answer to Exercise 3.23.

b. This is a difficult problem. This exercise is motivated by a real problem that we encountered in our research work: incremental compilation of object models (related to Chapter 18). As part of implementing incremental compilation, we need to maintain correspondence between the old and the new object models so that we can efficiently detect the differences. We debated this exercise among ourselves before devising our answer.

Our answer is based on Figure A3.27. Each vertex has many edges and each edge has two vertices. The homomorphism in Figure A4.10 maps a vertex-edge link from one undirected graph to a vertex-edge link from an isomorphic undirected graph. Note that Figure A4.12 also includes undirected graphs which are not isomorphic. In other words, the structure of the object model represents isomorphic undirected graphs but does not enforce the isomorphism constraint. In practice, this would be adequate, as the object model would be used to describe the data structure and programming code would enforce the isomorphism constraint.

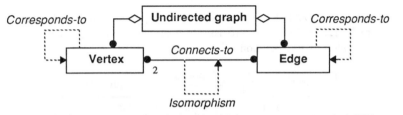

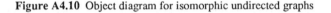

{graph1 (vertex connects to edge) ⇒ graph2 (vertex connects to edge) AND
graph2 (vertex connects to edge) ⇒ graph1 (vertex connects to edge)}

Figure A4.10 Object diagram for isomorphic undirected graphs

4.13 The object diagram given in the exercise does support multiple inheritance. If an instance of *Object class* is a subclass in more than one generalization relationship, there is an instance of *Generalization role*, with *role type* equal to *subclass* for each generalization relationship.

4.14 To find the superclass of a generalization using Figure E4.3, first query the association between *Generalization* and *Generalization role* to get a set of all roles of the given instance of *Generalization*. Then sequentially search this set of instances of *Generalization role* to find the one with *role type* equal to *superclass*. (Hopefully only one instance will be found with *role type* equal to *superclass*, which is a constraint that is not enforced by the model.) Finally, scan the association between *Generalization role* and *Object class* to get the superclass.

One possible revision which simplifies superclass lookup is shown in Figure A4.11. To find the superclass of a generalization, first query the association between *Generalization* and *Superclass role*. Then query the association between *Superclass role* and *Object class* to find the corresponding instance of *Object class*.

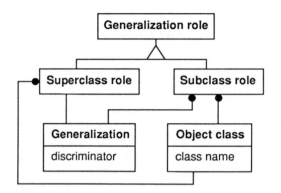

Figure A4.11 Metamodel of generalization relationships with separate
subclass and superclass roles

Another metamodel of generalization which supports multiple inheritance is shown in Figure A4.12. To find the superclass of a generalization using this metamodel, simply query the *Superclass* association.

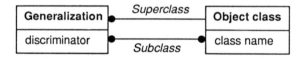

Figure A4.12 Simplified metamodel of generalization relationships

We do not imply that the metamodel in Figure A4.12 is the best model of generalization, only that it simplifies the query given in the exercise. The choice of which model is best depends on the purpose of the metamodel.

4.15 The metamodel in Figure E4.3 does not enforce the constraint that every generalization has exactly one superclass. In this figure, a *Generalization* has many *Generalization roles*; each *Generalization role* may have a *role type* of *superclass* or *subclass*. Figure A4.11 and Figure A4.12 are improved metamodels and enforce the constraint that every generalization has exactly one superclass.

4.16 Figure A4.13 is the instance diagram that corresponds to Figure E4.3 and Figure E4.4.

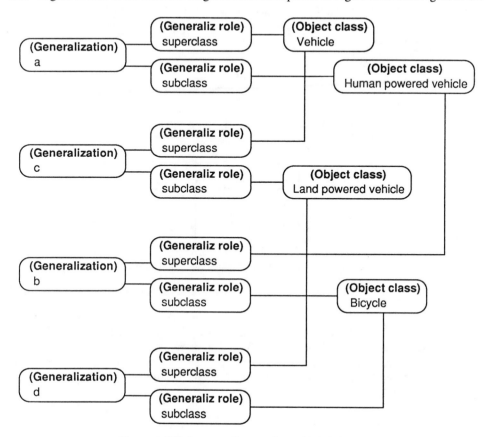

Figure A4.13 Instance diagram for multiple inheritance

4.17   There is a mistake in the exercise statement. The due date for a book would be best modeled as an ordinary attribute and the late charges for an overdue book can be modeled as a derived attribute. Note that *fine-per-day* is a class attribute as indicated by the '$' prefix. Figure A4.14 shows our answer to the exercise.

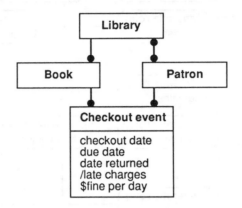

{late charges = (date-returned - due-date) * fine-per-day}

Figure A4.14 Object diagram for library book checkout system

4.18   Figure A4.15 presents one possible metamodel for BNF grammars. A BNF grammar consists of many production rules. Each production rule has many or-clauses which in turn reference many identifiers. An identifier may be a terminal such as a character string or a number or may be a non-terminal in which case it is defined by another production rule.

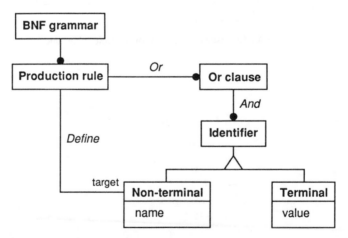

Figure A4.15 Metamodel for BNF grammars

In general, there are at least three ways to express BNF grammars: "railroad" diagrams as shown in the exercise, textual production rules, and state machine diagrams. The metamodel in Figure A4.15 describes the underlying meaning of a BNF grammar and is independent of the manner used to express it. Thus the metamodel applies equally well to each of these three ways of expressing a BNF grammar.

If you were developing software to automate the drawing of BNF "railroad" diagrams, you would need a model of the BNF logic as shown in Figure A4.15 and another model to store the corresponding graphic representation. The graphical model would describe the size of rectangles and circles, the placement of geometric shapes, and the stopping and starting position for lines and arrows. The same kind of architectural issue arose in our design of the OMTool program for automating the drawing of object diagrams and is discussed in Section 10.1.3.

5

Dynamic Modeling

5.1

    a. Assume that everything starts out on the east side and is to be moved to the west side. A scenario in which nothing gets eaten:

        (Farmer, fox, goose, corn all on W.)
        Farmer takes goose to E.
        Farmer returns alone to W.
        Farmer takes fox to E.
        Farmer takes goose to W.
        Farmer takes corn to E.
        Farmer returns alone to W.
        Farmer takes goose to E.
        (Farmer, fox, goose, corn all on E.)

    A scenario in which something gets eaten:

        (Farmer, fox, goose, corn all on W.)
        Farmer takes goose to E.
        Farmer returns alone to W.
        Farmer takes corn to E.
        Farmer returns alone to W.
        Goose eats corn.
        Farmer takes fox to E.
        (Farmer, fox, goose on E. Corn is gone.)

    b. There is ambiguity about what to include and how much detail to show. This is normal for specifications. One possible scenario:

Open door.
Get in car and sit down.
Close door.
Put key in ignition.
Put on seat belt.
Check that transmission is in park.
Depress and release accelerator pedal.
Turn key.
Engine starts.
Release key.
Depress brake pedal.
Release emergency brake.
Move transmission lever to drive.
Check for traffic in rear view mirror.
Turn on left directional light.
Move foot to accelerator pedal.
Depress pedal slowly and begin to drive.

c. Again there is considerable ambiguity about what to include.
Press "up" button.
Button lights up.
Bell sounds and "up" indicator lights.
Elevator door opens.
Get in elevator.
Press button for floor 6.
Button lights up.
Elevator door closes.
Elevator moves up.
Elevator stops at floor 3.
Elevator door opens.
Two passengers get on.
Elevator door closes.
Elevator moves up.
Elevator stops at floor 6.
Elevator door opens.
You and the other two passengers get out.
Note that specific incidents are properly part of a scenario.

d. This is similar to the previous part. Conditions are shown in parentheses:
(Traveling on the highway in drive.)
Accelerate to 90 km/hr.
Press "set" button on cruise control.
Cruise control engages control of accelerator.
Take foot off the accelerator pedal.
(Car operates accelerator under cruise control.)

Encounter slow moving car that you want to pass.
Depress accelerator and pass car.
Remove foot from accelerator.
(Cruise control continues to maintain speed.)
Encounter slow moving traffic that you cannot pass.
Depress brake pedal.
Cruise control disengages control of accelerator.
Maneuver past slow moving traffic.
Press "resume" button on cruise control.
Cruise control re-engages control of accelerator.
Take foot off accelerator.
Cruise control accelerates to preset speed.
(Car is operating under cruise control)

5.2   One of many possible scenarios:
Get into tub.
Turn on cold and hot water.
Water flows from faucet.
Adjust temperature.
Pull shower diverter.
Warm water flows from shower head.
Phone rings.
Turn off hot and cold water.
Water stops flowing.
Get out of tub.
Answer phone.
Talk.
Hang up phone.
Get into tub.
Turn on cold and hot water.
Push shower diverter.
Water flows from faucet.
Adjust temperature.
Pull shower diverter.
Warm water flows from shower head.
Wash yourself.
Turn off hot and cold water.
Water stops flowing.
Get out of tub.

5.3   The headlight and wheels each have their own state diagram. Note that the stationary wheel motion state includes several substates.

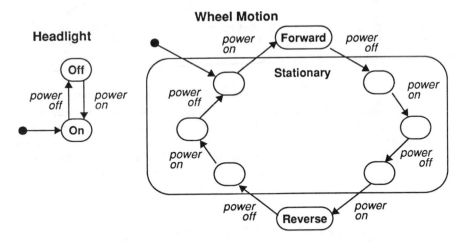

We have shown default initial states for the headlight and wheels. The actual initial state of the wheels may be arbitrary and could be any one of the power off states. The system operates in a loop and does not depend on the initial state, so you need not specify it. Many hardware systems have indeterminate initial states.

5.4

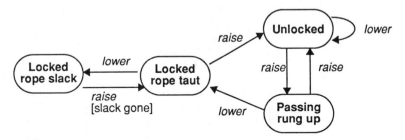

You could add detail with states for the ladder fully extended and fully contracted.

5.5

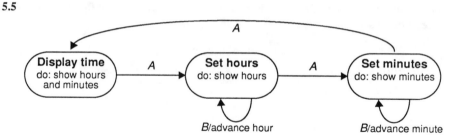

The event *A* refers to depression of the A button. In this diagram, releasing the button is unimportant and is not shown (although you must obviously release the button before you can press it again). The constraint that a new button event cannot be generated while any button is depressed can best be considered a constraint on the input events themselves and need not be shown in the state diagram (although it would not be wrong to do so).

5.6

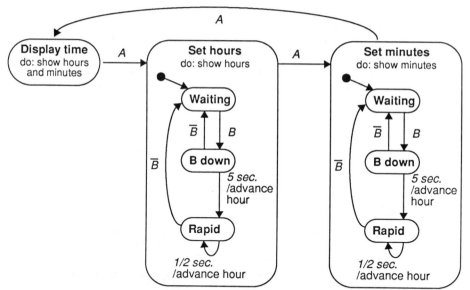

B means press button B while $\overline{B}$ means to release it. $B\overline{B}$ means to press and release it. The comments from the previous answer apply to button A.

5.7

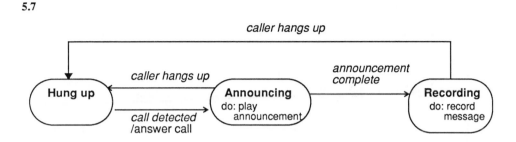

5.8 The number of rings could be kept in an internal counter that is reset on each new call and which is incremented on every ring.

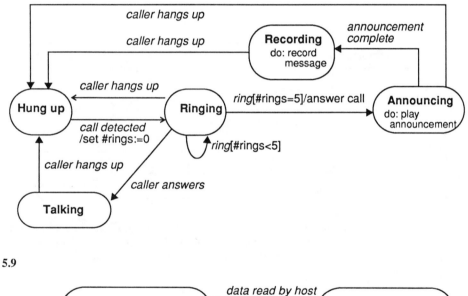

5.9

5.10   The completed state diagram for the motor control described in the exercise is shown.

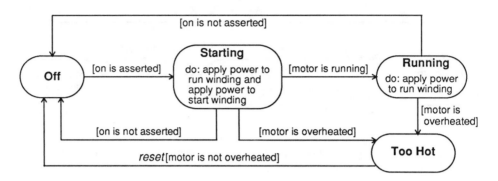

5.11

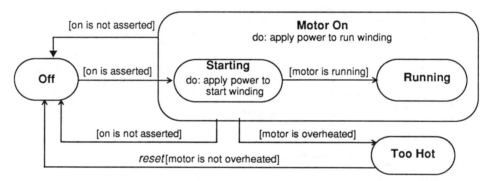

We have shown a transition from the off state to the starting state. We could instead have shown a transition from off to motor on and made starting the initial substate of motor on. Note how the action "apply power to run winding" has been factored out of both starting and running states.

5.12

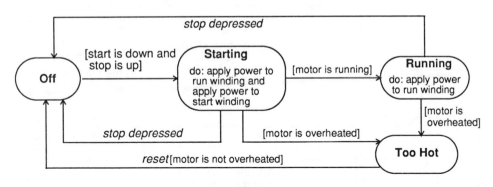

The stopping transition may be expressed as an event. The starting transition is most easily expressed as a condition on the start and stop buttons. It could be expanded in terms of start and stop buttons being depressed and released, but additional states would be required for little gain.

5.13

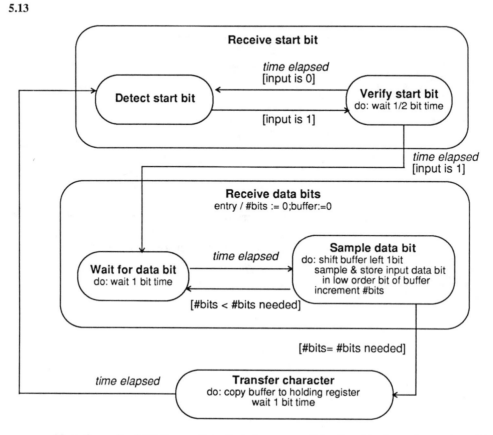

Note the wait of 1/2 time unit to find the center of the first bit, thereafter waits of 1 time unit per bit. We implicitly assume that the input will be 0 after the last bit is received. We could add an additional test for a 0 stop bit if desired.

5.14

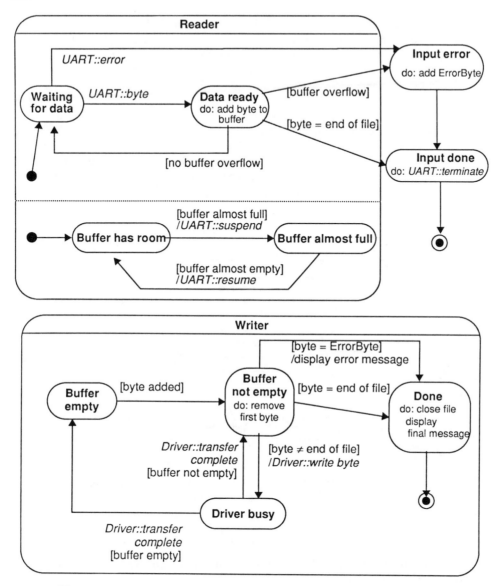

The program contains two concurrent but interacting subprograms, the reader and the writer. The reader reads data from the UART and stores it in the buffer. The writer takes data from the buffer and writes it to the disk driver. Communication is via the buffer, rather than direct events. A buffer may be regarded as a queue for events so that sending an event and receiving it can proceed asynchronously. This is the standard producer-consumer problem.

The reader contains two subparts, a main part that reads the characters from the UART and a secondary part that watches for the buffer to fill up. If the buffer gets too full, it sends a suspend message to the computer through the UART. However, there may be some delay until the computer stops sending characters, so the main part must continue to accept characters even when the buffer is getting full. This is why the main part cannot simply enter a suspend state. The threshold to resume transmission should be less than the threshold to suspend transmission to prevent thrashing and provide some hysteresis. In practice, the process to watch for buffer fill up could be merged with the read process. A flag would keep track of whether transmission had been requested to be suspended, so that a suspend message would not be sent twice. Note, however, that a two-state subprocess is a flag! Note also that when the reader terminates, the read subprocess causes both subprocesses to exit to a single done state.

5.15

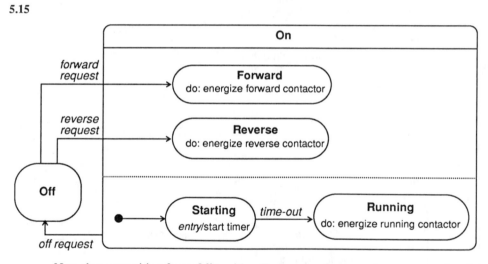

Note that a transition from *Off* to either *Forward* or *Reverse* also causes an implicit transition to *Starting,* the default initial state of the lower concurrent subdiagram. An off request causes a transition out of both concurrent subdiagrams back to state *Off*.

5.16a. Add an arrow labeled "[overheating detected]" from each non-*Off* state to state *Off*.

b. Add an arrow labeled "[overheating detected]" from state *On* to state *Off*. Because state *On* has substates, the transition applies to them.

5.17

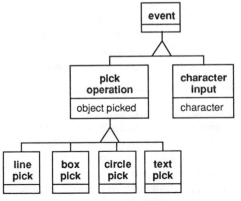

Additional event attributes could be added, depending on the application. The *pick operation* event could have a location, although it might then be made a subevent of a new event *locator event*. The various kinds of pick events could keep track of where on the object the pick occurred. The *text pick* event might note which character within the text was actually picked. Note of these additions would be wrong, but in the absence of any compelling reasons we would tend to omit them. Given the need to think about such possibilities, this problem is probably harder than a '2', maybe a '4'.

Do not confuse *text pick* with *character input*. Often *character input* will follow a *text pick* event that indicates which input object receives the input character.

5.18

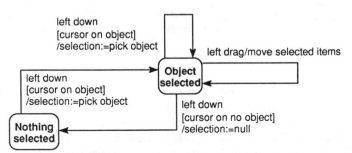

The question is ambiguous about whether a pick replaces the previous selection or adds to it. We have assumed replacement; otherwise the action on a left-down self-loop on *Object selected* becomes "add pick object to selection."

Some events can be ignored. In state *Nothing selected* event left down with cursor on no object has no effect and therefore is not shown. Similarly, left drag (that is moving the cursor while the left button is down) has no effect in the *Nothing selected* state.

This is only a small part of a complete editor. In the real editor there are more ways to pick items, therefore we assumed that a drag operation might move multiple items, even though there is no way to pick more than one item with the given fragment.

In the real editor, the right button is used to pop up a menu dependent on the selection state. There would be many selection substates, one for each kind of item (or combination of items) that can be selected. Similarly, there would be transitions to create new items.

5.19   There would be one concurrent state machine for each room, plus one each for the furnace control, blower control, and humidity control. They would have the following responsibilities:

Room control. Measures temperature in the room. Requests heat if temperature is too low. Cancels heat request if temperature is high enough. Controls flappers to the room based on room temperature. Allows user to set target temperature.

Furnace control. Turns on furnace if any room requests heat. Turns off furnace if no room requests heat. Turns off furnace if furnace temperature is too high.

Blower control. Turns on blower when furnace goes on. Turns off blower if furnace is off and furnace is cool enough.

Humidity control. Measures humidity and outside temperature. Allows user to set target humidity. Turns on humidifier if humidity is too low and blower is on.

5.20

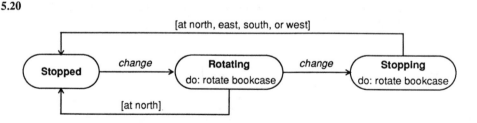

This exercise demonstrates that even simple state diagrams can lead to complex behavior. A state diagram that will explain the scenario given in the exercise is shown above. A *change* event occurs whenever the candle is taken out of its holder or whenever it is put back. The condition *at north* is satisfied whenever the bookcase is behind the wall. The condition *at north, east, south, or west* is satisfied whenever the bookcase is facing front, back, or to the side.

When you first discovered the bookcase, it was in the *Stopped* state pointing south. When your friend removed the candle, a *change* event drove the bookcase into the *Rotating* state. When the bookcase was pointing north, the condition *at north* put the bookcase back into the *Stopped* state. When your friend reinserted the candle, another *change* event put the bookcase into the *Rotating* state until it again pointed north. Pulling the candle out generated another *change* event and would have caused the bookcase to rotate a full turn if you had not blocked it with your body. Forcing the bookcase back is outside the scope of the control and does not have to be explained.

When you put the candle back again another *change* event was generated, putting the bookcase into the *Rotating* state once again. Taking the candle back out resulted in yet another *change* event, putting the bookcase into the *Stopping* state. After 1/4 turn, the condition *at north, east, south or west* was satisfied, putting the bookcase into the *Stopped* state.

What you should have done at first to gain entry was to take the candle out and quickly put it back before the bookcase completed 1/4 turn.

5.21a. Events are:

select	push select button
on-off	push on-off button
timed	push timed button
auto	push auto button
set	push set button
vcr	push vcr button
time-out	preset recording time has expired

Actions are:

next day	advance time setting display to next day of the week
next hour	advance time setting display to next hour
next minute	advance time setting display to next minute
next channel	advance channel setting display to next preset channel
initialize start time	set time setting display for start time to be current time
initialize stop time	set time setting display for stop time to be start time
more time	add fixed time increment to preset recording time

Activities are:

display time	display current time of day in time display
display start time	display start recording time in time display
display stop time	display stop recording time in time display
flash day	flash day segment of time display
flash hour	flash hour segment of time display
flash minutes	flash minutes segment of time display
flash channel	flash channel display
record	record the preset channel on the vcr tape
update time	change the time display as the current time changes
display auto	light the "auto" indicator on the display panel

b. A synopsis of the user manual is as follows:

To set the clock, push SELECT successively to set the day of the week, the hour, and the minutes in turn. Within each setting, push SET to advance the respective setting by 1 unit (15 minutes for minutes).

To set the record timer, push ON/OFF. The time to start recording is displayed. It is initially set to the current time. The start time may be set using the SELECT and SET buttons as described for setting the clock to set the day, hour, minutes, and channel to begin recording.

When the recording start time and channel have been selected, press ON/OFF again to set the recording stop time. The stop time is displayed. It is initially set to be the same as the start time. Press SELECT and SET to set the hours and minutes of the stop time as described for setting the clock.

When the stop time has been set, press ON/OFF a final time to return to the time-of-day display. To enable the automatic recording mode, press AUTO. The "auto" indicator lights up. When the preset recording start time is reached, the vcr automatically switches to the preset channel and begins recording. When the preset recording stop time is reached, the vcr automatically stops recording. The current time is displayed continuously in automatic mode. To disable automatic recording mode, press AUTO again; if the vcr is recording, then recording will cease.

To record for 15 minutes starting immediately, press TIMED. The vcr begins recording on the current channel. To extend the recording time by an additional 15 minutes, press TIMED one or more times. [Note that there appears to be no way to cancel timed recording before time expires. This is a bug in the state diagram and would be extremely annoying to vcr owners.]

Press the VCR button to toggle the output of the vcr between straight antenna input (to use the tuner on the TV set) and the output of the vcr (TV must be set on channel 3 or 4).

[The user's manual would also include descriptions of the manual control buttons omitted from the state diagram. The state diagram also omits controls for setting the current channel.]

c. The new state diagram (next page) is constructed by duplicating states *Set start time*r and *Set stop timer* for the second time and hooking the new states into the ON/OFF sequence. We have deleted the entry action to initialize the start time and stop time, because the user would not want to lose a previously set time in using the second setting.

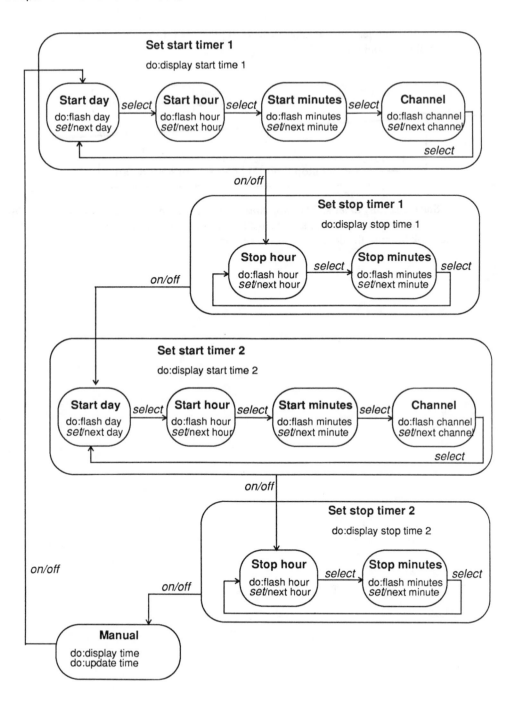

d. We could parameterize the states to avoid duplicating information in several places. For example, we could do as follows:

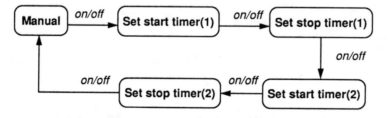

States *Set start timer* and *Set stop timer* would be defined by state diagrams with default initial states and formal arguments. Parameterization of states was not discussed in the book because the details are still uncertain.

6

Functional Modeling

6.1 Engineering analysis of a motor can be subdivided into electrical, mechanical, fan, and thermal analysis processes.

The electrical analysis process has multiple inputs. Electrical parameters, voltage, and frequency are external inputs. The temperature input comes from thermal analysis, and the speed comes from mechanical analysis. The output of electrical analysis is the electrical torque.

Mechanical analysis has an external input of load characteristics. Electrical torque and fan torque from other processes are also input. The output of mechanical analysis is the speed of the motor.

Fan analysis uses the motor speed to compute the fan torque and air flow.

Thermal analysis has external inputs of thermal parameters and ambient temperature. The losses from electrical analysis and the air flow from fan analysis are also inputs. The temperature of the motor is computed as a result.

6.2 In general there are at least two ways of solving systems with circular dependencies: solving a set of simultaneous equations or tearing and iteration. For this problem the dependencies are nonlinear and subroutines are provided for the subprocesses, so the best solution is tearing and iteration.

Tearing refers to the process of estimating values for one or more variables in order to break loops. For instance for Figure E6.1, the set of (speed, losses) is a tear set (sometimes called a cut point). If speed and losses were estimated then we could execute the subroutines in the following sequential order.

- Run fan analysis and compute air flow and fan torque.
- Run thermal analysis and compute temperature.

- Run electrical analysis and compute electrical torque as well as a new value of losses.

- Run mechanical analysis and compute a new value of speed.

We would repeat this cycle of computations until the new losses-value and speed-value matched the initial guessed-values. Various iteration schemes could be used to achieve convergence:

- fixed point. Use new computed values to seed the next round of computations.

- acceleration. Use numerical methods to analyze the past computed values and extrapolate the next values.

In general iterative problems have multiple possibilities for tear sets. For example, the following are also tear sets for the motor problem (electrical torque, fan torque, losses) and (temperature, speed). The choice of tear sets affects the ordering of the subroutines. Tear sets may have different behavior in terms of whether they converge, speed of convergence, and tolerance for error in initial conditions. Knowledge of the problem domain or observed numerical behavior guides the proper choice of tear sets.

6.3   Figure A6.1 and Figure A6.2 contain the data flow diagram for computing the net score for an athletic competition.

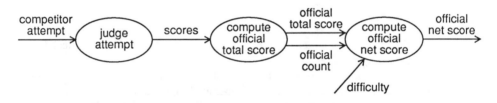

compute official total score process

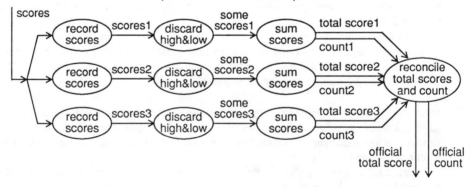

Figure A6.1 First portion of data flow diagram for judged athletic competition

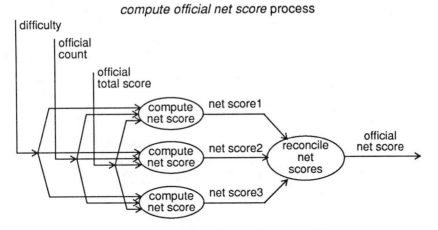

Figure A6.2 Remainder of data flow diagram for judged athletic competition

6.4 Figure A6.3 contains the data flow diagram for computing cylinder geometry.

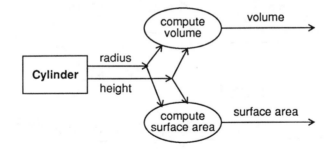

Figure A6.3 Data flow diagram for computing cylinder volume and surface area

Some different ways to compute volume and surface area for a cylinder are:

- *Using a formula.* Volume = $\pi r^2 h$. Surface area = $2\pi rh$. (r=radius, h=height)

- *Using a lookup table.* The volume and surface area are listed for standard values of radius and height.

- *Using numerical methods.* Calculate volume and surface area from the differential equation for a circle.

6.5 Figure A6.4 shows the data flow diagram for computing the mean for a sequence of input values.

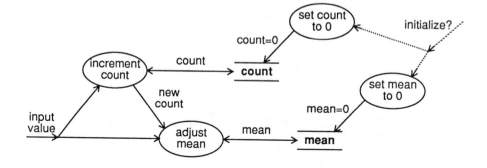

adjust mean process

(Note: n+1=new count, x_n=nth input value, $\bar{x}_n$=average after n values)

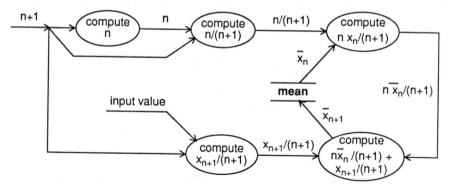

Figure A6.4 Data flow diagram for computing mean of a sequence of values

6.6   Figure A6.5 is a data flow diagram for computing the roots of a quadratic equation.

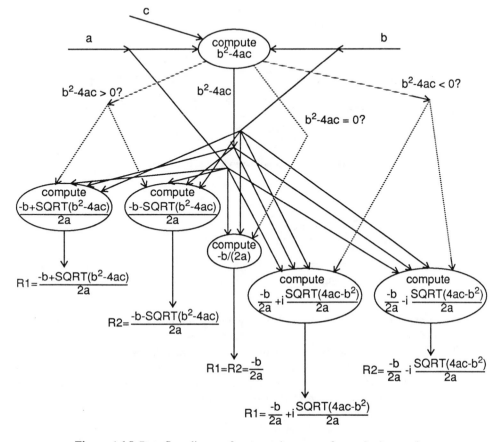

Figure A6.5 Data flow diagram for computing roots of a quadratic equation

6.7 a. Using conditional statements, the algorithm for T(x) can be expressed as:

```
IF (x>-3) AND (x<=-2) THEN T = 3+x
ELSEIF (x<=-1) THEN T = -x-1
ELSEIF (x<=0) THEN T = 1+x
ELSEIF (x<=1) THEN T = 1-x
ELSEIF (x<=2) THEN T = x-1
ELSEIF (x<=3) THEN T = 3-x
ENDIF
```

The above pseudo code can be simplified to the following.

```
t = x MOD 2 - 1
```

```
IF (t<0) THEN T = -t
ELSE T = t
ENDIF   /* compute absolute value */
```

b. Figure A6.6 shows a plot of T(x) for the interval -5 < x < 5.

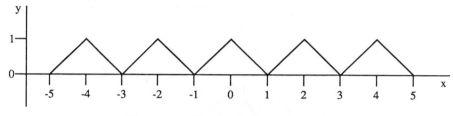

Figure A6.6 Plot of periodic function *T(x)*

c. The data flow diagram for T(x) in Figure A6.7 only uses functions and arithmetic.

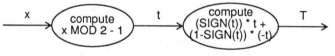

Figure A6.7 Data flow diagram for *T(x)*

6.8   Data flow diagrams are not helpful for explaining cutting and pasting in a simple diagram editor. We prefer to use pseudo code to describe these operations. In general, data
flow diagrams are most useful for expressing functional dependencies and packaging
programming code into modules. We restate this exercise as follows: *"Figure E6.2 is an
object diagram for a simple diagram editor. Explain how cutting and pasting works. Refer to exercise 4.7 for a synopsis of some operations."* For cutting the steps are:

```
selection::cut()
delete all boxes, links, line segments, and points from
    the buffer;
find all links that must be deleted because of the cut;
    /* call these bridging links - these are selected
    links which are connected to at least one unselected
    box or unselected links that are connected to at least
    one selected box */
undisplay bridging links;
delete bridging links;
disassociate selected links and boxes from sheet;
undisplay selected links and boxes;
associate selected links and boxes with buffer;
```

Pasting works as follows:

```
buffer::paste(sheet,offset)
for each box associated with buffer:
    make a copy of box, associate with original;
    move the copy of the box by offset;
    display the copy of the box;
    associate copy of box with sheet;
for each link associated with buffer:
    make a copy of link;
    associate copy of link with corresponding copies of
        boxes;
    for each line segment associated with link:
        copy line segment and associate with copy of link;
        for each point associated with line segment:
            copy point and move it by offset;
            associate copy of point with copy of line
                segment;
        display copy of line segment;
```

6.9 a. One possible metamodel for representing functional dependencies is shown in Figure
A6.8. We have generalized the classes *Actor*, *Process*, and *Data Store* into the class *Vertex*. We assume that each external data flow into and out from a functional model is attached to an actor. There are many similarities between a functional model and a graph. Each data flow is the output of exactly one vertex. A data flow can split and be used as an input for several vertices. Each vertex can have zero or more inputs and zero or more outputs. We assume that it is possible for a process to have no input and/or no outputs. Although the association in our metamodel between the classes *Functional Model* and *Vertex* is correct, it does not fully capture some constraints. More accurately, an *Actor* can be part of more than one *Functional Model*, but a *Process* cannot.

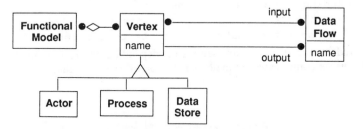

Figure A6.8 Metamodel for representing functional dependencies

b. The simplified metamodel shown in Figure A6.9 is adequate for this part. We assume
that a data flow that is not the output of a process is an output of an actor or a data store.
We do not assume that the functional dependencies form a directed acyclic graph. We

arbitrarily break ties in equally ranked processes. Processes can be arranged into an ordered list by the following procedure:

```
Initialize the output list to empty;
Place all processes in a set to be ordered;
For each process that has no inputs:
    Delete the process from the set of processes;
    Mark the process as known;
    Append the process to the output list;
    For each data flow that is an output of the process:
        Mark the data flow as known;
        Add the data flow to set of data flows to be
            considered;
For each data flow that is not the output of a process:
    Mark the data flow as known;
    Add the data flow to set of data flows to be
        considered;
While the set of data flows to be considered is not empty:
    Get and delete any data flow from the set;
    For each process that uses the data flow as an input:
        If process is not marked as known:
            add_to_list_if_possible(process);
If the set of processes to be ordered is not empty:
    Declare an error - not a directed acyclic graph;
```

The procedure *add_to_list_if_possible* behaves as follows:

```
add_to_list_if_possible(process)
If all inputs to process are marked as known:
    Delete the process from set to be ordered;
    Mark the process as known;
    Append the process to the output list;
    Add the data flows that are outputs of the process to
        the set of data flows to be considered;
```

Some students may devise a simpler answer depending on the assumptions they make. The answer is complicated by the consideration of processes that have no inputs or no output.

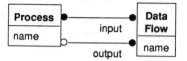

Figure A6.9 Simplified metamodel for representing functional dependencies

c. One possible ordering is p1, p3, p6, p2, p4, and p5. A data flow diagram is shown in Figure A6.10.

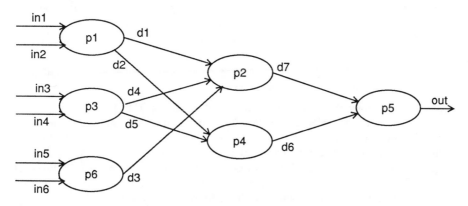

Figure A6.10 Data flow diagram for the processes described in the exercise

6.10a. absolute value: if $x \geq 0$ then $|x| = x$, else $|x| = -x$

b. trigonometric sine: $\sin \Theta = y/r$

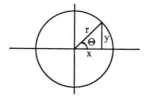

Figure A6.11 Definition of trigonometric sine

c. natural logarithm: $\ln(x) = \int_1^x (1/t)\, dt$

d. square root: $y = \mathrm{SQRT}\,(x)$ such that $x = y * y$

6.11a. pseudo code for absolute value

```
IF x ≥ 0 THEN RETURN x
ELSE RETURN -x
ENDIF
```

b. c. d. Two ways of implementing trigonometric sine, natural logarithm, and square root are by power series and fixed point iteration.

Mathematics can be used to derive an infinite power series ($a_0 x^0 + a_1 x^1 + a_2 x^2 + ...$) that is equivalent to the desired function. The function can then be approximated by evaluating the first portion of the power series and truncating the remainder. The sine, logarithm, and square root functions have an infinite number of power series; a desirable power series would converge quickly for the arguments of interest and bound the maximum error. Before computing a power series, the argument value is usually normalized to lie within a standard range. Thus for instance, the following property can be used to transform the sine argument to an equivalent argument that lies in the range of 0° to 360°

```
sin (Θ)  =  sin (Θ MOD 360°)
```

One could normalize the argument of the sin function even further by recognizing that

```
sin (Θ)  =  - sin (Θ - 180°)
```

and thus transform the sin argument to lie in the range of 0° to 180°.

Another way of implementing these functions is by fixed point iteration: Guess an initial value and then repeatedly apply an identity formula, until you are close enough to the correct answer. Special acceleration methods can be used to increase the rate of convergence of fixed point iteration. For example, an initial estimate of y = SQRT(x) is y = (1+x)/2; in fact this is a very good estimate of the square root for values of x close to 1. A new value of x can be computed with the following formula:

```
y (n+1)  =  (y (n)  +  x/y (n) )  / 2
```

PART 2: DESIGN METHODOLOGY

7

Methodology Preview

7.1 We have learned this lesson more times than we would care to admit. Carpenters have a similar maxim: "Measure twice, cut once." This exercise is intended to get the student to think about the value of methodologies in general. There is no single correct answer. It is probably too early in the book for the student to answer in detail about how the OMT methodology will help. Look for indications that the student appreciates the pitfalls of bypassing careful design.

The effort needed to detect and correct errors in the implementation phase of a software system is an order of magnitude greater than that required to prevent errors through careful design in the first place. Many programmers like to design as they code, probably because it gives them a sense of immediate progress. This leads to conceptual errors which are difficult to distinguish from simple coding mistakes. For example, it is easy to make conceptual errors in algorithms that are designed as they are coded. During testing, the algorithm may produce values that are difficult to understand. Analysis of the symptoms often produces misleading conclusions. It is not easy for the programmer to imagine that there is a conceptual error, because the focus is at a level that is too low. The programmer "cannot see the forest for the trees".

Careful design should be used with rapid prototyping as well as with the life cycle approach. You might ask the students to discuss this. The difference is that with the life cycle approach the entire system is designed before it is implemented. With rapid prototyping, portions of the system are designed, then implemented.

7.2 The intent of this exercise is get the student to think creatively about object-oriented techniques. There is no single correct answer. Look for ideas in areas given in the exercise or in other areas. We have some ideas which we have not yet pursued about extending object-oriented techniques into the given areas.

In language design, for example, a variation of object diagrams could be used to describe production rules. Production rules define how non-terminals are constructed from terminals and other non-terminals. There are two basic operators in the rules: *and* and *or*. The *or* operator combines constructs that produce a given non-terminal. The *and* operator expresses the sequence of terminals and non-terminals in a given production. There is a loose analogy between the and/or structure of production rules and the and/or nature of aggregation and generalization relationships. It might be possible to extend the object modeling notation to formalize the analogy. As an added benefit, the notion of multiplicity in object diagrams could be used to express lists and options in a more elegant fashion than the paradigms used to express them via production rules.

8

Analysis

8.1 [Do not worry if your answers do not exactly match ours since you had to make assumptions about the functional specifications. The point of the exercise is to make you think about the examples in terms of the three aspects of modeling. The authors even disagree among themselves concerning the correct answers to this question.]

a. *bridge player.* Functional modeling, object modeling, and dynamic modeling, in that order, are important for a bridge playing program because good algorithms are needed to yield intelligent playing. The game involves a great deal of strategy. Close attention to inheritance and method design can result in significant code reuse. The interface is not complicated, so the dynamic model is simple and could be omitted.

b. *change-making machine.* Functional modeling is the most important because the machine must perform correctly. A change making machine must not make mistakes; users will be angry if they are cheated and owners of the machine do not want to lose money. The machine must reject counterfeit and foreign money, but should not reject genuine money. The dynamic model is least important since user interaction is simple.

c. *car cruise control.* The order of importance is dynamic modeling, object modeling, and functional modeling. Because this is a control application you can expect the dynamic model to be important. There is a need to thoroughly understand scenarios and protocols for interaction. The functional model is simple because there are not many calculations.

d. *electronic typewriter.* The object model is the most important, since there are many parts which must be carefully assembled. The interaction between the parts also must be thoroughly understood. The dynamic model is next most important because an electronic typewriter must be easy to use. The functional model is least important.

e. *spelling checker.* The order of importance is object modeling, functional modeling, and dynamic modeling. Object modeling is important because of the need to store a great deal of data and to be able to access it quickly. Functional modeling is important because an efficient algorithm is needed to check spelling quickly. The dynamic model is simple because the user interface is simple: provide a chance to correct each misspelled word that is found.

f. *telephone answering machine.* The order of importance is dynamic modeling, object modeling, and functional modeling. The state diagram is non-trivial and important to the behavior of the system. The object model shows relationships between components that complement the dynamic model. The functionality that a telephone answering machine provides is straightforward.

8.2 [Student answers may vary widely from the answers given below. Each specification should be 75-150 words in length. (Specifications may be shorter than the 150-300 words specified in the exercise.)]

a. *bridge player.* Develop a computerized bridge playing system. The system will support as many as four players. From zero to four of the players will be computer generated. The computer must deal random hands, bid using standard conventions, play any hand, and keep score. All computer generated opponents must be "honest" and not take advantage of any knowledge of the hidden cards of opponents. There should be a setting for level of difficulty which the human user can adjust. The program must have an excellent, user-friendly interface with high resolution color graphics and quickly determine bids and plays. It is permissible for performance to degrade as the level of play becomes more difficult. The system should keep an optional log in which it records the cards dealt and the bids and plays for a given game. The system should also accept a predefined deal and bid and play list; this is useful for studying fine details of a bridge game.

b. *change-making machine.* Design the software for a machine that accepts paper currency and returns change. Important design goals in order of importance are: rejection of counterfeit and foreign currency, determination of denomination, correct dispensing of change, software versatility, and low cost. The software may be custom written for a particular microprocessor chip. Versatility refers to the fact that the software must be configurable to a variety of conditions. The software must be easy to reconfigure for international use with different types of currency and different formulas for dispensing change. The software must allow a fee to be imposed for change-making service.

c. *car cruise control.* Design a cruise control system for an automobile. The control has four buttons: *on/off*, *set*, *coast*, and *resume*. Once the control system is on, the driver accelerates to a desired speed and presses *set*. The speed will be maintained within a fixed tolerance until the driver hits the brake or presses the *off* button. The driver may accelerate above the preset speed by using the accelerator; once the accelerator is released the car will resume the preset speed. If the driver hits the brake, the cruise control is disabled until the driver presses the *resume* button at which time the car will resume the preset speed. If the driver holds the *coast* button, the car will decelerate until the button is released at which point the car's speed becomes the new desired speed. Abrupt changes or oscillations in speed will be avoided.

d. *electronic typewriter*. Design the software and hardware for an electronic typewriter. The typewriter need only support the standard *QWERTY* arrangement. Keys that are not letters and numbers can be arranged in the manner that seems most appropriate. Cost of the typewriter is paramount; intentions are to aim for the low end of the marketplace. The power supply need only handle the standard 120 volts of North America. Color of the typewriter is irrelevant—choose an inoffensive color that is inexpensive. The typewriter should be lightweight and easy to assemble; it need not be easy to repair. The typewriter should have a one-line electronic display; the line does not print until the carriage return is pressed. This buffering simplifies correction of minor typing errors.

e. *spelling checker*. Design the software for a spelling checker. The spelling checker must find incorrect words in a document and suggest corrections for all misspelled words. The spelling checker must use a word dictionary and permit the user to add new words. The software must run on IBM PCs and close compatibles and integrate with a variety of word processors. It must be memory resident and easily activated with a few keystrokes. The spelling checker must accept commands from both a mouse and keyboard; keyboard commands should be redefinable by modifying a configuration file. The software must be easy to use and present a polished pull-down menu interface. The user interface should take advantage of color and high resolution if it is present, but still be serviceable on a black and white low resolution system. It is important that the memory resident portion of the system occupy as little RAM as possible; it is acceptable for the software to overlay and access the disk and pull in additional code when it is activated.

f. *telephone answering machine*. Design the software for a telephone answering machine. The software must provide the following services as a minimum: answer the phone after a predetermined number of rings, play a recorded message, record the caller's message, and hang up after a predefined length of recording. The software should support remote dial-in and identification by password to hear any recorded calls. The software should be suitable for burning into ROM. As such it is important that the software be small in size and extremely reliable since it would be very costly to update the equipment once it is in a customer's hands. The software must operate in real-time but early projections are that this goal is easy to meet with modern microprocessors. You may choose any CPU chip for developing the software that you choose, but the wholesale quantity price of the CPU chip must be $10 or less.

8.3 a. A system to transfer data from one computer to another over a telecommunication line. The system should transmit data reliably over noisy channels with a failure rate of less than 1 in 10^9. Data must not be lost if the receiving end cannot keep up or if the line drops out. The system must operate at 300-19200 baud. The system should support several common error correcting protocols.

b. A system for automating the production of complex machined parts is needed. The parts will be designed using a three-dimensional drafting editor that is part of the system. The system will produce tapes that can be used by numerical control (N/C) machines to actually produce the parts. The system must be developed in x months and cost no more than y dollars. The system will support the following machining operations...

c. The software for a desktop publishing system is needed, based on a what-you-see-is-what-you-get philosophy. The system will support text and graphics. Graphics include lines, squares, rectangles, polygons, circles, and ellipses. The system should support interactive, graphical editing of documents. The system must run on the following hardware configurations... It must be capable of printout in *Postscript* format. The software must support the following operations... and be extensible and maintainable.

d. Software for generating nonsense is desired. The input is a sample document. The output is random text that mimics the input text by imitating the frequencies of combinations of letters of the input. The user specifies the order of the imitation and the length of the desired output. For order N, every output sequence of N characters is found in the input and at approximately the same frequency. As the order increases, the style of the output more closely matches the input. Working memory must be constant and not proportional to the size of input or output text, but the entire input document is randomly accessible at run time. Time performance should be proportional to N and to the number of output characters.

e. A system for distributing electronic mail over a network is needed. Each user of the system should be able to send mail from any computer account and receive mail on one designated account. There should be provisions for answering or forwarding mail, as well as saving messages in files or printing them. Also, users should be able to send messages to several other users at once through distribution lists. Messages must not be lost even if the target computer is down.

8.4   [Keep in mind that the requirements are incomplete, thus so are the object models.]

a. Multiple transmissions can occur at any given time. Each transmission has a baud rate and a transmission protocol. Transmissions are dynamically initiated and terminated. Each transmission has one source and one destination communication port. The source sends data and the destination receives data. Each port is dedicated to one transmission or is idle. (Note that the structure of the model does not strictly enforce the constraint that a port is associated with at most one transmission. Our model would permit both an *Input* and *Output* association when only one applies. We do not consider it worthwhile to modify the model to capture this constraint.) Each port has a name and is associated with one computer. A computer may communicate through many ports. A port transmits data through a communication line which may serve many ports.

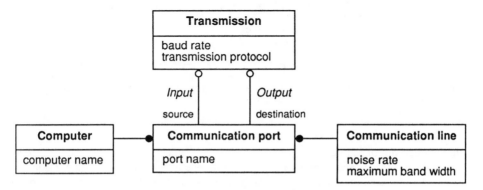

Figure A8.1 Object diagram for a data transfer system

b. A parts machining automation system designs parts. A design of a part produces many tapes, each of which is used to control one N/C machine. Each N/C machine may run different tapes over the course of a day. A N/C machine manufactures many parts, and a part may be machined by several N/C machines. Each tape is dedicated to a single part design.

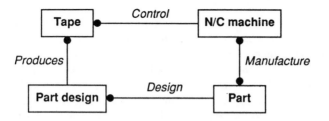

Figure A8.2 Object diagram for a parts machining automation system

c. Each desktop publishing document contains many text and graphics primitives. (In reality for any reasonable implementation of a desktop publishing system, a document would consist of several intermediate levels of structure. We do not show such structure because it is not obvious from the stated requirements.) Graphics primitives include lines, squares, boxes, polygons, circles, and ellipses. The *print* operation on the *Document* class interacts with *Printer* objects.

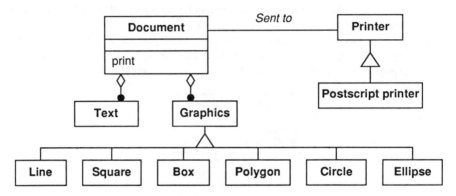

Figure A8.3 Object diagram for a desktop publishing system

d. For each run of the nonsense generator, the user can set two attribute values: *order of imitation* and *desired output length*. The nonsense generator takes an input document and generates an output document. An input document can be used for multiple runs of generating output.

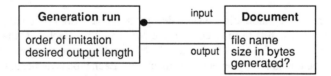

Figure A8.4 Object diagram for a nonsense generator

e. An electronic mail system must service multiple users and handle many individual mail messages. Each user has a set of email default parameters. Users may send and receive multiple mail messages. A mail message is sent by one user and received by one or more users. It is often convenient to send a mail message to multiple users via a distribution list. A distribution list is a list of users that has been predefined and named. A file may contain many mail messages. Users can perform many operations on mail such as save to file, print, send, and forward. A user has many computer accounts but receives mail at only one of these accounts. Each file is owned by some computer account. Multiple accounts may be supported by the same computer.

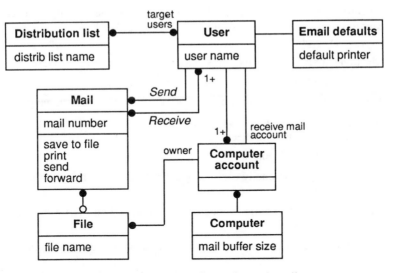

Figure A8.5 Object diagram for an electronic mail system

8.5   The following tentative classes should be eliminated.

- Redundant classes: *selected object, selected line, selected box, selected text* (redundant with *selection*), *connection* (redundant with *link*).

- Irrelevant classes: *computer* (it is implicit that we are developing a model for the purpose of computer implementation).

- Vague classes: *graphics object* (not sure precisely what this is; we do not need it as we have more specific classes).

- Attributes: *length, width, line segment coordinate, position, file name, name, origin, scale factor*.

- Implementation constructs: *x-coordinate, y-coordinate* (what about polar coordinates?, they are also really attributes), *menu* (but you could argue about whether *menu* should be a class), *mouse, button, popup, menu item* (a manner of implementing menus), *corner point, end point* (there are other ways to specify a box; these are also attributes), *character* (an implementation construct for text).

After eliminating improper classes we are left with *Line, Link, Collection, Selection, Drawing, Drawing file, Sheet, Point, Box, Buffer,* and *Text*.

8.6   We only need to prepare a data dictionary for proper object classes.

- Line—a graphical entity that connects two points; actually a line segment. Lines may be horizontal or vertical.

- Link—a connection path between two boxes. A link is represented as a series of joined alternating vertical and horizontal lines.

- Collection—a set of two or more lines and boxes, not necessarily connected. A collection is a grouping defined by the user and manipulated as a unit for moves and deletes, for example

- Selection—a set of boxes and links that the user selects with a mouse.

- Drawing—a set of sheets that contain boxes and links.

- Drawing file—a file that contains a stored representation of a drawing.

- Sheet—a set of boxes and links that fit on a standard piece of printer paper. Each box and link is on exactly one sheet.

- Point—a location on a sheet.

- Box—a rectangle optionally containing a single text. The sides of the rectangle are parallel to the axes.

- Buffer—a temporary holder for copied and cut selections. The paste operation uses the buffer contents.

- Text—a sequence of characters on a single horizontal line located within a box.

8.7   The following tentative associations should be eliminated because they are between eliminated classes:

- A *box has a position.* (*Position* is an attribute which has been eliminated. Replace by a *box has a point.*)

- A *character string has a location.* (*Location* is an attribute. We are using the term *text* and not *character string.*)

- A *line has length.* (*Length* is an attribute which has been eliminated.)

- A *line is a graphical object.* (For this problem, we do not consider *Graphical object* as a class worth modeling.)

- A *point is a graphical object.* (For this problem, we do not consider *Graphical object* as a class worth modeling.)

- A *point has an x-coordinate.* (*X-coordinate* is an attribute which has been eliminated.)

- A *point has a y-coordinate.* (*Y-coordinate* is an attribute which has been eliminated.)

The following tentative associations are irrelevant or implementation artifacts:

- A *character string has characters.* (This is not important enough to include in the model.)

- A *box has a character string.* (This is the same as a *box has text.*)

The following tentative associations are actions:

- A *box is moved.*

- A *link is deleted.*

- *A line is moved.*

The following associations are derived:

- *A link has points.*
- *A link is defined by a sequence of points.* (Replace by *a link corresponds to one or more lines.*)

The following associations were missing from the list given in the exercise:

- *A drawing has one or more sheets.*
- *A drawing is stored in a drawing file.*

We are left with the following correct associations and generalizations: *a box has text, a link logically associates two boxes, a link corresponds to one or more lines, a selection or a buffer or a sheet is a collection, a collection is composed of links and boxes, a line has two points, a drawing has one or more sheets, and a drawing is stored in a drawing file.*

8.8   [Our answers to these queries use a dot notation to indicate traversal of associations. The name after the dot is a role name or a class name across an association from the source. Thus the notation *link.box* means that given a *Link* object retrieve the associated set of *Boxes*. Note that the dot notation can be concatenated, thus *link.box.text* means that given a *Link* object retrieve the associated *Boxes*, and for each of these *Boxes* retrieve the associated *Text* object. An object-oriented language may not directly support this dot notation. In any case, the dot notation is unambiguous and clearly specifies the operations.

We used pseudo code in answering this exercise. An acceptable answer from a student may use pseudo code or a carefully written English explanation.]

a. *What are all selected boxes and links?*

```
Selection::retrieve_boxes_links (boxes, links)
    boxes:= self.box;
    links:= self.link;
```

b. *Given a box, determine all other boxes that are directly linked to it.*

```
Box::retrieve_direct_boxes () returns set of boxes
    boxes:= create_empty_set;
    for each link in self.link
        add set link.box to set boxes;
            /* link.box has two elements: */
            /* self & the linked box.     */
    end for each link
    remove self from set boxes;
    return boxes;
```

c. *Given a box, find all other boxes that are directly or indirectly linked to it.*

```
Box::retrieve_transitive_closure_boxes ()
returns set of boxes
   boxes:= create_empty_set;
   return self.TCloop (boxes);
Box::TCloop (boxes) returns set of boxes
   add self to set boxes;
   for each link in self.link
      for each box in link.box
         /* 2 boxes are assoc with a link */
         if box is not in boxes then
            box.TCloop(boxes);
         end if
      end for each box
   end for each link
```

d. *Given a box and a link, determine if the link involves the box.* This operation is symmetrical, thus it is arbitrary whether we assign it to class *Box* or class *Link*.

```
Box::check_connection (given_link) returns boolean
   if self is in given_link.box then return true
   else return false
   end if
```

e. *Given a box and a link, find the other box logically connected to the given box through the other end of the link.* This operation is symmetrical, thus it is arbitrary whether we assign it to class *Box* or class *Link*.

```
Box::retrieve_other_box (given_link) returns box
   if self is not in given_link.box then
      error;
      return nil
   else
      boxes:= given_link.box;
      remove self from set boxes;
      return (boxes.first_element);
         /* set boxes has a single element */
   end if
```

f. *Given two boxes, determine all links between them.* Multiple polymorphism, such as that provided by CLOS, would allow us to more naturally express this operation. See Section 15.8.4.

```
Box::retrieve_common_links (given_box2)
returns set of links
   links1:= self.link;
   links2:= given_box2.link;
   return (links1 intersect links2);
```

g. *Given a selection, determine which links are "bridging" links.*

```
Selection::retrieve_bridging_links ()
returns set of links
   selected_boxes:= self.box;
   bridges:= create_empty_set;
   for each box in selected_boxes
      for each link in box.link
         other_box:= box.retrieve_other_box (link);
         if other_box is not in selected_boxes then
            add link to set bridges;
         end if
      end for each link
   end for each box
   return bridges;
```

8.9   Figure E8.3 promotes the association between *Box* and *Link* to an object class. The connection between *Box* and *Link* should be modeled as a class if it has identity, important behavior, and relationships to other classes. The exercise only presents a fragment of the complete diagram and does not state the diagram's purpose, so we cannot assess the merits of the variation. The choice of implementation language may make one of the approaches more convenient.

a. *What are all selected boxes and links?* Same answer as Exercise 8.8a.

b. *Given a box, determine all other boxes that are directly linked to it.*

```
Box::retrieve_direct_boxes () returns set of boxes
   boxes:= create_empty_set;
   for each link in self.connection.link
      add set link.connection.box to set boxes;
         /* link.connection.box has two elements: */
         /* self & the linked box.              */
   end for each link
   remove self from set boxes;
   return boxes;
```

c. *Given a box, find all other boxes that are directly or indirectly linked to it.*

```
Box::TCloop (boxes) returns set of boxes
   add self to set boxes;
   for each link in self.connection.link
      for each box in link.connection.box
         /* 2 boxes are assoc with a link */
         if box is not in boxes then
            box.TCloop(boxes);
         end if
      end for each box
   end for each link
```

d. *Given a box and a link, determine if the link involves the box.* This operation is symmetrical, thus it is arbitrary whether we assign it to class *Box* or class *Link*.

```
Box::check_connection (given_link) returns boolean
    if self is in given_link.connection.box then
        return true
    else return false
    end if
```

e. *Given a box and a link, find the other box logically connected to the given box through the other end of the link.* This operation is symmetrical, thus it is arbitrary whether we assign it to class *Box* or class *Link*.

```
Box::retrieve_other_box (given_link) returns box
    if self is not in given_link.connection.box then
        error;
        return nil
    else
        boxes:= given_link.connection.box;
        remove self from set boxes;
        return (boxes.first_element);
            /* set boxes has a single element */
    end if
```

f. *Given two boxes, determine all links between them.* Multiple polymorphism, such as that provided by CLOS, would allow us to more naturally express this operation. See Section 15.8.4.

```
Box::retrieve_common_links (given_box2)
returns set of links
    links1:= self.connection.link;
    links2:= given_box2.connection.link;
    return (links1 intersect links2);
```

g. *Given a selection, determine which links are "bridging" links.*

```
Selection::retrieve_bridging_links ()
returns set of links
    selected_boxes:= self.box;
    bridges:= create_empty_set;
    for each box in selected_boxes
        for each link in box.connection.link
            other_box:= box.retrieve_other_box (link);
            if other_box is not in selected_boxes then
                add link to set bridges;
            end if
        end for each link
    end for each box
    return bridges;
```

8.10 There are an infinite number of correct answers to this exercise, one of which is listed below. Our scenario is certainly possible, but it is unlikely that a user would enter so many sheet operations in quick succession. Maybe the exercise should not have required inclusion of all operations from Exercise 8.5.

    User loads an existing drawing. The editor retrieves the document and sets the cursor to the last referenced sheet.

    User goes to the first sheet. The editor moves the cursor.

    User goes to the next sheet. The editor moves the cursor.

    User deletes this sheet. The editor requests confirmation. The user confirms.

    User goes to the last sheet. The editor moves the cursor.

    User goes to the previous sheet. The editor moves the cursor.

    User deletes all existing sheets. The editor requests confirmation. The user confirms.

    User creates a new sheet. The editor sets the cursor to this sheet.

    User creates a box. Editor highlights newly created box. User enters text "x".

    User copies x-box. Editor highlights new copy of box. User moves selected box.

    User selects text in box. Editor highlights text and unhighlights box. User cuts text. User selects empty box. Editor highlights empty box. User enters text "y".

    User copies y-box. Editor highlights new copy of box. User moves selected box. User edits the "y" and changes it to "+".

    User selects y-box. Editor highlights y-box. User copies y-box. Editor highlights new copy of box. User moves selected box. User edits "y" and changes it to "x+y".

    User cuts x+y-box. User changes his/her mind and pastes the x+y-box back in.

    User selects the x-box. Editor highlights x-box. User also selects the +-box. Editor also highlights +-box. User links the boxes.

    User selects the y-box. Editor highlights y-box. User also selects the +-box. Editor also highlights +-box. User links the boxes.

    User selects the +-box. Editor highlights +-box. User also selects the x+y-box. Editor also highlights x+y-box. User links the boxes.

    User selects all boxes and links. Editor highlights all boxes and links. User groups the selections. User aligns the grouped selection with regard to the left-right center of the page.

    User renames the drawing file and saves the drawing.

8.11 Error scenario 1:

    User enters command: *load existing drawing file* and supplies a file name. Command fails: file not found.

Error scenario 2:

    User selects the x-box. Editor highlights x-box.

    User also selects the y-box. Editor also highlights y-box.

    User also selects the +-box. Editor also highlights +-box.

    User tries to select the *link box* command.

    Command fails: must pick exactly two boxes for linking.

Error scenario 3:

    User selects the x-box. Editor highlights x-box.

    User tries to select the *enter text* command.

    Command fails: box already has text.

8.12 Of the classes we have discussed so far, only *User* and *Editor* have significant dynamic behavior. Figure A8.6 shows part of the event trace that corresponds to Exercise 8.10.

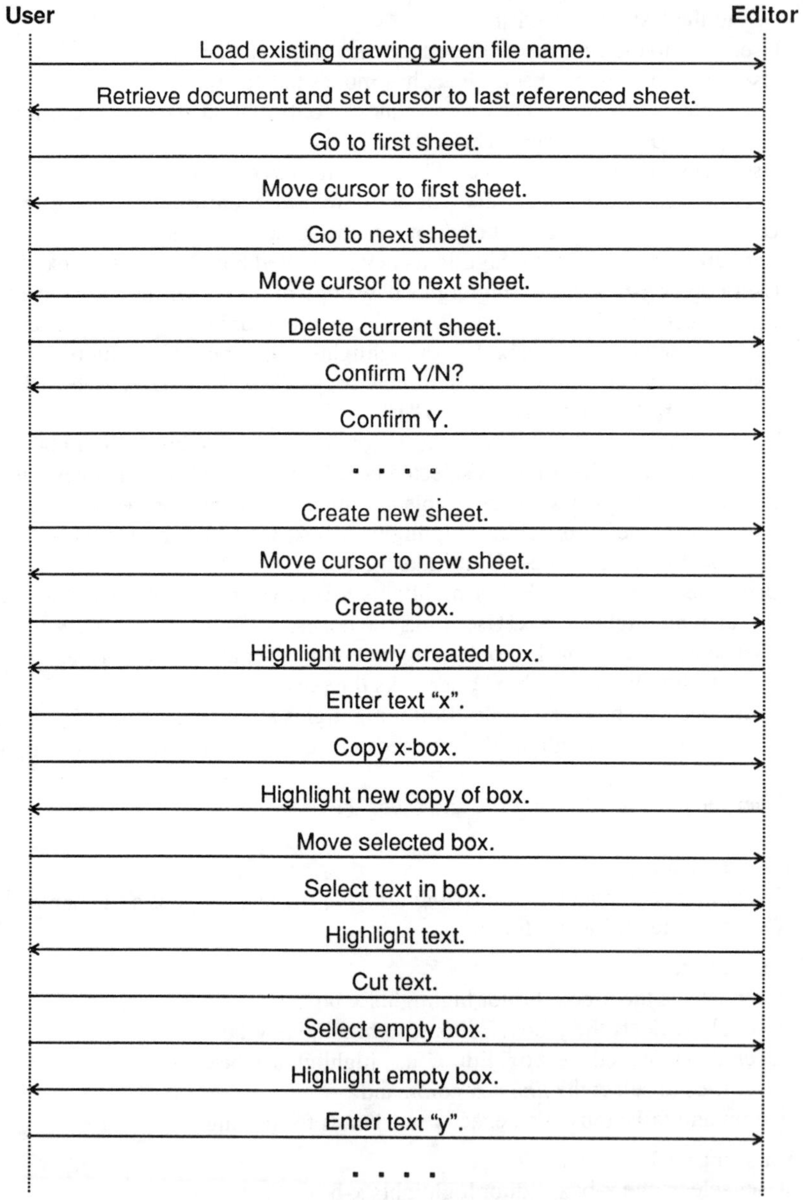

User		Editor
	Load existing drawing given file name.	→
←	Retrieve document and set cursor to last referenced sheet.	
	Go to first sheet.	→
←	Move cursor to first sheet.	
	Go to next sheet.	→
←	Move cursor to next sheet.	
	Delete current sheet.	→
←	Confirm Y/N?	
	Confirm Y.	→
	. . . .	
	Create new sheet.	→
←	Move cursor to new sheet.	
	Create box.	→
←	Highlight newly created box.	
	Enter text "x".	→
	Copy x-box.	→
←	Highlight new copy of box.	
	Move selected box.	→
	Select text in box.	→
←	Highlight text.	
	Cut text.	→
	Select empty box.	→
←	Highlight empty box.	
	Enter text "y".	→
	. . . .	

Figure A8.6 Partial event trace for a normal editor scenario

Figure A8.7 contains the event traces that correspond to Exercise 8.11.

Event trace for error scenario 1:

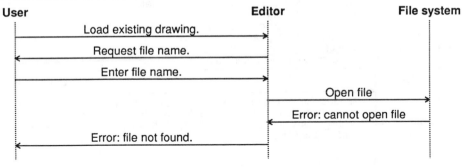

Event trace for error scenario 2:

User   **Editor**

Select x-box.

Highlight x-box.

Also select y-box.

Also highlight y-box.

Also select +-box.

Also highlight +-box.

Link boxes.

Error: must pick exactly 2 boxes for linking.

Event trace for error scenario 3:

User   **Editor**

Select x-box.

Highlight x-box.

Enter text.

Error: box already has text.

Figure A8.7 Event trace for error editor scenarios

8.13   Figure A8.8 contains an event flow diagram for the diagram editor.

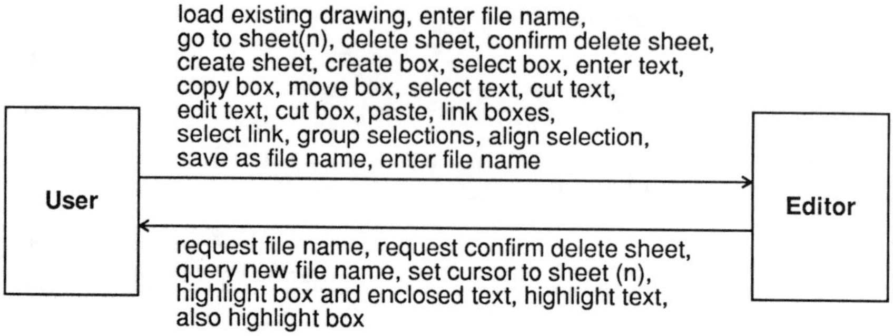

load existing drawing, enter file name,
go to sheet(n), delete sheet, confirm delete sheet,
create sheet, create box, select box, enter text,
copy box, move box, select text, cut text,
edit text, cut box, paste, link boxes,
select link, group selections, align selection,
save as file name, enter file name

User

Editor

request file name, request confirm delete sheet,
query new file name, set cursor to sheet (n),
highlight box and enclosed text, highlight text,
also highlight box

Figure A8.8 Event flow diagram for the simple diagram editor

8.14   [This exercise is much more difficult than indicated in the text. We would rate this exercise as difficulty (10). We recommend that the exercise be simplified as follows: specify what classes require state diagrams and describe some states and events relevant to these classes.]

The following object classes require state diagrams: *Editor, Mouse, Buffer,* and *Selection.*

The *Editor* state diagram coordinates the other state diagrams. Some *Editor* states are: *No active diagram, Active diagram,* and *Confirm action. Editor* events include: *display sheet(n), create sheet, delete sheet, create box,* and *create link.*

The *Mouse* state depends on what combination of buttons are pressed. However the state of the mouse is not important for this problem. The statement that "a three button mouse will be used..." in the description prior to Exercise 8.5 is really an improper software requirement and should be challenged by the developer of the diagram editor. A variety of input devices could be used to convey editing information, such as ASCII text, a mouse, a track ball, and a light pen.

The *Buffer* is used for *copy, cut,* and *paste* operations. The state of the buffer is simple: either it is empty or it is full.

The *Selection* state diagram indicates whether one or more objects are selected. Thus there are two states: *Something selected* and *Nothing selected.* The object model contains important information for the *Something selected* state: precisely which boxes and links are selected. The *pick* operation would need to distinguish between picking the first object selected and picking subsequent objects.

8.15   [This question is too vague and should not be assigned.]

8.16 The following tentative classes should be eliminated.

- Redundant classes. *child, contestant, individual, person, registrant* (all are redundant with competitor).
- Vague or irrelevant classes. *back, card, conclusion, corner, individual prize, leg, pool, prize, team prize, try, water ballet.*
- Attributes. *address, age, average score, child's name, date, difficulty factor, raw score, net score, score, team name*
- Implementation constructs. *file of team member data, list of scheduled meets, number, group.*
- Operations. *compute average, register.*

After eliminating improper classes we are left with *Age category, Competitor, Event, Figure, Judge, League, Meet, Routine, Scorekeeper, Season, Station, Team,* and *Trial.*

The astute reader will notice some of the remaining classes do not appear in Figure E8.4. That is because Figure E8.4 is only a partially completed object diagram. (See our answer to Exercise 8.19 for an improvement to Figure E8.4 regarding *raw score*.)

8.17 We only need to prepare a data dictionary for proper object classes.

- Age category—a sequence of ages into which children are grouped for the purpose of awarding prizes. There is more than one age category. Age categories do not overlap.
- Competitor—a child who participates in a swimming meet.
- Event—a figure performed by a contestant at a swimming meet. For each competitor and figure there is one event and one or more trials.
- Figure—a standard sequence of actions performed by each competitor at a swim meet.
- Judge—a person who rates the quality of a trial at a swimming meet.
- League—a group of teams that compete against one another at swimming meets.
- Meet—a series of events that are performed by two or more swimming teams on a particular date at a specific site.
- Routine—a swimming maneuver which is performed by an entire team at the same time. A high quality routine has a high level of coordination between team members.
- Scorekeeper—a person who records scores at a swimming meet.
- Season—a series of swimming meets that occur in the same summer.
- Station—a location around a swimming pool where each contestant performs a figure. All events for a figure at a given meet are held at one station.
- Team—a group of children who compete at a swimming meet. Each child belongs to exactly one team. A team is treated as a unit for the purpose of awarding team prizes.
- Trial—an attempt by a competitor to perform an event at a swimming meet.

8.18 The following tentative association should be eliminated because it involves an eliminated class:

- *A competitor is assigned a number.* (*Number* is an attribute which has been eliminated.)

The following tentative associations are implementation artifacts:

- *The highest score is discarded.*
- *The lowest score is discarded.*
- *Prizes are based on scores.*
- *Competitors are split into groups.*

The following tentative associations are actions:

- *A competitor registers.*
- *A number is announced.*
- *Raw scores are read.*
- *Figures are processed.*

The following association is derived:

- *A trial of a figure is made by a competitor.* (Replace by *a figure has many events, an event has many trials,* and *a competitor performs many trials.*)

The following associations were missing from the list given in the exercise:

- *A judge may serve at several stations.*
- *A station has many scorekeepers.*
- *Scorekeepers may work at more than one station.*

We are left with the following correct associations and generalizations: *a season consists of several meets, a meet consists of several events, several stations are set up at a meet, several events are processed at a station, several judges are assigned to a station, routines and figures are types of events, a league consists of several teams, a team consists of several competitors, a figure has many events, an event has many trials, a competitor performs many trials, a trial receives several scores from the judges, a judge may serve at several stations, a station has many scorekeepers,* and *scorekeepers may work at more than one station.*

8.19 The object model presented in Figure E8.4 can be improved by making *raw score* a link attribute instead of an object class. *Raw score* does not have significant behavior, properties, or identity; thus it is better represented as an attribute than as an object class. This improvement to the model is shown in Figure A8.9. Our answers to the remaining exercises are based on Figure A8.9. Some of the query statements for this exercise are vague and require interpretation. Our answers to Exercise 8.19 use the same dot notation as the answers to Exercise 8.8.

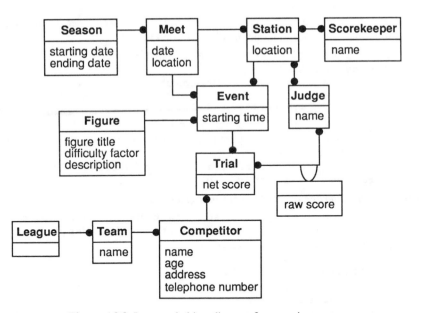

Figure A8.9 Improved object diagram for a scoring system

[Some of our answers to these problems traverse a series of links (such as *season.-meet.event.trial* in answer d). Section 10.9 on page 249 of the textbook states that each class should have limited knowledge of an object model and that operations for a class should not traverse associations that are not directly connected to it. We have violated this principle here to simplify our answers. A more robust answer would define intermediate operations to avoid these lengthy traversals.]

a. *Find all the members of a given team.*

```
Team::retrieve_team_members ()
returns set of competitors
   return self.competitor;
```

b. *Find which figures were held more than once in a given season.*

```
Season::find_repeated_figures () returns set of figures
   answer:= create_empty_set;
   figures:= create_empty_set;
   for each event in self.meet.event
      if event.figure in figures then
         add event.figure to set answer;
      else add event.figure to set figures;
      endif
   end for each event;
   return answer;
```

c. *Find the net score of a competitor for a given figure at a given meet.* There are several ways to answer this question, one of which is listed below.

```
Competitor::find_net_score (figure, meet)
returns net_score
    event:= meet.event intersect figure.event;
        /* the above code should return exactly one    */
        /* event (otherwise there is an implementation */
        /* error). This is a constraint implicit in the */
        /* problem statement which is not expressed in  */
        /* the object model.                            */
    trial := event.trial intersect self.trial;
    return trial.net_score;
```

d. *Find the team average over all figures in a given season.*

```
Team::find_average (season) returns average_score
    trials:= season.meet.event.trial intersect
     self.competitor.trial;
    sum:=0; count:=0;
    for each trial in trials
       add trial.net_score to sum; count++;
    end for each trial
    return sum/count;
```

e. *Find the average score of a competitor over all figures in a given meet.*

```
Competitor::find_average (meet) returns average_score
    trials:= meet.event.trial intersect
        self.trial;
    compute average as in answer (d)
    return average;
```

f. *Find the team average in a given figure at a given meet.*

```
Team::find_average (figure, meet) returns average_score
    trials:= meet.event.trial intersect
        figure.event.trial intersect
        self.competitor.trial;
    compute average as in answer (d)
    return average;
```

g. *Find the set of all individuals who competed in any events in a given season.*

```
Season::find_competitors_for_any_event ()
returns set of competitors
    return self.meet.event.trial.competitor;
```

h. *Find the set of all individuals who competed in all of the events held in a given season.*

```
Season::find_competitors_for_all_events ()
returns set of competitors
    answer:= create_empty_set;
    events:= self.meet.event;
    competitors:= self.meet.event.trial.competitor;
```

```
        for each competitor in competitors
            if competitor.trial.event = events
                /* test for set equality */
                then add competitor to set answer;
            end if
        end for each competitor
        return answer
```

i. *Find the judges who judged a given event in a given season.* [The exercise statement does not fully make sense. Specifying an event implicitly specifies the season. (In the object model, starting with an *Event* and traversing towards *Season* yields a single answer.) We will restate this exercise as: Find the judges who judged a given *figure* in a given season.]

```
    Figure::find_judges (season) returns set of judges
        judges:= create_empty_set;
        stations:= season.meet.station intersect
            self.event.station;
        for each station in stations
            add station.judge to set judges;
        end for each station
        return judges;
```

j. *Find the judge who awarded the lowest score during a given event.*

```
    Event::find_low_scoring_judge () returns judge
        low_score:= INFINITY;
        answer:= NIL;
        for each trial in self.trial
            for each judge in trial.judge
                if link(trial,judge).raw_score < low_score then
                    low_score:= link(trial,judge).raw_score;
                    answer:=judge;
                end if
            end for each judge
        end for each trial
        return answer;
```

k. *Find the judge who awarded the lowest score for a given figure.*

```
    Figure::find_low_scoring_judge () returns judge
        low_score:= INFINITY;
        answer:= NIL;
        for each trial in self.event.trial
            for each judge in trial.judge
                if link(trial,judge).raw_score < low_score then
                    low_score:= link(trial,judge).raw_score;
                    answer:=judge;
                end if
            end for each judge
        end for each trial
        return answer;
```

1. *Modify the diagram so that the competitors registered for an event can be determined.*

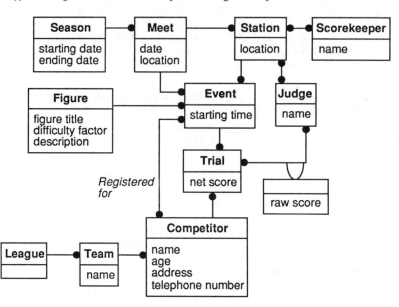

Figure A8.10 Object diagram for a scoring system that supports event registration

8.20 [The exercise statement has a slight error: Difficulty factors are not entered for events, but are entered for figures.]

Scenarios are intrinsically less interesting for the swimming league than for the earlier diagram editor exercise. The diagram editor is an interactive application that has an important dynamic model. The diagram editor has a simple object model and complex user interaction scenarios. In contrast, the swimming league is a data management problem, where most operations merely store and retrieve data. The swimming league has a complex object model and a rich variety of queries, but relatively simple scenarios for acquiring data.

At the beginning of the 1991 swimming season, the following data was entered into the system. The two teams were the Dolphins and the Whales. The six competitors were Heather Martin, Elissa Martin, Cathy Lewis, Christine Brown, Karen Solheim, and Jane Smith. The name, age, address, and telephone number of each competitor was entered into the system. Heather Martin, Elissa Martin, and Cathy Lewis were members of the Dolphins team. The other three competitors were members of the Whales team. The three judges were Bill Martin, Mike Solheim, and Jim Morrow.

The meets were scheduled for July 6 at Niskayuna, July 20 at Glens Falls, and August 3 in Altamont. In each of the three meets the same four figures were scheduled to be performed for a total of twelve events. These figures are the Ballet Leg (1.0), the Dolphin

(1.2), the Front Pike Somersault (1.3), and the Back Pike Somersault (1.5). Difficulty factors for figures are parenthesized.

For the July 6 meet at Niskayuna, the Ballet Leg event was scheduled to begin at 9:00 AM, the Dolphin at 9:00 AM, the Front Pike Somersault at 10:00 AM, and finally the Back Pike Somersault at 10:00 AM.

For the July 20 meet at Glens Falls, the Back Pike Somersault begins at 9:00 AM, the Front Pike Somersault at 9:00 AM, the Dolphin at 10:00 AM, and the Ballet Leg at 10:00 AM.

For the August 3 meet at Altamont, the Ballet Leg event was scheduled to begin at 9:30 AM, the Dolphin at 9:30 AM, the Front Pike Somersault at 10:30 AM, and the Back Pike Somersault at 10:30 AM.

8.21 First error scenario. Someone tries to schedule a meet for July 20 at Voorheesville. This is not permitted, since there is already a meet scheduled for that date at Glens Falls.

Second error scenario. Competitor Karen Solheim tries to give the registrar two phone numbers, one for her home and another for her father's office. The current object model cannot accept this data, since *telephone number* is a simple attribute of *Competitor*.

Third error scenario. Competitor Cathy Lewis informs the registrar that she would like to compete with the Dolphins team on July 6 and 20 and the Whales team on August 3. Christine Brown and Jane Smith will miss the meet on August 3 due to vacation plans, and Cathy Lewis would like to even up the teams. The object model forbids this data entry, since a *Competitor* is specified as belonging to exactly one *Team*.

8.22 Printing forms. For each competitor currently in the system:

- print out the current name, age, address, and telephone number, then
- mail the form to each competitor.

Processing forms. There are a number of possibilities, such as adding a new competitor, deleting an old competitor, keeping records for a competitor but deactivating the competitor for the upcoming season, and changing information for a competitor. Note that *age* is a poor choice of base attribute for the *Competitor* class. The model would be improved by making *birthdate* a base attribute and *age* a derived attribute from the *current date* and *birthdate*.

Karen Solheim returned her form and changed her address from 722 State Street to 1561 Northumberland Drive in anticipation of an upcoming move.

Heather Martin called up to complain because her sister Elissa Martin received a form and she did not. After some checking, it became apparent that the wrong address was entered in the computer for Heater Martin. Heather's address was corrected.

Both Ann Davis and Loren Jones called and said they would be unavailable to compete in the 1990 season. They were kept as competitors in the system, but were no longer assigned to a team. This required a minor change to the object model to make team optional for a competitor.

The object model also requires extension to track contestant number. We decided to add another attribute to the *Competitor* class called *number* to accomplish this. Heather Martin was assigned number 3; Elissa Martin was assigned number 4; and Cathy Lewis was assigned number 1. Christine Brown was assigned number 5; Karen Solheim was assigned number 1; and Jane Smith was assigned number 9. All these numbers were the same as last year. Two competitors may have the same number as long as they are members of different teams.

8.23 The 2 teams were the Dolphins and the Whales. The 4 competitors were Heather Martin, Elissa Martin, Cathy Lewis, and Christine Brown. Stations were set up on the northwest and southeast corners of the pool with three judges each. The 4 events were the Ballet Leg, the Dolphin, the Front Pike Somersault, and the Back Pike Somersault. Heather was number 3. When Heather approached the station to try the Ballet Leg the computer operator called her number as it appeared on the display. When Heather verified her number the operator confirmed it with the computer which was then ready to accept scores. After Heather performed the Ballet Leg the 3 judges held up the scores 3.8, 3.6, and 3.7. A scorekeeper read the scores. As they were read the computer operator entered them into the computer. Another scorekeeper wrote them down and checked the numbers on the computer display after they were entered. In this case the operator made a mistake and the judges were asked to repeat the scores. When everyone was satisfied the operator verified the scores and the computer stored them in a database.

When all of the events were over, the scores from the two stations were merged into a single database. Then the raw scores were converted into net scores for each trial, the overall scores were computed for each competitor, the competitors were sorted by overall score, and the results were printed. The print outs included an ordered listing of the winners and summary sheets for each competitor. The summary sheet for each competitor included raw scores, degree of difficulty, and net scores for each event.

8.24 No classes require object diagrams. The swimming league exercises are a data management type of problem. These types of problems have little interesting dynamic behavior. Even the scenarios are little more than random combinations of data.

8.25 This question is too vague and should not be assigned.

8.26 A partial shopping list of operations is shown in Figure A8.11.

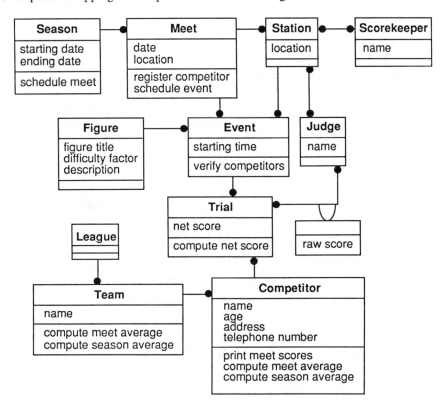

Figure A8.11 Partial object diagram for a scoring system including operations

8.27 The following bullets summarize what the operations should do.

- *schedule meet.* If the meet is not already known, add it to the system along with its required link. (The object model specifies that a meet must have exactly one season.) Specify a date and location for the meet.

- *register competitor.* Given the name of a competitor, make sure that a *Competitor* object is entered into the system. Make sure that the competitor is assigned a team. Note that there is no explicit association between *Meet* and *Competitor*; thus we can make sure that a competitor is known to the system, but the model contains nothing special registering a competitor for a meet.

- *schedule event.* If the event is not already known, add it to the system along with its required links. (The object model specifies that an event must have exactly one figure, meet, and station.) Assign the event a starting time.

- *verify competitors.* Make sure all attributes are filled in for each competitor. Make sure that each competitor is assigned a team.

- *compute net score.* For a given trial, retrieve the set of raw scores from the judges. Delete the high and low score. Average the remaining scores.

- *compute meet average.* For the given team, retrieve *team.competitor.trial.net_score.* For the given meet, retrieve *meet.event.trial.net_score.* Intersect these two sets of scores and compute the average of the resulting set. (Note that we have described the *compute-meet-average* operation with a procedure. The operation need not be computed in the manner that we have specified but may be computed with any algorithm that yields an equivalent result.)

- *compute season average.* For the given team, retrieve *team.competitor.trial.-net_score.* For the given season, retrieve *season.meet.event.trial.net_score.* Intersect these two sets of scores and compute the average of the resulting set.

- *print meet scores.* For the given competitor and meet, retrieve the set of trials. For each trial, print the competitor name, meet date, meet location, and net score.

- *compute meet average.* For the given competitor and meet, retrieve the set of trials. Compute the average of the net scores for these trials.

- *compute season average.* For the given competitor and season, retrieve the set of trials. Compute the average of the net scores for these trials.

8.28 The revised diagrams are shown in Figure A8.12-Figure A8.15. Note that Figure A8.12 could be simplified by combining *Appointment* and *Date-time* and treating *Date-time* as an attribute. Figure A8.15 could be simplified by combining *Edge* and *Incidence.* In general a ternary association can always be converted into a class. Some thought may be required to get the multiplicities right.

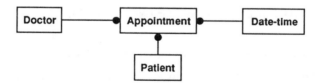

Figure A8.12 Object diagram for appointments

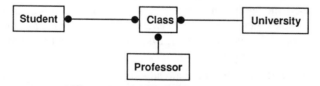

Figure A8.13 Object diagram for classes

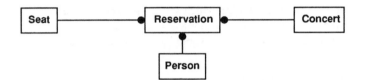

Figure A8.14 Object diagram for reservations

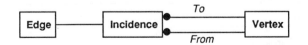

Figure A8.15 Object diagram for graphs

8.29 The event trace for the given scenario is shown in Figure A8.16.

Sender   **Receiver**

Start of transaction

Acknowledge

Start of file

Acknowledge

File data

Acknowledge

File data

Acknowledge

File data

Acknowledge

End of file

Acknowledge

End of transaction

Acknowledge

Figure A8.16 Event trace for a data transmission protocol

8.30 The event trace for a scenario in which several packets are garbled is shown in Figure A8.17. Note that the exercise did not ask for errors caused by corruption of receiver packets. In an actual protocol, this would have to be taken into account.

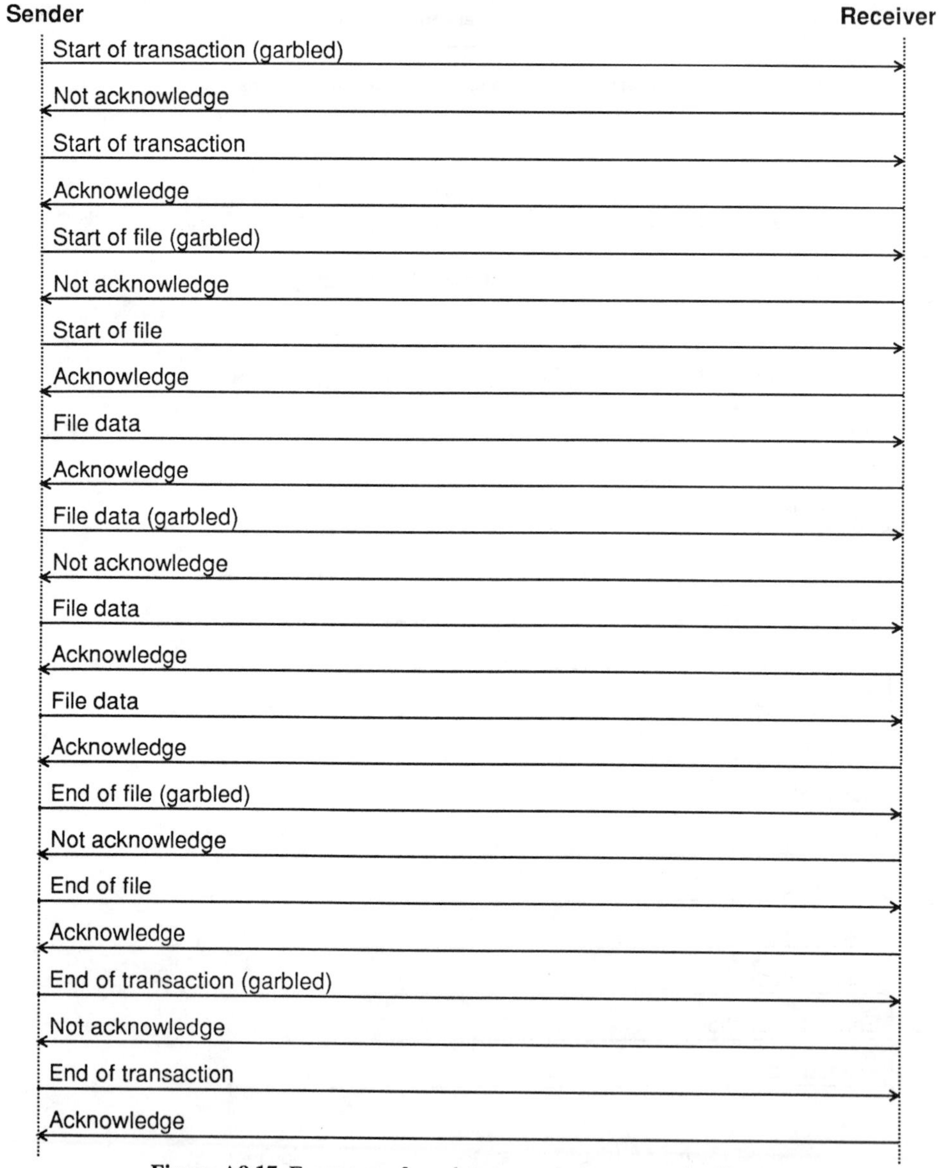

Sender   **Receiver**

Start of transaction (garbled) →

Not acknowledge ←

Start of transaction →

Acknowledge ←

Start of file (garbled) →

Not acknowledge ←

Start of file →

Acknowledge ←

File data →

Acknowledge ←

File data (garbled) →

Not acknowledge ←

File data →

Acknowledge ←

File data →

Acknowledge ←

End of file (garbled) →

Not acknowledge ←

End of file →

Acknowledge ←

End of transaction (garbled) →

Not acknowledge ←

End of transaction →

Acknowledge ←

Figure A8.17 Event trace for a data transmission protocol with errors

8.31   State diagrams are needed for both the sender and the receiver. We assume that a separate process supplies the sender with files to be sent and that another process stores the data on the receiver end. A simplified state diagram for the sender is shown in Figure A8.18. The state diagram for the receiver is shown in Figure A8.19. The abbreviations *ack* and *nack* are used for acknowledged and not acknowledged. The states needed to control the flow of data to processes that supply the sender and service the receiver are not shown in the diagrams. Note that neither of the state diagrams deals very well with complete system failure. In practice, time outs and retry counts would probably be used to make the system more robust.

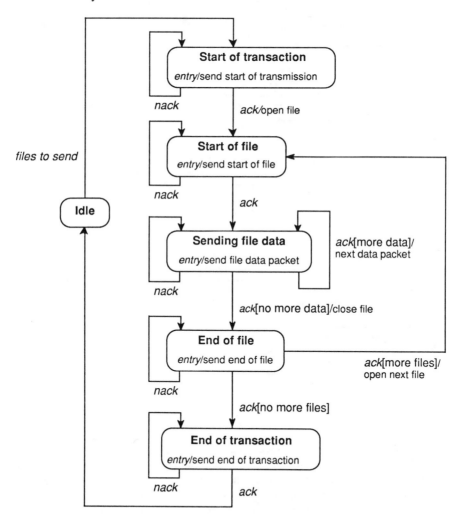

Figure A8.18 State diagram for the sender

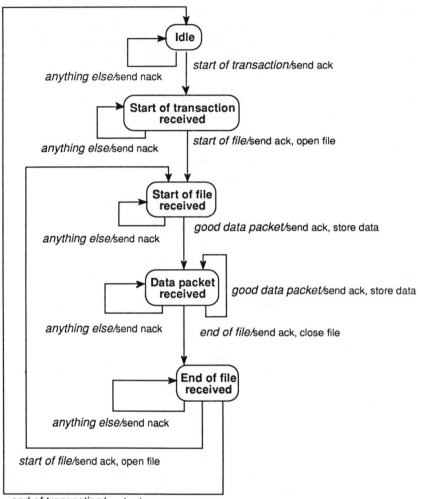

Figure A8.19 State diagram for the receiver

8.32 Figure A8.20 shows a simple state diagram for a cashier station. On beginning work a cashier inserts a key, enters the cashier's code number, and enters the amount of cash in the cash drawer. The cashier may obtain the purported cash drawer balance by hitting the "balance" key or may hit the "transaction" key to begin a transaction. The first part of the transaction is the entry of the customer's ID number, after which a series of withdrawal or deposit entries can be made. When all the entries have been made, the cashier

hits "process" to execute the transaction. The cashier may hit "cancel" to cancel a transaction and discard any entries.

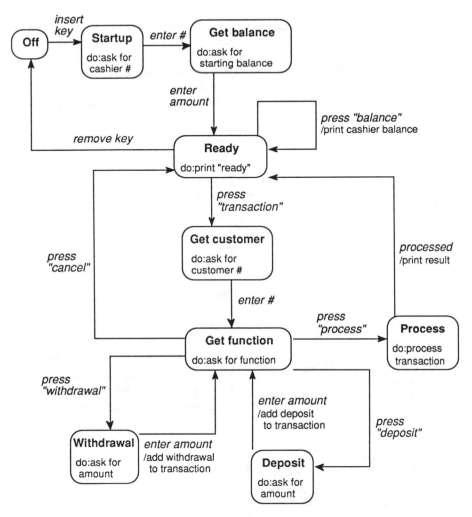

Figure A8.20 State diagram for a cashier station

This is a minimal dynamic model. It could be improved in various ways: Enclose all
of the states except *Off* in a superstate called *On* and draw the *remove key* transaction
from *On* to *Off*, so that removal of the key in any state turns off the machine. Nest some
of the other states so that *cancel* can be entered at any state, such as in the *Withdrawal*
or *Deposit* states. Add more functions, such as a closedown operation in which the cashier enters the amount of cash in the drawer for reconciliation.

8.33a. Candidate keys are *Flight + Seat* and *Flight + Person.*

    b. The only candidate key is *Flight + Seat.*

8.34 There are several ways to use generalization to improve the object diagram given in this exercise. One possibility is shown in Figure A8.21. We recommend that you discuss with the students whether the attributes and methods are correctly placed. For example, strictly speaking, the operation *open file* is misplaced in the class *File.* After all, an instance of a file is not actually available until after the file is opened. It would be better if it were renamed *open* and placed in the class *File descriptor.* Similarly, *create file* and *create descriptor* are probably misplaced.

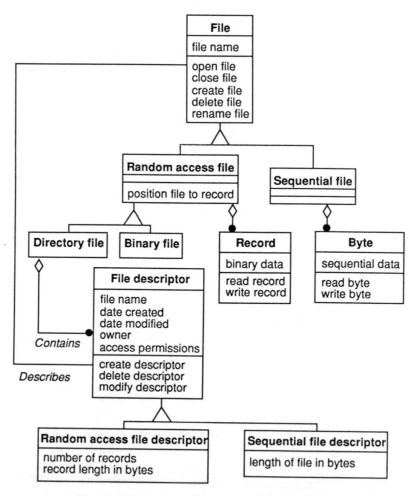

Figure A8.21 An improved object diagram for a file system

9

System Design

9.1 a. An electronic chess companion combines features of interactive interface and batch transformation architectures. Entering and displaying moves is dominated by interactions between the chess companion and the human user. Once a human has entered a move, the activity of the chess companion is a batch transformation in which the positions of the pieces on the board are used to compute the next move.

b. An airplane flight simulator for a video game system combines features of interactive interface and dynamic simulation architectures. Interactive features include interpreting the joystick input and displaying cockpit information and the view of the terrain. Simulation involves computing the motion of the airplane. Another acceptable answer is interactive interface and continuous transformation, since computing the motion of the airplane is done by a continuous transformation of the joystick input.

c. A floppy disk controller chip is predominately a real-time system. With the possible exception of computing a cyclic redundancy code, there are practically no computations. Strict timing constraints must be satisfied to avoid losing data. The most important part of the design is the state diagram.

d. A sonar system is mainly a continuous transformation with some real time and some interactive interface aspects. Converting a continuous stream of pulses and echoes into range information is a continuous transformation. Because the system must process the data as fast as it comes in, there is a real-time flavor. Display of the range information involves interactive interface issues.

9.2 a. Procedural control is adequate for the chess companion since the user interface is simple.

b. Event driven control is recommended for the flight simulator, to accept push button events and a timing interrupt to pace the display update so that the apparent flight velocity does not change with the complexity of the calculations. Procedural control can be used, but the quality of the simulation will suffer. We assume that the terrain is static; otherwise we would consider concurrent control to handle the motion of other objects.

c. A floppy disk controller requires hardware control, not software control. Hardware controls are typically designed using state diagrams, which are relatively easy to convert into hardware. One way to do this is to use micro-coding. The state diagrams are converted into a procedure which in turn is implemented as a sequence of micro-instructions. Each output of the controller is typically controlled by one of the bit fields in an instruction. Instructions for branching and looping based on inputs and controller registers are usually available.

d. The real time aspect of the sonar system makes concurrent control desirable.

9.3   It is totally out of the question to store the data samples without buffering. For example, during the 10 milliseconds that the read/write head takes to move from one track to the next, 160 bytes would be lost. It is clear that a buffer is needed. We will discuss some of the constraints and control issues. Then we will present a couple of approaches.

A system architect would probably question the decision to limit the buffer size to 64000 bytes. Memory is cheap, and 160000 bytes would be enough to store all of the samples, greatly simplifying the design. However, within the context of this problem, 64000 bytes is a constraint.

Careful system design can reduce the size of the buffer. It is a good idea to store the data in sequential tracks to minimize the time spent in moving from one track to the next. Beyond that, there are special track formats to reduce the time lost moving between tracks. For example, if only a portion of a track is used or if the tracks are carefully arranged, the beginning of one track could be at the read/write head just as the head has completed an adjacent track.

Another dimension to consider is whether or not the buffer can be emptied while a track is being written. If it can, there is some hope of making the buffer only as large as required to store data that would be lost during the head motion between tracks. Otherwise the buffer may have to hold several tracks of data. First, estimate the rate that data can be written to the disk. The average time to find the beginning of a track, 83 milliseconds, is approximately equal to the time for the disk to turn one half of a revolution, so it takes about 166 milliseconds to make a complete turn. Therefore, the disk is revolving 6 times in a second. The number of bytes per track is approximately equal to the total storage, 243000 bytes, divided by the number of tracks, 77, or about 3155 bytes per track. (51 tracks are needed, leaving 26 tracks on the disk for other functions.) The rate at which data could be written to the disk is equal to the bytes per track times the spinning rate, or about 18935 bytes per second. This is greater than the rate of data input so there is some hope of sizing the buffer for a single track.

There are two control aspects to consider: initiating data storage and servicing the analog to digital converters and the disk drive.

We must assume that the initiation of data storage is to be controlled externally, because there is no reason for us to believe that our product will be able to control the events that are generating the data.

Another aspect of control is servicing the converters and the disk drive. Two common approaches are polling and interrupt driven. Polling involves continuously checking the status of both devices and transferring data as needed. This approach simplifies the hardware design at the expense of tying up the CPU during the capture of data. The interrupt driven approach relies on a hardware interrupt controller to notify the CPU when external devices need servicing, freeing up the CPU to do other tasks in the meantime. Our choice will depend on whether or not there is anything to do while data is being collected. It is also entirely possible that the interrupt driven approach has been selected to satisfy the requirements of other functions of the product, so we would want to explore further before making a decision.

We now analyze a couple of approaches:

- Sequential tracks, standard formatting with a buffer that holds several tracks

The simplest solution is to not use any special disk formatting, for which a worst case analysis is indicated. For each 3155 byte track that is written, it will take 10 milliseconds to position the head, up to 166 milliseconds for the beginning of the track to come around, and 166 milliseconds to write the track. During this time, 5488 bytes come in, so the buffer is filling faster that it can be emptied.

Without special formatting, it takes 342 milliseconds to complete a track. During the 10 seconds that it takes for all data to come in, a little over 29 tracks can be written. To be on the safe side, plan on writing 91495 bytes to the disk in 10 seconds. This leaves over 68000 bytes for the buffer, so this approach will not work unless we increase the amount of memory in the system.

- Sequential tracks, special disk formatting with a buffer for one track

If the disk is formatted carefully, the time to find the beginning of a track after completing an adjacent track can be reduced. This time will not be zero, because we will want some margin for error. The problem statement does not give any information about variations in disk speed, but 5 milliseconds (representing a 3 percent variation in disk speed) should give us sufficient margin for error. By careful formatting, the total time to write a track could be cut to 181 milliseconds. During this time, only 2896 bytes is input, which is less than a track, so the strategy could work. Because the system has no control over when the data starts coming in, it must be prepared to buffer one complete track of data. This approach will work with a buffer of 3155 bytes.

9.4   This system combines features of an interactive interface with a batch transformation. An interactive interface is needed to edit drawings. Converting a drawing to an N/C tape is a batch transformation. Determining an efficient sequence of drilling operations is a form of the traveling salesman problem. The optimum solution would take a long time to compute, and is not really needed for this application. There are several engineering solutions that produce a reasonably efficient sequence of operations without using a lot of computing resources. An excellent algorithm is given by John D. Litke in "An Improved Solution to the Traveling Salesman Problem with Thousands of Nodes", *Communications of the ACM*, Volume 27, Number 12, December 1984, 1227-1236.

It is convenient to break the system into three major subsystems: editor, planner, and puncher. The editor could be subdivided into user interface, graphics display and file interface. Everything runs on a PC, so there is no question of assigning subsystems to hardware devices. The editor is used to prepare drawings. The planner determines a sequence of operations to accomplish the drilling. The puncher, which incorporates a driver for operating a punch, prepares an N/C tape.

There are no concurrency issues. A sequential approach is adequate. Experience has shown that a PC is adequate for two dimensional drafting.

Control must be considered for the editor and the puncher. Either procedural control or event driven control is suitable for the puncher. The editor should be event driven. Global resources are adequately handled by the operating system of the PC.

9.5   The interface is simplified by being line oriented, leaving the bulk of the work to be done on the batch transformations required to execute the commands.

There are three major subsystems: user interface, file interface and expression construction. There is no inherent concurrency. It is assumed that the system operates on a sufficiently powerful computer. Files are adequate to store previous work. During the design phase a language for representing expressions should be designed. Global resources are adequately handled by the operating system of the computer. A procedural approach is adequate for control.

9.6   Figure A9.1 shows one possible partitioning.

command processing						
user interface	construct expression				file interface	
line semantics	apply operation	substitute	rationalize	evaluate	save	load
line syntax						
operating system						

Figure A9.1 Block diagram for an interactive polynomial symbolic manipulation system

9.7   A single program provides faster detection and correction of errors and eliminates the need to implement an interface between two programs. With a single program, any errors that the system detects in the process of converting the object diagram to a database schema can be quickly communicated to the user for correction. Also, the editing and the conversion portions of the program can share the same data, eliminating the need for an interface such as a file to transfer the object diagram from one program to another.

Splitting the functionality into two programs reduces memory requirements and decouples program development. The total memory requirement of a single program would be approximately equal to the sum of the requirements of two separate programs. Since both programs are likely to use a great deal of memory, performance problems could arise if they are combined. Using two separate programs also simplifies program development. The two programs can be developed independently, so that changes made in one are less likely to impact the other. Also, two programs are easier to debug than one monolithic program. If the interface between the two programs is well defined, problems in the overall system can be quickly identified within one program or the other.

Another advantage of splitting the system into two programs is greater flexibility. The editor can be used with other back ends such as generating language code declarations. The relational database schema generator can be adapted to other graphical front ends.

9.8 a. A single geometrical model completely describes an object diagram, but would be too low level a representation. It is tedious to construct object diagrams by drawing lines, boxes, text, and so forth. Deriving the logical model from the physical representation is possible, but is time consuming and ambiguous.

b. Two separate models. This is the best solution, because it decouples two independent views of an object diagram, making both views less cluttered and easier to understand during system design. The geometrical model is useful for preparing printouts. The logical model is useful for semantic checking and interacting with the backend programs which need to know what the diagram means but do not care about the precise manner in which it is drawn.

9.9 The fastest way to implement the system is to use a commercially available desktop publishing system to edit the object diagrams, the approach that was taken in the application described in Chapter 18. This eliminates the need to design and implement interactive graphics software, a step that is time consuming and error prone. As a bonus, there will be probably be good user documentation for the desktop system and vendor support. The impact of future enhancements made by the vendor is uncertain. On the one hand, the added functionality may make the overall system more attractive. On the other hand, future releases of the commercial system may change the markup language.

Implementing your own editor will result in a more robust system because the system can be designed to allow the user to draw only valid object diagrams. With the desktop editor, it is possible to draw pictures which cannot be interpreted as object diagrams. Also, because your own editor can be customized to the semantics of object diagrams, it will be easier and faster to use than the general-purpose desktop publishing system.

9.10 A block diagram of the transformation is shown in Figure A9.2. The first transformation performs syntactical and semantic analysis of the input file, creating instances in the document model for each item encountered. The second transformation converts the raw information in the document model into networks by determining intersections. The third transformation analyzes the connectivity information in the connection model. The fourth transformation decides how to implement the object model in the form of database tables. The last transformation is simply a printing operation. See Chapter 18 for more details. Note that two steps in this exercise have been combined into one step in Chapter 18.

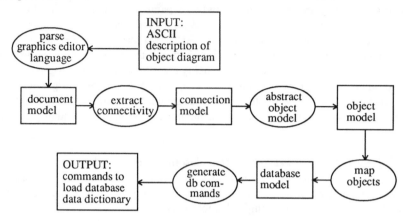

Figure A9.2 Transformation of a desktop publishing system file into a relational database schema

9.11   The reader should note that this problem does not give an exhaustive list of solutions.

   a. *Do not worry about it at all. Reset all data every time the system is turned on.* This is the cheapest, simplest approach. It is relatively easy to program, since all that is needed is an initialization routine on power up to allow the user to enter parameters. However, this approach cannot be taken for systems which must provide continuous service or which must not lose data during power loss.

   b. *Never turn the power off if it can be helped. Use a special power supply, including back-up generators, if necessary.* This approach is used for critical systems which must provide continuous service no matter what. This kind of power supply is called an UPS (uninterruptible power supply) and is relatively expensive. A bonus of this approach is that the application program is simplified, since it is assumed to be always running.

   c. *Keep critical information on a magnetic disk drive. Periodically make full and/or incremental copies on magnetic tape.* This approach is moderately expensive and bulky. In the event of a power failure, the system stops running. An operating system is required to cope with the disk and tape drive. An operator is required to manage the tapes, which would preclude applications where unattended operation is required.

   d. *Use a battery to maintain power to the system memory when the rest of the system is off. It might even be possible to continue to provide limited functionality.* This solution is relatively cheap, compact, and requires no operator. The main drawback of this approach is having to remember to change the battery periodically. In many applications, the user may not be aware that there is a battery that needs to be changed.

e. *Use a special memory component.* This approach is relatively cheap and is automatic. However, the system cannot run when power is off. Some restrictions may apply such as a limit on the number of times data can be saved or on the amount of data that can be saved. A program may be required to save important parameters as power is failing.

f. *Critical parameters are entered by the user through switches.* This approach is very well suited to certain types of data, such as options, that are set only once, and is relatively cheap. Usually only a limited amount of data can be entered this way. Of course, the program cannot save any data through this scheme.

9.12a. *Four function pocket calculator.* Do not worry about permanent data storage at all. All of the other options are too expensive to consider. This type of calculator sells for a few dollars and is typically used to balance checkbooks. Memory requirements are on the order of 10 bytes.

b. *Electronic typewriter.* Memory requirements are on the order of 10,000 to 100,000 bytes per document. The system does not need to function when power is off, but the work in progress should not be lost. Commercially available electronic typewriters typically use floppy disk drives, backup batteries or special memory components. Each of these methods will preserve data for more than a year. The advantage of floppy disk drives is that they can be used to store many documents. Backup batteries or special memory components cost less than disk drives, and are used in some of the less expensive models even though they have limited storage capacity. Some electronic typewriters use memory modules that can be removed from the typewriter. Memory modules are more expensive than floppy disks, but are more immune to the hazards that smoke, dirt, bending and liquid spills present to floppy disk drives, so are better suited to users who are not familiar with floppy disk drives.

c. *System clock for a personal computer.* Only a few bytes are required, but the clock must continue to run with the main power off. Battery backup is an inexpensive solution. Clock circuits can be designed that will run for 5 years from a battery.

d. *Airline reservation system.* The amount of data to be stored is very large. Use a combination of uninterruptible power supplies, disk drives and magnetic tapes. This application requires that the system always is available. Expense is secondary consideration.

e. *Digital control and thermal protection unit for a motor.* On the order of 10 to 100 bytes are needed. This application is sensitive to price. An uninterruptable power supply is too expensive to consider. Tape and disk drives are too fragile for the harsh environment of the application. Use a combination of switches, special memory components, and battery backup. Switches are a good way to enter parameters, since an interface is required anyway. Special memory components can store computed data. A battery can be used to continue operation with power removed but presents a maintenance problem in this application. We would question this requirement, seeking alternatives such as assuming that the motor is hot when it is first turned on or using a sensor to measure the temperature of the motor.

9.13a. A description of the diagram, assuming that tabs, spaces, and line feeds are ignored, is:

```
(DIAGRAM
    (CLASS
        (NAME "Polygon"))
    (CLASS
        (NAME "Point")
        (ATTRIBUTE "x")
        (ATTRIBUTE "y"))
    (ASSOCIATION
        (ROLE (NAME "Polygon") ONE)
        (ROLE (NAME "Point") MANY)))
```

b. Data in storage and data in motion are similar in that they can convey the same information. The same format can be used to store data or to transmit it from one location to another. In fact, many operating systems provide services that work equally well on files or on streams of data. The answer to the first part of this problem could be interpreted as either a format for a file or for a data transmission. Both data in storage and data in motion have semantics and syntax that can be described using the same tools. The point is, the distinction between data stores and data flows in data flow diagrams is not all that sharp.

c. We give both production rules and a diagram for the language to describe polygons. Each production rule is a nonterminal, followed by ::=, followed by a (possibly empty) string of nonterminals and terminals. Nonterminals are lower case identifiers. The productions rules for the language are:

```
diagram ::= ( DIAGRAM list_of_polygons_opt );
list_of_polygons_opt ::=
                          | list_of_polygons;
list_of_polygons ::= polygon
                          | list_of_polygons polygon;
polygon ::= ( POLYGON list_of_points );
list_of_points ::= point
                     | list_of_points point;
point ::= ( POINT x y );
```

We have chosen to allow an empty list of polygons but a polygon must contain at least one point. Other definitions are possible. The nonterminals x and y are integers. The corresponding BNF is shown in Figure A9.3.

An example of a square in this language is:

```
( DIAGRAM
    ( POLYGON
        ( POINT 0 0 )
        ( POINT 10 0 )
        ( POINT 10 10 )
        ( POINT 0 10 )))
```

An example of a triangle in this language is:

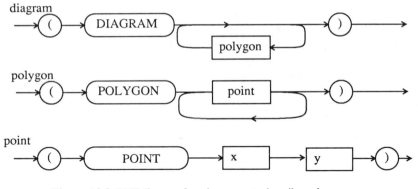

Figure A9.3 BNF diagram for a language to describe polygons

```
( DIAGRAM
    ( POLYGON
        ( POINT 10 0 )
        ( POINT 10 10 )
        ( POINT 0 10 )))
```

In both cases the points are listed in the order of their connectivity.

9.14 The hardware approach is fastest, but incurs the cost of the hardware. The software approach is cheapest and most flexible, but may not be fast enough. Use the software approach whenever it is fast enough. General purpose systems favor the software approach, because of its flexibility. Special purpose systems can usually integrate the added circuitry with other hardware.

Actually, there is another approach, firmware, that may be used in hardware architectures. Typically, in this approach a hardware controller calculates the CRC under the direction of a microcoded program that is stored in a permanent memory that is not visible externally. We will count this approach as hardware.

a. Use a hardware approach for a floppy disk controller. Flexibility is not needed, since a floppy disk controller is a special purpose system. Speed is needed, because of the high data rate.

b. Use a software approach for a system to transmit data files from one computer to another over telephone lines. This system is a general purpose one, capable of running on a variety of computers. Data rates are relatively modest.

c. Use hardware to check memory. This is an example of a very specific application, where the function can probably be integrated with the circuitry in the memory chips. The data rate is very high.

d. Use hardware or software for a magnetic tape drive, depending on the data rate and quality of the tape drive, and the application. If the drive is tightly integrated into a larger, specialized system, and the data rate is not too high, it may be cheaper to compute the CRC in software. On the other hand, if the tape drive is a general purpose one, or if the data rate is high, a hardware approach is better.

e. Use a software approach to validate an account number. The data rate is very low. The system handling the account number is probably running on a general purpose computer.

9.15   (Project)

10

Object Design

10.1a. For a circle of radius R centered at the origin, we have $x^2 + y^2 = R^2$. Solving for y, we get $y = \pm\sqrt{(R^2 - x^2)}$. We can generate a point for each x coordinate by scanning x from $-R$ to R in steps of one pixel and computing y. The center point of the circle must be added to each generated point. This simple algorithm is both inefficient and leaves large vertical gaps in the circle near $x = \pm R$ where the slope is great. More sophisticated algorithms compute 8 points at once, taking advantage of the symmetry about the axes, and also space the points so that there are no gaps. See *Fundamentals of Interactive Computer Graphics* by Foley and Van Dam for details.

b. For an ellipse centered at the origin with axes A and B parallel to the coordinate axes, we have $(x/A)^2 + (y/B)^2 = 1$. We can solve for y in terms of x as for the circle. The equations are more complicated if the axes are not parallel to the coordinate axes. The same objections apply to this simple algorithm as to the previous one, and better algorithms exist.

c. Drawing a square is simply drawing a rectangle whose sides are equal. Unlike a circle, there is little advantage to treating a square as a special case. See Part d.

d. To draw a rectangle of width $2A$ and height $2B$ with sides parallel to the coordinate axes centered at (X, Y), fill in all pixels with ordinates $Y-B$ and $Y+B$ between abscissas $X-A$ and $X+A$, and fill in all pixels with abscissas $X-A$ and $X+A$ between ordinates $Y-B+1$ and $Y+B-1$. If the rectangle is not parallel to the coordinate axes, then line segments must be converted to pixel values. This is more complicated than it seems because of the need for efficiency, avoiding gaps, and avoiding a jagged appearance ("aliasing").

[This problem is either very easy or very hard. Since the problem was rated as a "3" then very simple answers such as the ones given here should be acceptable. In reality converting real-valued functions to pixels is a subtle and difficult topic because of the incompatibility of mapping real numbers into integers. It is covered at length in most graphics texts under the title of "scan conversion."]

10.2 Certainly any algorithm that draws ellipses must draw circles, since they are ellipses, and any algorithm that draws rectangles must draw squares. The real question is whether it is worthwhile providing special algorithms to draw circles and squares. There is little or no advantage in an algorithm for squares, because both squares and rectangles are made of straight lines anyway. An algorithm for circles can be slightly faster than one for ellipses. This may be of value in applications where high speed is required, but is probably not worthwhile otherwise.

10.3 A general n-th order polynomial has the form $\sum_{i=0}^{n} a_i x^i$. Each term requires i multiplications and one addition (except the 0-th term), so computing the sum of the individual terms requires $\sum_{i=1}^{n} i = \frac{n(n+1)}{2}$ multiplications and n additions. Computing the sum by successive multiplication and addition requires one multiplication and one addition for each degree above zero, or a total of n multiplications and n additions. The second approach is not only more efficient than the first approach, it is better behaved numerically, because there is less likelihood of subtracting two large terms yielding a small difference. There is no merit at all to the first approach and every reason to use the second approach.

10.4 [This question is unfortunately backwards. It would have been better to give models containing associations and ask how to implement them in terms of data structures. As it stands, the question asks how to model something already implemented in terms of various data structures. The question could also be read to ask for a model of the *implementation* of each of these data structures. This is not our intent but a student answering that question should not be penalized.]

a. to d.

All of these first four data structures implement an ordered something-to-many association. The distinctions among them are the operations they support which may be considered implementation distinctions that can be used to optimize access but which are not part of the logical model.

e. Here is a simple although slightly incorrect model of a binary tree.

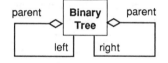

The problem is that a subtree cannot be both a left subtree and a right subtree but can participate in only one parent association. The following model is more precise:

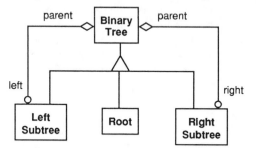

A given binary tree may or may not have a left or right subnode (one might quibble about whether a node is allowed to have only a single subnode and if so, what kind it should be). A given binary tree can either be a root node or a left subtree or a right subtree of a larger tree.

10.5 The following model enforces a constraint that is missing in Figure E10.1: Each boundary corresponds to exactly one ellipse or rectangle. One measure of the quality of an object diagram is how well its structure captures constraints.

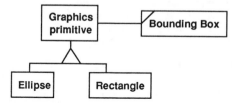

Another improvement is renaming "Boundary" as "BoundingBox." One might expect the boundary to be the perimeter of the figure. Choosing names carefully is important to avoid confusion and misunderstanding. Be careful not to use familiar words in an unconventional way.

We have also shown BoundingBox as a derived object, because it would be computable from the parameters of the graphic figure and would not supply additional information.

[This answer has been expanded slightly from the answer in the book. Don't penalize students for not renaming or deriving the class, because it was not asked for.]

10.6 [This question is poorly phrased in the book. A better phrasing would be: "Which class(es) in the object diagram must supply a delete operation visible to the outside world? Delete means to destroy an object and remove it from the application."]

All of the classes will probably implement a delete method, but the GraphicsPrimitive class must define *delete* as an externally-visible operation. Very likely an application will contain mixed sets of GraphicsPrimitive objects. A typical operation is to delete a GraphicsPrimitive component from a set. The client program need not know the class of a component; all that matters is that it supplies a delete operation. Of course, it may be that Ellipse and Rectangle have to implement the operation as distinct methods, but they inherit the operation protocol from the origin class GraphicsPrimitive. Class Boundary (or BoundingBox) must also define a delete operation, but this should not be visible to the outside world. A Boundary (or BoundingBox) object is a derived object and may not be deleted independently of its GraphicsPrimitive. The delete operation is visible only as an implementation method visible to class GraphicsPrimitive.

10.7 Text is a String. Each of the other attributes is a Coordinate. Coordinate is a type that represents a measure of length. It may be defined as an integer or a real value. Defining a separate type Coordinate is better than expressing these attributes directly as Integer or Real values because a separate type permits us to change the definition of the type or the units of measure (pixels, millimeters, picas, etc.).

10.8 As it stands, line objects need not be moved when a column is moved, because their positions are relative to the location of the column they are in.

For efficiency, we might add the location of each line as an attribute of the Line class. Let us also assume that things must be redisplayed after they are moved. Then the algorithm to move a column would look like:

```
Column::move(newx:Coordinate,newy:Coordinate) is
    set location of column to new values;
    set current line location to column location;
    for each line:Line in the column do
        display the line at the current line location;
        add line height to the current line location;
    end
```

10.9 Each page has an explicit PageSize object that tells how big it is. Each PageSize object has an associated PageMargins object that specifies the default margin settings for pages of that size. Any page can explicitly specify a PageMargins object to override the default margin settings.

It would also be acceptable to have a single PageMargins object for the entire newspaper, but the solution we have given is somewhat more versatile, because the margin settings are likely to be affected by page size. The PageMargins values could also be embedded in the PageSize class as attributes.

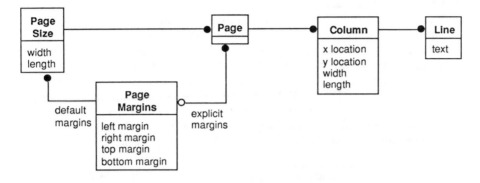

10.10 The answer depends on whether the model is used only to generate output (going from a document to the individual lines) or whether the model is also used to take input (the user picks a line at random and operates on it). In the latter case, it is probably best to implement each association in both directions. If the model is used only for output, then the associations might only be traversed in one direction, from page to column and from column to line. However, from line to column and from column to page is of multiplicity "one" so there is little to be gained by not implementing the association in both directions.

The lines within a column should be ordered. We need to know more about the problem to determine if the columns on a page should be ordered. If text is to flow from page to page when changes are made, columns should be ordered, otherwise there is little advantage to having ordered columns.

To implement the associations using pointers: Each Page object has an attribute that is a Set of Column objects. Each Column object has an attribute that is a List of Line objects and an attribute that is the Page containing the column. Each Line object has an attribute that is the Column containing the line.

10.11 A derived association supports direct traversal from *Page* to *Line*. In general derived entities present a trade-off: They speed execution of certain queries but incur an update cost to keep the redundant data consistent with the base data whenever the base data is changed.

The line-page association is derived by composing the line-column and column-page associations. Since it is present for optimization, it would probably be traversed only from lines to pages and could therefore be implemented as a pointer attribute within class *Line*.

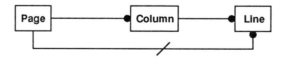

10.12 We assume an ordinary 52-card deck. Type *Rank* is an enumeration of {Ace, King, Queen, Jack, 10, 9, 8, 7, 6, 5, 4, 3, 2}. The ranks are ordered but the order varies from game to game (some games rank the ace highest, some lowest). Depending on the games to be supported, the enumeration could be ordered or unordered. If the enumeration is unordered, then an ordering function must be provided to rank values in a particular game. (In some games, the ranking varies by suit.) Type *Suit* is an enumeration of {Spade, Club, Heart, Diamond}. For many games, suits are unordered; the order of suits varies in other games, so an ordering function on suit values is probably best. Suit and rank could also be implemented as objects rather than pure values, given the complexity of the ordering functions and other peculiarities of real card games.

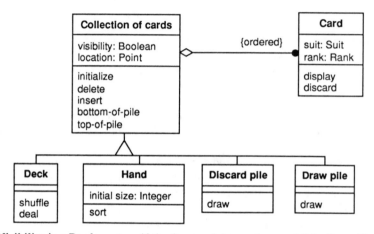

Visibility is a Boolean, true if the fronts of the cards are visible. It could also be implemented as an enumeration type with values {Front, Back}, in which case its name should be changed to *visibleSide* or something like that.

10.13 While writing pseudocode, we discover the need for some modifications to the object model. We introduce a new abstract class *Pile* to include *Deck, DiscardPile,* and *Draw-Pile.* We also add some internal methods to help in implementation. We also discover that a couple of operations, such as *bottom-of-pile* and *top-of-pile*, are misplaced in the class hierarchy. We also note some abstract operations on the diagram.

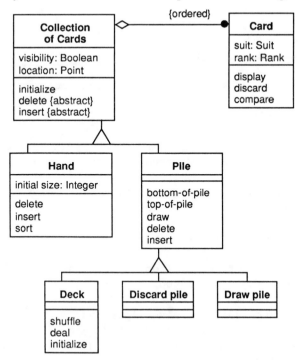

Note: The notation Collection-Card[collection] means to traverse the Collection-Card association from a given collection object to card objects, in this case returning a set of cards. The value returned is a set or scalar accordingly as the multiplicity is many or one.

```
CollectionOfCards :: initialize ()
{
    // This default method is inherited by all classes except
       Deck
    Clear the set Collection-Card[self]
}
Deck :: initialize ()
{
    // This method overrides the default inherited method
    // to set up the deck.
    // The deck still needs to be shuffled explicitly.
    Clear the set Collection-Card[self];
    for each suit in the enumerated set Suit do:
```

```
        for each rank in the enumerated set Rank do:
            create card := Card (suit, rank);
            add (deck, card) to Collection-Card;
        end;
    end;
    visibility := FALSE;// assume a deck is face down
    location := default_deck_location;
    // place deck on a default screen location
}
Pile :: delete (card: Card)
{
    if card ≠ self.topOfPile() then report an error and return;
    delete (self, card) from Collection-Card association;
    topcard := self.topOfPile();
    topcard.display (self.location, self.visibility);
    // the new top picture overwrites the old one
}
Hand :: delete (card: Card)
{
    delete (self, card) from Collection-Card association;
    if nothing was deleted, then report an error and return;
    // we assume that a hand is displayed from left-to-right
    // starting at the given location
    erase the image of the deleted card;
    shift the images of any remaining cards one position to the
        left;
}
Pile :: insert (card: Card)
{
    // insertions onto piles go on the top
    append (self, card) to the end of the Collection-Card
        association;
    card.display (self.location, self.visibility);
}
Hand :: insert (card: Card)
{
    add (self, card) to the Collection-Card association
        according to the sort order of cards;
    shift the images of any cards to the right of the insert
        point one position to the right;
    display the image of the inserted card;
}
Pile :: top_of_pile (): Card
```

```
{
    if the pile is empty, then return nil;
    return Collection-Card[self].last;
}
Pile :: bottom_of_pile (): Card
{
    if the pile is empty, then return nil;
    return Collection-Card[self].first;
}
Deck :: shuffle ()
{
    ncards := number of cards in Collection-Card[self];
    generate a random permutation of size ncards;
    rearrange array Collection-Card[self] using the random
        permutation;
}
Deck :: deal (nhands: Integer, hsize: Integer): Array of Hand
// Deals nhands hands of hsize cards each.
// Returns the hands.
// Any leftover cards remain in the deck.
{
    if nhands * hsize > size of the deck, then report an error
        and return nil;
    create and initialize an array of nhands empty Hand objects;
    for isize := 1 to hsize do:
            for ihand := 1 to nhands do:
                delete the top card from the deck and add it to
                    hand ihand;
    return the array of hands;
}
Hand :: sort ()
{
    sort array Collection-Card[self] using the comparison
function Card::compare;
}
// We assume that there is a generic sort routine to sort
// arrays taking as argument a comparison function between
// pairs of array elements.
// The comparison function returns
// LESS_THEN, EQUAL_TO, or GREATER_THAN.
Card :: compare (other_card): ordering
// Compares two cards by suit, then by rank
// suits and ranks are ordered according to their enumeration
values
```

```
        {
            if self.suit < other_card.suit then return LESS_THAN
            else if self.suit > other_card.suit then return
    GREATER_THAN
            else if self.rank < other_card.rank then return LESS_THAN
            else if self.rank > other_card.rank then return
    GREATER_THAN
            else return EQUAL_TO;
        }
        Pile :: draw (hand: Hand)
        {
            card := self.top_of_pile();
            self.delete (card);
            hand.insert (card);
        }
        Card :: discard (pile: DrawPile)
        {
            collection:CollectionOfCards := Card-Collection[self];
            collection.delete (card);
            pile.insert (card);
        }
        Card :: display (location)
        {
            Render a card on the screen at the given location with
                self.suit and self.rank;
        }
```

10.14 This association would likely be traversed in both directions. Operations on a collection of cards, such as *insert*, require access to the ordered set of cards. On the other hand, the user may be able to select a card from the screen, in which case the collection containing the card must be found. The association is ordered because the cards in a collection form either a pile or a fan.

A typical implementation is to store a list of cards in each collection object and to store a pointer to the enclosing collection in each card object.

10.15 We have also changed *rawScore* to be a link attribute, which more accurately captures the dependencies between *Trial* and *Judge*.

One might define types *Address* and *TelephoneNumber*, but they can take many variant forms and this application probably does not need anything beyond a simple text string.

10.16 The simplest approach is to implement every association in both directions. The cost is not so great and many times you will later regret having implemented an association in a single direction. In the rest of this answer we attempt to indicate when a one-way im-

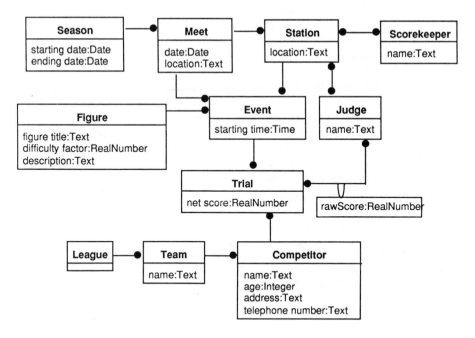

plementation of an association might be feasible, but traversal directionality depends highly on the details of the application. We state the assumptions that we make. Many of these decisions are arguable. An arrow indicates that the association is implemented in the given direction.

Season -> ordered many Meet. Probably want to order meets by date. Probably do not need to go from meet to season, but not costly to do so.

Meet -> unordered many Station. There is no reason to order stations nor any basis to do so. An implementation might introduce station numbers but they are not an inherent part of the logical model. Probably do not need to go from station to meet, but not costly.

Many Station <-> unordered many Scorekeeper. Need to go both ways. Need to know which scorekeepers are assigned to a station, each scorekeeper needs to know the stations assigned during the day.

Many Station <-> unordered many Judge. Same comments as previous entry.

Station <-> ordered many Event. Probably want to keep them in order by time because each station can support only one event at a time. We will probably want to query an event to see what station it is on.

Meet <-> unordered many Event. This event is derived from Meet->Station and Station->Event. Because a meet (unlike a station) may have simultaneous events, ordering is not so useful. We may need the back pointer to answer questions such as "Which meets did a competitor participate in during a season?"

Figure <-> many ordered Event. We need to go both ways; an event needs to know its figure, and we may want to know the meets at which a figure is held. Events could be ordered by meet date.

Event <-> many ordered Trial. We will need to go both ways. The trials are held in a specific sequence that is very important for scheduling.

Trial -> unordered many (Judge, rawScore). You could possibly omit the judge. No need to order the scores. No reason to go backwards from judge to (Trial, rawScore), unless possibly we need to audit each judge's performance.

Competitor <-> ordered many Trial. Obviously a competitor can only do one thing at a time, and the trials are ordered by time.

League <-> unordered many Team. Need to go both ways, no obvious ordering.

Team <-> unordered many Competitor. Same as previous entry.

10.17

```
Trial::computeNetScore ()
    Scan all raw scores in a trial finding the sum of scores,
        minimum score, maximum score, and number of scores;
    If number of scores is less than or equal to 2, report an
        error and stop;
    Subtract minimum and maximum scores from the sum of scores;
    average score := adjusted sum / (number of scores - 2);
    net score := average score * self.event.figure.difficulty;
```

10.18a. We need to add a many-to-many association *registered_for* between a set of events and an ordered list of competitors to keep track of who is registered for which events. We will use the registration order in scheduling trials. We use figure as an argument, rather than trial; event is really an internally-computed object that must be determined.

```
Competitor::register (meet: Meet, figure: Figure)
    Scan the events at the given meet to find the one for the
        given figure.
    If no suitable event is found, report an error.
    If the competitor is already registered for the event,
        return.
    Append the competitor to list registered_for[event].
```

When the event is held, the *registered_for* association is used to generate the list of competitors, in the order of registration. After each competitor competes in the event, a trial is created and scored for the competitor.

b.

```
Competitor::registerAllEvents (meet: Meet)
    For all events at the meet:
        If the competitor is already registered for the event,
            go on to the next event;
        Append the competitor to the list registered_for[event];
```

c. We presume that scheduling is manual. Someone must decide which events are to be held at which meets. To keep track of the decisions, we need an operation:

```
Meet::addFigure (figure: Figure)
    Create an event object.
    Associate it with the meet.
    Associate it with the figure.
```

We will not assign starting times until all the figures are selected. A simple scheduling algorithm assuming equal blocks of time for each event is:

```
Meet::scheduleAllEvents ()
    while events have not been scheduled do:
        for each available station do:
            get the next unscheduled event;
            if no more events, then return;
            append the event to Station-Event[station];
```

A more sophisticated algorithm would take into account the number of competitors registered for an event and the average time required for a trial of the given figure.

d. We again assume that scheduling is manual and that what is wanted is an operation to keep track of decisions. We also assume that simultaneous meets are not held.

```
Season::addMeet (date: Date, location: Location)
    If there is already a meet on the date, report error
    Create a new Meet object with the date and location
    Insert it in the ordered list of meets by date
```

e. We assume that a set of available judges and a set of available scorekeepers is provided. We also assume that there is a minimum and a maximum number of judges and scorekeepers permitted for a station (the two numbers may be the same). We assume that there is some priority rule for selecting personnel if there are too many volunteers for a meet.

```
Meet::assignPersonnel (judges, scorekeepers)
    Sort the judges and scorekeepers in priority order.
    averageJudges = number of judges/number of stations
    averageScorekeepers = number of scorekeepers/number of
        stations
    if averageJudges < minimum permitted, report an error
    if averageScorekeepers < minimum permitted, report an error
    neededJudges = minimum (averageJudges, maximum permitted)
    neededScorekeepers = minimum (averageScorekeepers, maximum
        permitted)
    for each station:
        assign the next neededJudges judges and
            neededScorekeepers scorekeepers.
    Notify any remaining judges and scorekeepers that they are
        not needed.
```

10.19 The code listed below sketches out a solution. This code lacks internal assertions that would normally be included to check the correctness of the metadata. For example, error code should be included to handle the case where the role is a subclass and the relationship is not Generalization. In code that interacts with users or external data sources, it is usually a good idea to add an error check as an else clause for conditionals that "must be true."

```
trace_inheritance_path (class1, class2): Path
{
    path := new Path;
// try to find a path from class1 as descendent of class2
    classx := class1;
    while classx is not null do:
        add classx to front of path;
        if classx = class2 then return path;
        classx := classx.get_superclass
// didn't find a path from class1 up to class2
// try to find a path from class2 as descendent of class 1
    path.clear;
    classx := class2;
    while classx is not null do:
        add classx to front of path;
        if classx = class1 then return path;
        classx := classx.get_superclass
    // the two classes are not directly related
    // return an empty path
    path.clear
    return path
}
Class::get_superclass (): Class
{
    for each role in self.connection do:
        if the role is a Subclass then:
            relationship := role.relationship;
            if relationship is a Generalization then:
                other_roles := relationship.end;
                for each other_role in other_roles do:
                    if other_role is a Superclass then:
                        return other_role.class
    return nil;
}
```

10.20

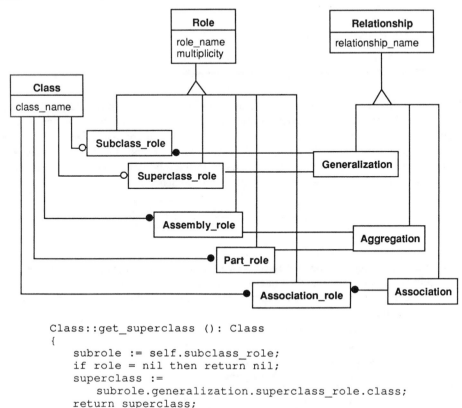

```
Class::get_superclass (): Class
{
    subrole := self.subclass_role;
    if role = nil then return nil;
    superclass :=
        subrole.generalization.superclass_role.class;
    return superclass;
}
```

The remainder of the algorithm is the same as in the previous answer. This is a good example of modular code, as a change to the model affected only one routine.

10.21 We make the following assumptions: The length of a name is unrestricted, names consist of alphanumerics and underscores, input names do not contain double underscores but generated association names may have double underscores. The algorithm:

```
If the association has a relationship_name,
then return the name,
else do:
    Get the two roles in the association.
    Get the two class names from the classes in the roles.
    Sort the two class names in alphabetical order.
    Form a string class1.class_name & "__" & class2.class_name
```

```
If the string is unique among explicit association names and
there are no other associations between the two classes,
Then return the string,
Else form the string class1.class_name & "_" &
role1.unique_role_name() & "_" & class2.class_name & "_" &
role2.unique_role_name() and return the string.
```
(The operator & indicates string concatenation.)

10.22 Political party membership is not an inherent property of a voter but a changeable association. The revised model better represents voters with no party affiliation and permits changes in party membership. If voters could belong to more than one party, then the multiplicity could easily be changed. Parties are instances, not subclasses, of class *Political party* and need not be explicitly listed in the model; new parties can be added without changing the model and attributes can be attached to parties.

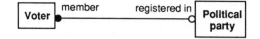

10.23 The algorithm may best be expressed as two coroutines, one which scans the passengers requiring reassignment and the other which scans the empty seats to reassign. A coroutine is a subroutine that keeps its internal state and internal location even after a call or return statement.

```
old_row_count = number of rows in the old plane
new_row_count = number of rows in the new plane
// By specification, new_row_count < old_row_count.
Coroutine reassign_passengers ()
    for each row from new_row_count+1 to old_row_count do
        for each seat in a row from left to right:
            if a passenger is assigned to the seat do
                new_seat := get_empty_seat();
                if new_seat ≠ nil
                then reassign it to the passenger
                else put the passenger on standby
Coroutine get_empty_seat (): seat
    for each row from 1 to old_row_count do
        for each seat in a row from left to right do
            if no passenger is assigned to the seat,
            then return it,
            else go on to the next seat
    report a seat shortage error
    return nil to indicate we have run out of seats
```

10.24 The left figure shows an index on points using a doubly-qualified association. The association is sorted first on the *x* qualifier and then on the *y* qualifier. Because the index is an optimization, it contains redundant information also stored in the point objects. The right figure shows the same diagram using singly-qualified associations. We had to introduce a dummy class *Strip* to represent all points having a given x-coordinate. The second model would be easier to implement on most systems because a data structure for a single sort key is more likely to be available. The actual implementation could use B-trees, linked lists, or arrays to represent the association.

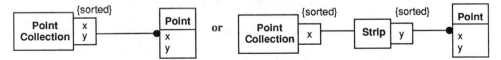

The code listed below specifies search, add, and delete methods.

```
PointCollection::search (region: Rectangle) : Set of Point
{
    make a new empty set of points;
    scan the x values in the association until x ≥ region.xmin;
    while the x qualifier ≤ region.xmax do:
        scan the y values for the x value until y ≥ region.ymin;
        while the y qualifier ≤ region.ymax do:
            add (x,y) to the set of points;
            advance to the next y value;
        advance to the next x value;
    return the set of points;
}
PointCollection::add (point: Point)
{
    scan the x values in the association until x ≥ point.x;
    if x = point.x then
        scan the y values for the x value until y ≥ point.y
    insert the point into the association at the current
location;
}
PointCollection::delete (point: Point)
{
    scan the x values in the association until x ≥ point.x;
    if x = point.x then
        scan the y values for the x value until y ≥ point.y
        if y = point.y then
            for each collection point with the current x,y value:
                if collection point = point, delete it and return
    report point not found error and return
}
```

Note that the scan operation should be implemented by a binary search to achieve logarithmic rather than linear times. A scan falls through to the next statement if it runs out of values.

10.25 The analysis is a bit complicated. We can look at several different cases.

There is an initial search in x of cost = log (number of columns containing points) ≤ log N, where N is the total number of points. We must search every column between the top and bottom of the target rectangle. Within each column, there is an initial search cost of log (number of points in the column). There is no additional cost within a column, except to scan out the points within the target rectangle, but there is no waste in doing this, because we stop after the first non-output point. So the total cost is log (#columns) + (#columns in rectangle) * log (#points in column) + #output points. Note that the middle term is really a sum over the column because the number of points in the column is not constant, but you get the idea.

We can ignore the first term, which will be small compared to the other terms for most practical cases. We will also separate out the final term, which is the number of output points and represents the useful work, and concentrate on the wasted searches represented by the middle term. For an algorithm like this, we really want to know the ratio between the wasted work and the useful work. The time will vary a lot depending on the number of output points and not just N, so it is not productive to characterize it by just N.

In the worst case, every point will be on a different column. If the target rectangle spans the entire y dimension, the total cost will be N, the number of points. To make matters worse, if the rectangle is wide and thin, it might contain no points at all, so the yield is 0 output points. The cost per output point is infinite! (Of course, this is a bit unfair, because the cost per point of any algorithm is infinite in this case.) This algorithm is good for tall narrow rectangles but not so good for short wide ones.

In a medium case, assume that points are randomly but sparsely distributed, with less than one point per column on average. Then we essentially end up searching all the points between the left and right lines of the rectangle. The x-ordering helps us avoid searching unnecessary columns, but the y-ordering within the column doesn't help because there is only a single point per column. On average, the fraction of points that fall within the rectangle is equal to its height divided by the total height of the search space, so the cost per yield point is the reciprocal of that fraction. It is still bad to have short rectangles.

In a dense case, assume that there are many points per column, Pcolumn, on average in the search space and the target rectangle contains many points per column, Phit, although Phit may be much less than Pcolumn. Then the waste of searching each column is log Pcolumn for a yield of Phit, so the waste is small provided Pcolumn < exp(Phit). For example, assume 100 points per column, then log(100) = 7 is the waste per column; a target rectangle that is 10% of the height will yield 10 points, so the waste is less than the cost and an order of magnitude better than searching all the points.

What can we say about this algorithm? It is highly asymmetric with respect to the x and y axes, and not very good if the target rectangles will be horizontal lines. It is also not very good if there are not many points per column, but in that case we can increase the interval of x-values per column so that more points are included. In general, we would like the column interval to be approximately the width of the rectangle, so that we need to scan as few columns as possible yet do not scan unnecessary points. Then the waste will be fairly small. If the shapes of the target rectangles vary a lot, then this algorithm will not always be so good.

To summarize, ordering points and using binary search works well for one-dimensional searches, but not so well for two-dimensional searches, because the points may be ordered first on the wrong dimension, reducing the search to a linear search. The proper approach to 2-d searching is not to nest two 1-d searches but to build a new 2-d algorithm, called a quadtree. Details may be found in graphics texts.

10.26a. In the worst case, if we search the wrong way first by chance, then the search will go to the top of the class hierarchy, so the cost is linear in the depth. If we modify the algorithm so that we search up from both classes at the same time, then the search cost will be no more than twice the difference in depth of the two classes and will not depend at all on the depth of the class hierarchy (except as a limit on the difference in depths). If the class hierarchy is very deep, then the algorithm should be modified to limit the cost, otherwise the added complexity is probably not worth the bother.

b. The algorithm we described is proportional to the number of seats in the old plane (we must scan the "missing" seats for passengers to reassign and the "common" seats for potential reassignment). It does not depend at all on the number of passengers. Any attempt to be more clever is misplaced zeal because this algorithm is fast enough for any practical purpose.

10.27 Pseudo code for a garage door opener is listed below. Statement labels are enclosed in angle brackets.

```
<closed>      wait for depress event
<opening>     start opening door
              wait for door open event
<open>        wait for depress event
<closing>     start closing door
              wait for either depress or door closed event:
                  if depress event then goto opening
                  if door closed event then goto closed
```

Don't be afraid to use gotos! They have a legitimate use in representing exceptional flow of control, such as exceptions and interrupts.

11

Methodology Summary

[All of the exercises in Chapter 11 are projects and are therefore not answered here.]

12

Comparison of Methodologies

12.1 There are two points to this exercise. The first point is that doubly qualified many-to-many associations can occasionally arise. The other point is to show how the ER notation loses semantic content when representing advanced object modeling constructs. There are several ways to convert the object diagram given in the exercise to an ER diagram, depending on how the qualifiers are treated. We have chosen to promote the qualifiers into classes as shown in Figure A12.1. Students may discover other valid interpretations.

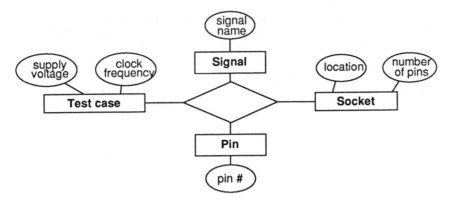

Figure A12.1 ER diagram for an integrated circuit tester

12.2 The point of this exercise is that object diagrams are well suited to generalization.

a. One possible modification of the object diagram to include a nose wing and an elevator
is shown in Figure A12.2. *Fixed surface* encompasses *Nose wing* and *Glider wing*. *Control surface* specializes to *Rudder* and *Elevator*. The methods on the class *Glider* for
computing and integrating accelerations do so by summing up the contributions from all
associated control surfaces.

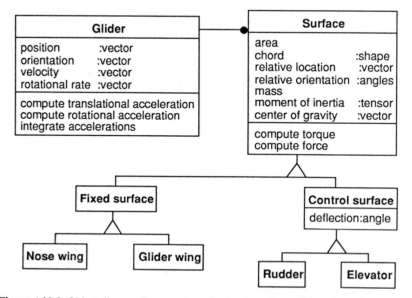

Figure A12.2 Object diagram for a portion of a simulator for a glider with additional surfaces

The modification of the data flow diagram to accommodate an elevator and a nose
wing is shown in Figure A12.3.

b. No modification of the object diagram would be required to simulate combinations of
control surfaces falling off. All that would be needed would be to change instances of
the association between the classes *Glider* and *Surface*. The data flow diagram could be
revised by redefining some of the processes. For example, to simulate a glider with a
missing elevator, the process *Compute Elevator Forces* must be redefined to produce no
force or torque.

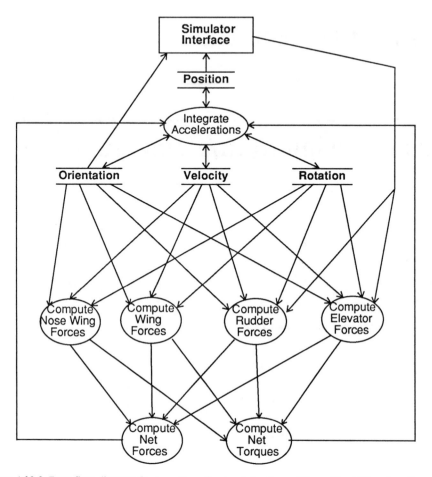

Figure A12.3 Data flow diagram for a portion of a simulator for a glider with additional surfaces

13

From Design to Implementation

[There are no exercises in Chapter 13.]

14

Programming Style

14.1 [We could not think of many unary operations where the order of traversal actually matters. We considered extending the exercise to binary operations, but then the answer gets more complicated than we intended.] The operations will depend on the class of the node. For classes with an attribute that contributes to a total, the operation *Total( )* is appropriate. For geometrical classes, the operations *Move(offset)* and *Rotate(angle)* could be applied.

We did not say in the problem statement how any arguments were to be passed to the operations. This could be done via a global variable or by passing arguments in a data structure. We will assume the latter, and have modified *Ordered_visit* accordingly. The following is the pseudocode for one way for performing *Ordered_visit*:

```
Ordered_visit(node, method, arguments)
{
    if node is not NIL
    {
        Ordered_visit(node.left_subtree, method,
                arguments);
        apply method(arguments) to node;
        Ordered_visit(node.right_subtree, method,
                arguments);
    }
}
```

14.2 The first operation is a special case of the second operation. The distinction between the two types of accounts can be eliminated by treating a normal account as a reserve account with a reserve limit of zero. Attributes needed to track accounts include *balance*, *reserve_balance*, and *reserve_limit*.

14.3a. This is an example of poor programming style. The assumption that the arguments are legal and the functions called are well behaved will cause trouble during program test and integration.

   The following statements will cause the program to crash if the argument to *strlen* is zero:

```
root_length = strlen(root_name);
suffix_length = strlen(suffix);
```

The following statement will assign zero to *sheet_name* if the program runs out of memory, causing a program crash during the call to *strcpy* later in the function:

```
sheet_name = malloc(root_length + suffix_length + 1);
```

The following statements will cause the program to crash if any of the arguments are zero:

```
sheet_name = strcpy(sheet_name, root_name);
sheet_name = strcat(sheet_name, suffix);
```

If *sheet_type* is invalid the switch statement will fall through leaving *sheet* without an assigned value. Also, it is possible that the call to *vert_sheet_new* or the call to *horiz_sheet_new* could return zero for some reason. Either condition would make it possible for the following statement to crash:

```
sheet->name = sheet_name;
```

b. The revised function is given below. The function *report_error(message)* reports errors.

```
Sheet create_sheet (sheet_type, root_name, suffix)
Sheet_type sheet_type;
char *root_name, *suffix;
{   char *malloc(), *strcpy(), *strcat(), *sheet_name;
    int strlen(), root_length, suffix_length;
    Sheet sheet, vert_sheet_new(), horiz_sheet_new();
    if(root_name)
        root_length = strlen(root_name);
    else
    {
        root_name = "";
        root_length = 0;
    }
    if(suffix)
        suffix_length = strlen(suffix);
    else
    {
        suffix = "";
        suffix_length = 0;
```

```
    }
    sheet_name = malloc(root_length + suffix_length + 1);
    if(sheet_name)
    {
        sheet_name = strcpy(sheet_name, root_name);
        sheet_name = strcat(sheet_name, suffix);
    }
    else
    {
        sheet_name = "";
        report_error("Out of memory.");
    }
    switch(sheet_type)
    {   case VERTICAL:
            sheet = vert_sheet_new();
            break;
        case HORIZONTAL:
            sheet = horiz_sheet_new();
            break;
        default:
            sheet = vert_sheet_new();
            break;
    }
    if(sheet)
        sheet->name = sheet_name;
    else
        report_error("Failure to create sheet.");
    return sheet;
}
```

The revised function will not crash under error conditions. If a sheet is not created, zero is returned, and it is up to the calling routine to properly handle the failure.

14.4   [There is a flaw in the code given in the exercise. The statements which retrieve attribute values from the variable *term* are incorrect because attributes belong to the subclass of *Term*. C provides no intrinsic support for inheritance so we must explicitly code the desired behavior. We have corrected this flaw in the answer.] The following uses better names.

```
Value evaluate_expression(term)
Term term;
{
    Value value, first_operand, second_operand;
    Value apply_operator(), evaluate_variable();
    Expression expression;
```

```
        Variable variable;
        Constant constant;
        switch(term->term_type){
        case CONSTANT:
            constant = term;
            value = constant->value;
            return value;
            break;
        case VARIABLE:
            variable = term;
            value = evaluate_variable(variable->name);
            return value;
            break;
        case EXPRESSION:
            expression = term;
            first_operand = evaluate_expression(
                expression->first_operand);
            second_operand = evaluate_expression(
                expression->second_operand);
            value=apply_operator(first_operand,
                    second_operand,
                    expression->binary_operator);
            return value;
            break;
        }
    }
```

14.5 [Most of this exercise was already answered if you assigned Exercise 8.19. Our original intent was that the answer to Exercise 8.19 should be a concise natural language explanation and that the answer to this exercise should be more precise and contain more detail than the answer to 8.19. When we answered 8.19 we found we had to furnish more detail than we intended to avoid being vague.]

[The operations are too short to separate policy from implementation. Note that we traversed multiple links in our answer to Exercise 8.19, which violates one of the guidelines given in this chapter. We violated the principle of information hiding to simplify our answers and make them easier to understand. In any case, it is straightforward to define intermediate operations which eliminate the need to traverse a long series of links.]

15

Object-Oriented Languages

15.1 The solution of this problem relies upon one of the workarounds or substitutes for multiple inheritance described in Section 4.4.3 on page 67. For this problem, we prefer the technique labeled "nested generalization." In the revised object diagram below, a new subclass of AC called AC/DC is added combining the features of AC and DC. Any methods defined on DC must be repeated on AC/DC, but since DC has no attributes the new class does not need any. Universal_motor class inherits from the AC/DC class.

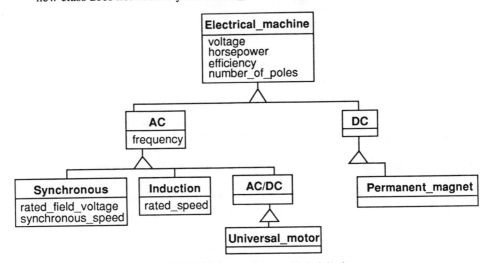

Figure A15.1 Workaround for multiple inheritance

We solved this problem using the Smalltalk/V programming environment by Digitalk. Smalltalk/V lacks multiple inheritance, but we can use the nested generalization technique as a substitute, as shown in the following class declarations:

```
Object subclass: #ElectricalMachine
    instanceVariableNames:
        'voltage horsepower efficiency numberOfPoles '
    classVariableNames: ''
    poolDictionaries: '' !

ElectricalMachine subclass: #AC
    instanceVariableNames: 'frequency '
    classVariableNames: ''
    poolDictionaries: '' !

AC subclass: #Synchronous
    instanceVariableNames:'ratedFieldVoltage synchronousSpeed'
    classVariableNames: ''
    poolDictionaries: '' !

AC subclass: #Induction
    instanceVariableNames: 'ratedSpeed '
    classVariableNames: ''
    poolDictionaries: '' !

AC subclass: #ACDC
    instanceVariableNames:''
    classVariableNames: ''
    poolDictionaries: '' !

ACDC subclass: #UniversalMotor
    instanceVariableNames:''
    classVariableNames: ''
    poolDictionaries: '' !

ElectricalMachine subclass: #DC
    instanceVariableNames: ''
    classVariableNames: ''
    poolDictionaries: '' !

DC subclass: #PermanentMagnet
    instanceVariableNames:''
    classVariableNames: ''
    poolDictionaries: '' !
```

We have not shown the methods. We must copy some methods from DC to ACDC in using this technique, but that is the price of not having multiple inheritance.

15.2a. The one to one association is implemented symmetrically as a pointer in each class. If the programming language permits, direct access to the object pointers should be restricted. Setting of the association should be done through an operation. Each participant in the association maintains its own side of the association and calls on the associated object to maintain the other side. The logic is symmetric. Each object contains an internal attribute, _update_in_progress_, that breaks the potential infinite recursion. C++ allows classes to be declared friends of a class, restricting access of features to classes that are declared as friends. Here we describe (in C++) a one-one association between two classes A and B.

The answers use a library class *Set* to store sets of associated objects. Operations on *Set* include *add(Object)* and *remove(Object)*. We used the National Institutes of Health Class Library (NIHCL) as described in *Data Abstraction and Object-Oriented Programming*, by Gorlen, Orlow and Plexico, John Wiley and Sons, 1990, but we do not show NIHCL details that are irrelevant to the implementation of associations. Note that we do not show the other attributes or methods of the classes which would be present in an actual application.

Other implementations are possible. This implementation is symmetric but forces the associated classes to be mutual friends. An alternate approach is to write a separate function that is a member of neither class but a friend of both to actually update the pointers on both sides.

```cpp
// class A with a one to one association with class B
class A: public Object {
    B* b;
    int _update_in_progress;
public:
    void add_B (B&);
    void remove_B (B&);
};

// class B with a one to one association with class A
class B: public Object {
    A* a;
    int _update_in_progress;
public:
    void add_A (A&);
    void remove_A (A&);
};

// association methods on class A with one to one association
void A::add_B (B& aB)
{
    // break mutual recursion on updates
    if(_update_in_progress) return;
    // remove current b since association is one-to-one
    if (b != NULL) {
        remove_B (*b);
    }
    // update this end of association
    _update_in_progress = 1;
    b = &aB;
    // update other end of association
    aB.add_A (*this);
    _update_in_progress = 0;
}
```

```
void A::remove_B (B& aB)
{
   if (_update_in_progress) return;
   _update_in_progress = 1;
   if (&aB != NULL) aB.remove_A (*this);
   b = NULL;
   _update_in_progress = 0;
}

// association methods on class B with one to many association

void B::add_A (A& anA)
{
   // break mutual recursion on update
   if (_update_in_progress) return;
   // remove current a since association is one-to-one
   if (a != NULL) {
      remove_A (*a);
   }
   // update this end of association
   _update_in_progress = 1;
   a = &anA;
   // update other end of association
   anA.add_B (*this);
   _update_in_progress = 0;
}

void B::remove_A (A& anA)
{
   if (_update_in_progress) return;
   _update_in_progress = 1;
   if (a != NULL) {
      anA.remove_B (*this);
   }
   a = NULL;
   _update_in_progress = 0;
}
```

b. The one-to-many association is asymmetric, unlike the one side implemented in 15.2a. For each A object there is a Set of pointers to B objects. The Set class supports the operations *add(Object&)* and *remove(Object&)*. The question stated that the association is traversed only in the one-to-many direction, therefore it is unnecessary to keep a pointer to A within class B. We assume that all additions and removals to the association are done from the A end and that we need not worry about possible reuse of a B object in multiple A objects (otherwise we do have to keep an A pointer in each B). Because only one end of the association need be modified, there is no need for mutual recursion.

```
// class A with a one to many unordered association with class B
class A: public Object {
   Set Bs; // set of pointers to related B objects
public:
```

```
        void add_B (B&);
        void remove_B (B&);
};

// class B with a one to one association with class A
class B: public Object {
};

// association methods on class A to many related B objects

void A::add_B (B& aB)
{
    // update this end of association
    (this->Bs).add (aB);
    // no need to update other end of association
}

void A::remove_B (B& aB)
{
    (this->Bs).remove(aB);
}
```

   c. This is the same as 15.2b but the set of related objects is now ordered. Instead of a Set
      object we used an OrderedCltn object to hold the ordered list of B objects. We assume
      that new B objects are added to the end of the list, which is the behavior of library meth-
      od OrderedCltn::add. The methods are exactly the same as in part b and are not repeated
      here.

```
    // class A with a one to many unordered association with class B
    class A: public Object {
        OrderedCltn Bs; // list of pointers to related B objects
    public:
        void add_B (B&);
        void remove_B (B&);
    };

    // class B with a one to one association with class A
    class B: public Object {
    };
```

   d. This is implemented with a set on one side of the association and an ordered collection
      on the other side. The methods look the same on both A and B, because both Set and
      OrderedCltn support the add and remove operations.

```
    // class A with a many to many association with class B
    // The association is unordered in the A-to-B direction
    class A: public Object {
        Set Bs;
        int _update_in_progress;
    public:
            void add_B (B&);
            void remove_B (B&);
    };
```

```
// class B with a many to many association with class A
// The association is ordered in the B-to-A direction
class B: public Object {
    OrderedCltn As;
    bool _update_in_progress;
public:
    void add_A (A&);
    void remove_A (A&);
};

// association methods on class A with many to many association
void A::add_B (B& aB)
{
    // break mutual recursion on updates
    if(_update_in_progress) return;
    // update this end of association
    _update_in_progress = 1;
    (this->Bs).add(aB);
    // update other end of association
    aB.add_A (*this);
    _update_in_progress = 0;
}

void A::remove_B (B& aB)
{
    if (_update_in_progress) return;
    _update_in_progress = 1;
    if (&aB != NULL) aB.remove_A (*this);
    (this->Bs).remove(aB);
    _update_in_progress = 0;
}

// association methods on class B with many to many association
void B::add_A (A& anA)
{
    // break mutual recursion on update
    if (_update_in_progress) return;
    // update this end of association
    _update_in_progress = 1;
    (this->As).add(anA);
    // update other end of association
    anA.add_B (*this);
    _update_in_progress = 0;
}

void B::remove_A (A& anA)
{
    if (_update_in_progress) return;
    _update_in_progress = 1;
    if (&anA != NULL) anA.remove_B (*this);
    (this->As).remove (anA);
    _update_in_progress = 0;
}
```

15.3 Strong typing permits the detection of object class mismatches at compile time, thus eliminating surprises during run time. Strong typing gives semantic information known to the programmer to the compiler as well, permitting earlier detection of bugs as well as documenting the program. Operations are usually applied to objects that share some common behavior, such as a draw operation for geometric primitives. As long as the objects to be operated on can be kept within the same generalization hierarchy, strong typing does not limit the designer. In other words, the objects to be operated on must have a common origin class at some point in the class hierarchy.

If, however, multiple inheritance exists within the object model and the implementation language does not directly support it, a common origin class may not exist for different sets of operations. Here, strong typing restricts the operations that can be applied.

Strong typing also forces more recompiles than weak typing, so weak tying may be more desirable during development, which strong typing may be better for production.

15.4a. *Sorted dictionary.* Implement as an Array of pairs. The first element of each pair is the name, the second element is the object that the name maps into. The array is kept sorted on the name value. Binary searches are used for efficiency. Inserting or deleting an entry requires that subsequent entries in the array be moved up or down by one position each. If many insertions are expected and efficiency is a problem, then a B-tree data structure can be implemented, but the present implementation will serve for many purposes and does not require implementation of a new fundamental data structure.

[Note: the sorted dictionary as described in the problem was not so well thought out.]

- find (name) - use a binary search to find the correct entry in the sorted array. Return the second part of the entry.

- delete (name) - use a binary search to find the position of the correct entry in the array, then delete it from the array (Array::delete). If the name is not found, don't delete anything.

- find_first () - get the first entry from the array (Array::index) and return it. [In spite of the question, a caller might want both name and object.]

- find_last () - get the last entry from the array (Array::index) and return it.

- find_previous (object), find_next (object) - [These operations are not well supported by a sorted dictionary that maps from name to object, because the dictionary does not support mapping from object to name. The question should have asked instead for find_previous (name) and find_next (name).]

- find_previous (name) - use a binary search to find the position of the correct entry in the array. If found, decrement the position. If not found, use the position before the point where the search failed. Index the array (Array::index) and return the pair.

- find_next (name) - similar to find_previous

- insert (name, object) - use a binary search to find the position of the name in the array. If it is there, replace the second value of the pair. If it is not there, then insert a new pair into the array at the point where the search failed (Array::insert).

- initialize () - Create a zero-length array and store it in the sorted dictionary.

b. *Polygon.* Implement as an Array of Point. The Polygon needs a pointer to the Array of points and each Point needs a pointer to its Polygon.

- Polygon::delete () - for each Point in the array, delete the Point. Then delete the array and the polygon object itself.

- Polygon:: get_points () - return a copy of the array of points.

- Polygon::create (Array of Points) - copy the array and store it in a new empty polygon object. Scan the array of points and update the polygon pointer in each one.

- Point::delete () - Search point.polygon.array to find the point and delete it from the array. Set point.polygon pointer to nil. (This algorithm is not fast but is probably fast enough for most small polygons.)

- Point::append (polygon) - append the point to the array in the polygon (Array::append). Set the polygon pointer in the point.

- Point::get_polygon () - return the polygon pointer in the point.

c. *Index.* Implement using a Dictionary of Sets. Each Set contains objects of the given target type.

- add (object_selector, object_target) - if the selector is not in the dictionary, create a set, add (object_selector,set) to the dictionary. Otherwise, use the selector to get the set from the dictionary. Add the target to the set.

- delete (object_selector, object_target) -if the selector is not in the dictionary, return. Otherwise, use the selector to get the set from the dictionary. Remove the target from the set. If the set becomes empty, remove it from the dictionary.

- find (object_selector) - if the selector is not in the dictionary, return an empty set. Otherwise, use the selector to get the set from the dictionary. Return a copy of the set.

15.5a. An interpreter is a convenient way to quickly find out how a subroutine in a library behaves, bypassing the edit, compile, link, and execute cycle encountered in compiled languages. Some languages have both a compiler and an interpreter. The interpreter is used for rapid program development and the compiler is used to produce an efficient final version of the program. Use the interpreter to try out operations and see how they work. Experiment with different arguments to subroutines.

b. System builders prevent this kind of error. They perform all of the required steps and only the required steps to rebuild an application after you modify one or more source files. If you don't use a system builder, you are faced with the choice of repeating all of the steps in the build process, which is time consuming, or trying to remember which steps are affected by your changes, which is error prone. *Make* is a popular system builder available on Unix systems. Always use a system builder, even if the program exists in a single file. Interruptions often cause the programmer to forget the last thing done even for simple projects.

c. First try an interpreter if you have one. Interpreters often detect errors, such as memory access errors, that are hard to find during execution. The program appears to be storing wild pointers to memory.

If you don't have an interpreter, then a symbolic debugger is a useful tool for diagnosing this type of problem. It allows you to run your program until the fault condition occurs and then see the line where the fault is occurring as well as the values of program variables. However, a data-dependent memory access failure may have been caused by a much earlier error, so some investigation may be necessary. Check all array dimensions and add code to make sure you are not violating constraints.

d. A change control system is an excellent way of coordinating a team software project. Even for a one-person project, a change control system keeps a history of changes and permits rollback in case of disaster. Most modern operating environments have tools to maintain control of source code. In Unix, SCCS and RCS are available. DEC VMS has CMS (Configuration Management System). Other more extensive configuration control systems are commercially available. Educate your development team early on the use of these tools and require their use from the start of the project.

e. Use a system builder such as Unix *make*. Complex dependencies can be built that will only rebuild those portions of a system that changed the last time the system was built. See the answer to part b.

f. Have your preprocessor generate a source code line number and source code file name on each debug statement you generate. In the C language, the #line directive tells the symbolic debugger to use the original line numbers in reporting locations.

15.6a. Because of the tight memory requirements all text segments should be deallocated when they are no longer needed. The problem is to develop a uniform policy to determine when they are no longer needed. Classes and methods provide a convenient framework for a solution. One set of guidelines is to place the responsibility for memory reclamation with the methods which modify text segments. Access to text segments outside of the object which owns them should be read only. Temporary text segments should be deallocated as soon as possible. One way to combine text segments follows:

```
determine total size of the segments that are to be combined.
allocate enough memory for the result.
copy the original text segments into the allocated memory.
deallocate the memory assigned to the original text segments.
```
We assume that the old segments are no longer accessible.

b. (1) Even with efficient swapping and unlimited memory, performance in a virtual system is bound to degrade after time. If, however, objects tend to be accessed and created sequentially, this approach may be acceptable, because references to contiguous objects will cluster and physical memory pages can be reused.

(2) Deallocation of objects eventually requires garbage collection to recover unused memory fragments. Frequent dereferencing may result in fragments that will be time consuming to recover. This approach may work if objects are all the same size. Another approach is to allocate a large block of memory for all the objects in a pass and deallocate it all at once (if possible).

c. It is not recommended to let the operating system allocate a large amount of virtual memory and forget about garbage collection all together in systems that run indefinitely. Eventually all of the memory will be used up. Memory must be deallocated when objects are no longer referenced. Consider writing your own memory allocation/deallocation function to replace the library function, taking the characteristics of your own objects into account.

d. The first approach works only in special circumstances in which the lifetime of the object is short. It is a dangerous approach that builds many assumptions into the code. A safer approach is for the caller to explicitly destroy the object.

15.7   When a point is deleted, it must notify its polygon to remove the point. Likewise, when a polygon is deleted, it must tell each of its points that it no longer exists. Points that find themselves no longer referenced should delete themselves.

15.8   [*Note to the Instructor:* If this exercise is assigned together with Exercise 15.9, which requires the student to implement the Binary_Tree class, then you should encourage the students to modify the specifications of the operations to be consistent with the conventions of the language being used. For an example, in our answer to 15.9 below we have modified the specification to be consistent with the naming conventions of Smalltalk. The answer that follows is a direct interpretation of the problem as specified, and is independent of implementation language.]

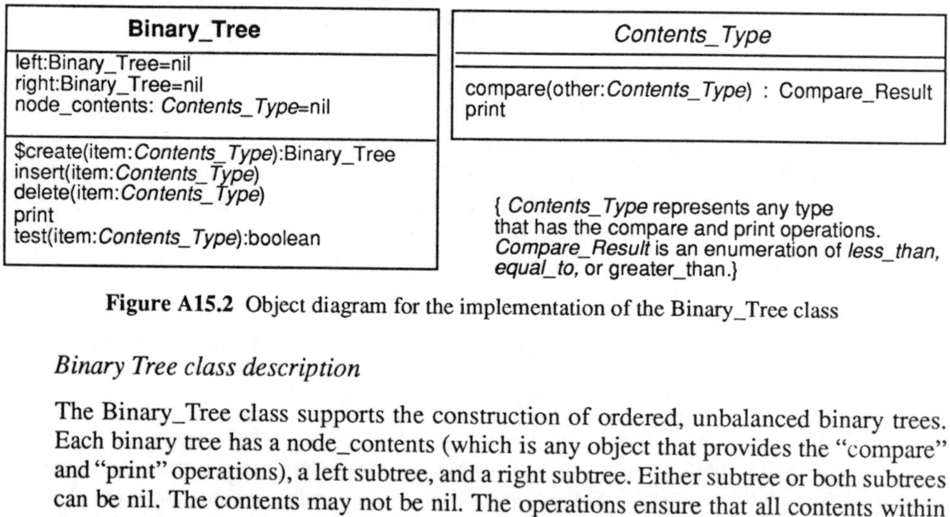

Binary_Tree
left:Binary_Tree=nil right:Binary_Tree=nil node_contents: *Contents_Type*=nil
$create(item:*Contents_Type*):Binary_Tree insert(item:*Contents_Type*) delete(item:*Contents_Type*) print test(item:*Contents_Type*):boolean

Contents_Type
compare(other:*Contents_Type*) : Compare_Result print

{ *Contents_Type* represents any type that has the compare and print operations. *Compare_Result* is an enumeration of *less_than*, *equal_to*, or greater_than.}

Figure A15.2 Object diagram for the implementation of the Binary_Tree class

Binary Tree class description

The Binary_Tree class supports the construction of ordered, unbalanced binary trees. Each binary tree has a node_contents (which is any object that provides the "compare" and "print" operations), a left subtree, and a right subtree. Either subtree or both subtrees can be nil. The contents may not be nil. The operations ensure that all contents within the left subtree are less than the contents of the current node, and all contents within the right subtree are greater than or equal to the current node contents. Duplicate content values are allowed in the tree. The user of the class is prevented from directly modifying the node_contents attribute so that the ordering of the tree can be preserved.

Operations

create (item : Contents_type) : Binary_Tree
> Returns a new instance of Binary_Tree consisting of a single node with "item" stored as its node_contents.

insert (item : Contents_type)
> Inserts "item" within a new node of the tree being operated upon, insuring that the ordering of items within the tree is preserved.

delete (item : Contents_type) : boolean
> Deletes the first occurrence of "item" from the tree being operated upon. Returns True iff an occurrence of the item was found. Deallocates the node that contained the item, if it has no subtrees.

print
> Prints the tree with its contents, in the order of node contents.

test (item : Contents_type) : boolean
> Returns True if and only if "item" is within the contents of any node of the tree.

Assertions and Constraints

In the following, if a subtree is nil then assertions involving comparison are automatically satisfied.

create:
> return_value.node_contents = item
> return_value.left = nil
> return_value.right = nil

insert:
> For some subtree S of self, S.node_contents = item
> For all subtrees S of self,
> S.left.node_contents < S.node_contents ≤ S.right.node_contents

delete:
> If "item" is contained in the BinaryTree "self" when "delete" is invoked, then the number of node_contents within self that match "item" will be reduced by one after the "delete" operator has been executed, and return_value will be "True".
> If no node_contents within self matched "item", then the return_value will be "False".

print:
> The contents of the tree are displayed in the order implied by the comparison operator.

test:
> return_value = True iff for some subtree S of self, S.node_contents = item

15.9 The following is an implementation of the Binary Tree class in Digitalk's Smalltalk/V language.

```
Object subclass: #BinaryTree
    instanceVariableNames:
        'left right nodeContents '
    classVariableNames: ''
    poolDictionaries: '' !
```

We have renamed the "create" operation specified above to conform to Smalltalk naming conventions. The class operation "BinaryTree with: item" returns a BinaryTree node with "item" as its contents. This method must call a private instance method to set the node contents. This is because instance variables in Smalltalk are private, and a class method may not access the instance variables–even of an instance that it has just created.

```
!BinaryTree class methods !

with: anObject
        "Answer a new BinaryTree node with anObject
        as nodeContents."

    | newNode |
    newNode := self new.
    newNode setContents: anObject.
    ^ newNode
```

The delete method avoids leaving an empty node in the tree by "pulling up" a node from a subtree, substituting it for the deleted node. If either subtree is nil, the node to be pulled up is just the other subtree. But if both subtrees are non-nil, the node to be pulled up is the maximal element in the left subtree. We have defined another method (*findMaxValue*) to find the maximal element. The delete method calls itself recursively if the object to be deleted isn't found in the current node.

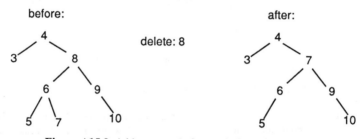

Figure A15.3 A binary tree before and after a deletion

```
!BinaryTree methods !

delete: anObject
    "Delete one occurrence of anObject from the receiver,
     a BinaryTree. Answer the new root node of the tree."

    nodeContents = anObject ifTrue: [
        left isNil ifTrue: [
            right isNil ifTrue: [ ^nil ].
            ^ right ].
        right isNil ifTrue: [
            left isNil ifTrue: [ ^nil ].
            ^ left ].
        nodeContents := left findMaxValue.
        left := left delete: nodeContents.
        ^self ].
```

```
anObject < nodeContents ifTrue: [
    left notNil ifTrue: [
        left := left delete: anObject ] ]
  ifFalse: [
      right notNil ifTrue: [
          right := right delete: anObject ] ].
^self!

findMaxValue
    "Answer the maximum of all nodeContents values in tree."
    right isNil ifTrue: [ ^nodeContents ].
    ^ right findMaxValue!
```

To insert a node, we search down the tree comparing values and going left or right accordingly until we find an empty subtree, which is replaced by a new node containing the target value:

```
insert: anObject
        "Insert an object that supports magnitude comparison
         into self, an ordered binary tree. Answer self."

    anObject < nodeContents
        ifTrue: [ left isNil
            ifTrue: [ left := BinaryTree with: anObject .
                    ^self ]
            ifFalse: [ left insert: anObject .
                    ^self ]
            ]
        ifFalse: [ right isNil
            ifTrue: [ right := BinaryTree with: anObject .
                    ^self ]
            ifFalse: [ right insert: anObject .
                    ^self ]
            ]
```

In Smalltalk, objects do not generally print themselves, but instead they provide the printOn: operation that is called by many tools within the Smalltalk environment to display the contents of an object. In our implementation, we print the nodes and subnodes of the tree in a nested parentheses format (see examples below).

```
printOn: aStream

"Print a string representation of the tree and its contents
        on aStream. Answer self."

    aStream nextPutAll: '( ' .
    left notNil
        ifTrue: [ aStream nextPutAll: (left printString) ] .
    nodeContents notNil

ifTrue: [ aStream nextPutAll: (nodeContents printString) .
            aStream nextPut: $ ] .
    right notNil
```

```
        ifTrue: [ aStream nextPutAll: (right printString) ] .
    aStream nextPutAll: ' ) ' .
    ^self

setContents: anObject
      "Private -
       set nodeContents of self to anObject. Return self."

    nodeContents := anObject.
    ^ self

test: anObject
      "Answer True iff anObject is contained in self."

    nodeContents = anObject ifTrue: [ ^true ] .
    left = nil ifFalse: [
        (left test: anObject) ifTrue: [ ^true ] ] .
    right = nil ifFalse: [
        (right test: anObject) ifTrue: [ ^true ] ] .
    ^false
```

Now that the BinaryTree class is defined, we implement two other classes to test it. The first of these classes is Person, with attributes "name" and "ssn" (social security number). Rather than defining the "compare" method, we again conform to Smalltalk conventions by providing the "<" operation instead. (Other comparison operations such as ">" and ">=" could also be provided, but only "<" and "=" are required for our test.)

```
Object subclass: #Person
    instanceVariableNames:
        'name age ssn '
    classVariableNames: ''
    poolDictionaries: '' !
```

The name:ssn: operation creates a new Person object with the given name and social security number:

```
!Person class methods !

name: nameString ssn: ssnString
      "Answer a new Person with name and ssn initialized"

    | newPerson |
    newPerson := Person new.
    newPerson
        setName: nameString;
        setSsn: ssnString.
    ^newPerson

!Person methods !

< aPerson
      "Answer true iff the name of the recipient
       is less than the name of aPerson"
```

```
     ^( name < (aPerson name) )

= aPerson
        "Answer true iff the receiver has the same name
        as aPerson.The test must be consistent with <."
     ^( name = (aPerson name))

name
        "Answer the name of the recipient."
     ^name

printOn: aStream
        "Print a representation of the Person on aStream.
        Answer self."

     name notNil ifTrue: [ name printOn: aStream ] .
     ^self.

setName: aString
        "Private method to set recipient's name."
     name := aString copy .
     ^aString

setSsn: aString
        "Private method to set recipient's ssn."
     ssn := aString copy .
     ^aString

ssn
        "Answer the social security number of the recipient."

     ^ssn
```

We use the Person class to perform a series of tests on the BinaryTree class. Informal testing within the Smalltalk environment can be accomplished by selecting an expression with the cursor and choosing either the *Show it* or the *Inspect it* menu operation. This causes the expression to be evaluated, and either displays the result in the workspace or calls the object inspector to inspect the structure of a more complex object. In the following examples, we used *Show it* repeatedly to evaluate a series of test expressions. The results of the *Show it* are in bold-face type.

```
ATree := BinaryTree new.
    ( )
ATree insert: (Person name: 'Bill' ssn: '111-22-3333') .
ATree insert: (Person name: 'Harriet' ssn: '555-11-8888') .
ATree insert: (Person name: 'Bob' ssn: '777-99-0011') .
ATree insert: (Person name: 'Fred' ssn: '145-64-9876') .
ATree insert: (Person name: 'Sally' ssn: '001-64-7356') .
    ( 'Bill' ( ( 'Bob' ( 'Fred' ) ) 'Harriet' ( 'Sally' ) ) )

ATree:= ATree delete: (Person name: 'Bill' ssn: '999-99-9999')
```

```
    ( `Bill' ( ( `Bob' ( `Fred' ) ) `Harriet' ( `Sally' ) ) )
ATree := ATree delete: (Person name: `Bill' ssn: `111-22-3333')
    ( ( `Bob' ( `Fred' ) ) `Harriet' ( `Sally' ) )
ATree := ATree delete: (Person name: `Fred' ssn: `145-64-9876')
    ( ( `Bob' ) `Harriet' ( `Sally' ) )
ATree := ATree delete: (Person name:`Sally' ssn:`001-64-7356')
    ( ( `Bob' ) `Harriet' )
ATree:=ATree delete:(Person name:`Harriet' ssn:`555-11-8888')
    ( `Bob' )

ATree test: (Person name: `Harriet' ssn: `555-11-8888'). false
ATree test: (Person name: `Bob' ssn: `777-99-0011'). true
ATree test: (Person name: `Bob' ssn: `999-77-1100'). false

ATree delete: (Person name: `Bob' ssn: `777-99-0011') nil
```

The Page class can be defined similarly and used to test BinaryTree. The following simple example defines a page as having a page number and some contents (which is just a long string of text in this simple example). Only the pagenumber is considered in defining the comparison operators. The "printOn" method only prints the page number. New pages must be constructed by using the "new" operation inherited from the Object class, and then using "setPageNumber:" and "setContents:" to set the attributes.

```
Object subclass: #Page
    instanceVariableNames:
        'pageNumber contents '
    classVariableNames: ''
    poolDictionaries: '' !

!Page methods !

< aPage
        "Answer true if the pageNumber of self < the pageNumber
            of aPage. "

    pageNumber isNil ifTrue: [ ^true ] .
    ^ pageNumber < aPage pageNumber

= aPage
        "Answer true iff the pageNumber of self = the pageNumber
            of aPage. "

    pageNumber isNil ifTrue: [ ^false ] .
    ^ pageNumber = aPage pageNumber

contents
    ^ contents

pageNumber
    ^ pageNumber

printOn: aStream
```

```
      "Print a representation of self on aStream. Answer
          self."

   pageNumber notNil ifTrue: [
      aStream nextPutAll: 'Page ' .
      pageNumber printOn: aStream ] .
   ^self.

setContents: aString
   contents := aString .
   ^self

setPageNumber: anInteger
   pageNumber := anInteger .
   ^self
```

Testing BinaryTree with the Page class would be done in a manner similar to the tests using the Person class.

15.10 We would like to define a Deck class that provides methods to shuffle itself and deal four hands. First a new Deck object will have to be created, and it must be initialized to contain one card of each suit and rank. We ignore for the moment the definition of what a Card is.

This problem will be solved using the Smalltalk/V language from Digitalk. The code to create, shuffle and deal the hands will look like the following Smalltalk statement.

```
Deck new initialize
   shuffle;
   deal.
```

The results of executing this statement and other test statements are show after Problem 15.13.

A Deck is a CollectionOfCards. Because the order of the cards in a deck or pile must be preserved, we decide that our CollectionOfCards class should inherit from Smalltalk's OrderedCollection class. This gives us a rich set of operations to iterate over the collection and access its members.

```
OrderedCollection subclass: #CollectionOfCards
   instanceVariableNames:
      'visibility location '
   classVariableNames: ''
   poolDictionaries: '' !

CollectionOfCards subclass: #Deck
   instanceVariableNames: ''
   classVariableNames: ''
   poolDictionaries: ''
```

The "shuffle" method of class Deck is written in three statements. First we determine the size of the Deck. Next, we create an OrderedCollection of the same size, called "swapIndices" containing random numbers with values in the range from 1 up to the size of the Deck. Then each card in the deck is swapped with some other card, using the corresponding member of the swapIndices collection to select which other card to swap with. For example, if the 23rd element of swapIndices is 49, then we swap the 23rd card in the deck with the 49th card. This ensures that each card is swapped with at least one other card in the deck. (We could define a new operation to swap the i'th and j'th cards in a CollectionOfCards if that operation is deemed useful in other contexts.)

```
!Deck methods !

shuffle
    "Shuffle the receiver deck into a random order."
    | sizeInterval swapIndices anItem |

    sizeInterval := 1 to: self size .
    swapIndices := sizeInterval collect: [ :x |
        ( SmallInteger random: self size ) + 1 ] .
    sizeInterval with: swapIndices do: [ :i :j |
        anItem := self at: i .          "Swap card i with card j"
        self at: i put: ( self at: j ) .
        self at: j put: anItem ]
```

Another operation on a deck of cards is to deal from the deck to create a "hand" for each of the players. The problem statement calls for dealing the entire deck into four hands. An interesting generalization would be to deal a given number of hands each consisting of a given number of cards, but the implementation below sticks to the original problem statement.

We have decided to return the four Hands as an Array of four elements, each of which is an instance of the Hand class. The algorithm for dealing does exactly what a real dealer would do. One card at a time is deleted from the deck and dealt to one of the four hands. The i'th card in the deck goes into the hand selected by the operation (i modulo 4) plus one.

```
deal

"Answer an Array of 4 Hands resulting from dealing the deck.
      The deck is left empty."

| hands aCard |
hands := Array with: Hand new with: Hand new
        with: Hand new with: Hand new .
( 1 to: (self size) ) do: [ :i |
    aCard := self delete .
    ( hands at: ( i \\ 4 + 1) ) insert: aCard ] .
^ hands
```

15.11 The association between CollectionOfCards and Card is partially implemented as a consequence of our decision to make CollectionOfCards a subclass of OrderedCollection. We thereby give CollectionOfCards the capability of containing other objects, which we intend to restrict to Card objects in this case. This also gives us the ability to access the cards that are contained in a CollectionOfCards. But the problem calls for implementing the association in the opposite direction as well, going from a particular card to find the CollectionOfCards (Deck, Hand, Pile) that it is contained in, if any.

First we need to define the class Card. Each Card object has the attributes "suit" and "rank", implemented as instance variables. There is also an instance variable that tells which CollectionOfCards the card belongs to. This instance variable gives us the ability to traverse the association between CollectionOfCards and Card in the reverse direction.

```
Object subclass: #Card
    instanceVariableNames:
        'suit rank collection '
    classVariableNames:
        'Suits Ranks '
    poolDictionaries: ''
```

We need to represent the ranks (ace, 2, 3, ... jack, queen, king) and the suits (spades, hearts, diamonds, clubs) internally. We use the numbers from 1 to 13 to represent rank, and instances of the Symbol class (a subclass of the String class) to represent suits. This has the merit that the ranks have a natural ordering, and most such objects will print out as desired, but we will have to make special provisions for the ordering of the suits, and for printing ace, jack, queen, and king.

The methods need to know what the valid suits and ranks are. Rather than hard-coding this knowledge within several methods of the class, we put it in one place as class method "Suits" and "Ranks", each of which returns a sequence of the appropriate objects.

```
!Card class methods !

ranks
        "Answer an Interval containing the card ranks."
    Ranks isNil ifTrue: [
       Ranks := 1 to: 13 ] .
    ^Ranks


suits

"Answer an OrderedCollection containing the card suits."
    Suits isNil ifTrue: [
        Suits := OrderedCollection with: #spade with: #heart
            with: #club with: #diamond ] .
    ^Suits
```

We also define a class method that creates a card with a given suit and rank.

```
suit: aSuit rank: aRank
    "Answer a new card with suit aSuit and rank aRank."
    ^( self new )
    suit: aSuit ;
    rank: aRank ;
    yourself
```

The above class method relies on the following private instance methods that initialize the suit and rank of a newly-created card.

```
!Card methods !

suit: aSuit
        "Private -
        Set receiver's suit to aSuit. Answer the receiver."
     suit := aSuit .
     ^self

rank: aRank
        "Private -
        Set receiver's rank to aRank. Answer the receiver."
     rank := aRank .
     ^self
```

To access the instance variables of the Card class, we will need the following trivial methods.

```
suit
        "Answer the recipients suit."
     ^suit

rank
        "Answer the recipients rank."
     ^rank

collection

"Answer the CollectionOfCards that this card belongs to,
        or answer nil if it isn't in a collection."
     ^ collection

collection: aCollectionOfCards
        "Set the collection that this card belongs to."
     collection := aCollectionOfCards
```

Finally we need a method to return a readable string representation of any Card. This will be used whenever a Card is printed by the Smalltalk user interface. We solve the problem of printing out the special cases of rank by writing a separate method that returns the representation of a rank as a string.

```
printOn: aStream
        "Print a representation of the receiver on aStream.
        Answer aStream."

     aStream
        nextPutAll: self rankAsString ;
        nextPutAll: ' of ' ;
        nextPutAll: suit ;
        nextPut: $s .
```

```
^ self

rankAsString
        "Answer the receiver's rank as a string, decoding the

numerical representation of ace, jack, queen, and king."
    rank = 1 ifTrue: [ ^ 'ace' ].
    rank = 11 ifTrue: [ ^ 'jack' ].
    rank = 12 ifTrue: [ ^ 'queen' ].
    rank = 13 ifTrue: [ ^ 'king' ].
    ^ rank printString
```

15.12 In order to sort the cards in a Hand, we need to provide the ability to compare two cards and determine which is greater than the other. Looking at other classes in the Smalltalk environment, we see that comparison is conventionally provided by operations such as <= (less than or equal) which return a Boolean value. We define such a method for the Card class, taking care to sort aces high:

```
<= aCard
        "Answer true iff the recipient sorts before aCard.
        Aces (represented by rank = 1) are higher than
        any other rank."

    | otherRank otherSuit |
    otherSuit := aCard suit.

suit = otherSuit ifFalse: [    "Determine if suit <= otherSuit"

Suits do: [ :nthSuit |    "Scan Suits collection for match."
        suit = nthSuit ifTrue: [ ^true ].
        otherSuit = nthSuit ifTrue: [ ^false ] ]
    ].
    suit = otherSuit ifTrue: [
        otherRank := aCard rank.
        rank = 1 ifTrue: [ ^ true ].       "Ace is high."
            otherRank = 1 ifTrue: [ ^ false ].
            ^ otherRank <= rank ].
    ^ false
```

The Hand class inherits most of its capability from the CollectionOfCards class, so it is trivial to define:

```
CollectionOfCards subclass: #Hand
    instanceVariableNames: ''
    classVariableNames: ''
    poolDictionaries: ''
```

The sort method of the Hand class will rely on the above method of comparing Cards. In Smalltalk, there is a SortedCollection class which maintains the ordering implied by the <= operation provided by its members. The fact that SortedCollection works for any class providing some (possibly unusual) implementation of <= is one of the beauties of object-oriented polymorphism.

We can write our sort method in two statements. First we transform the Hand into a SortedCollection, then we replace the cards in the Hand with the corresponding sorted cards.

```
!Hand methods !

sort

"Sort the hand according to rank in suit in descending order.

Members are sorted in the order implied by their <= method."
    | sorted |
    sorted := self asSortedCollection.
    self replaceFrom: 1 to: (self size) with: sorted.
```

15.13 The "deal" method depends on the operations "insert" and "delete", which will be provided by CollectionOfCards so that they are inherited by both the Deck and the Hand classes. Here, we determine that the top card of a Deck will be represented by the last card of the OrderedCollection object that it is based on. These two methods also update the relationship between the Card and CollectionOfCards classes, which was discussed in the answer to Problem 15.11.

```
!CollectionOfCards methods !

delete
        "Remove the top (last) card from the collection.
         Answer the card being deleted."

    ^ self removeLast collection: nil .

insert: aCard

"Insert a Card at the top of the receiver CollectionOfCards."

    aCard collection: self .
    ^self add: aCard
```

Results of Problems 15.10 through 15.13

The classes DiscardPile and DrawPile have not been discussed, but can be implemented simply as subclasses of CollectionOfCards.

The code written for Problems 15.10 through 15.13 can be tested by using the *Show it* and *Inspect it* commands in the Smalltalk environment. Below we show the results of executing the methods defined in these problems. The output of the *Show it* command is shown in bold face.

```
Card suit: #spade rank: 9        9 of spades

Hand new insert: ( Card suit: #club rank: 1 ) ;
    insert: ( Card suit: #spade rank: 2 ) ;
    insert: ( Card suit: #heart rank: 3 ) ;
    yourself
    Hand(ace of clubs 2 of spades 3 of hearts )
```

```
DiscardPile new insert: ( Card suit: #club rank: 1 ) ;
    insert: ( Card suit: #spade rank: 2 ) ;
    insert: ( Card suit: #heart rank: 3 ) ;
    yourself
    DiscardPile(ace of clubs 2 of spades 3 of hearts )

DrawPile new insert: ( Card suit: #club rank: 1 ) ;
    insert: ( Card suit: #spade rank: 2 ) ;
    insert: ( Card suit: #heart rank: 3 ) ;
    yourself
    DrawPile(ace of clubs 2 of spades 3 of hearts )

(Hand new insert: ( Card suit: #club rank: 1 ) ;
    insert: ( Card suit: #club rank: 9 ) ;
    insert: ( Card suit: #club rank: 3 ) ;
    insert: ( Card suit: #club rank: 8 ) ;
    asSortedCollection )
SortedCollection(ace of clubs 9 of clubs 8 of clubs 3 of clubs)

(Deck new initialize
    shuffle;
    deal ) do: [ :aHand | aHand sort ]

    ( Hand (king of spades 10 of spades 4 of spades
    6 of hearts 3 of hearts ace of clubs king of clubs
    9 of clubs 7 of clubs 2 of clubs ace of diamonds
    7 of diamonds 4 of diamonds )
    Hand (queen of spades 7 of spades king of hearts
    jack of hearts 10 of hearts 8 of hearts 7 of hearts
    4 of hearts jack of clubs 10 of clubs 5 of clubs
    queen of diamonds 3 of diamonds )
    Hand(8 of spades 6 of spades 5 of spades ace of hearts
    2 of hearts 8 of clubs 3 of clubs king of diamonds
    jack of diamonds 10 of diamonds 9 of diamonds
    5 of diamonds 2 of diamonds )
    Hand(ace of spades jack of spades 9 of spades 3 of spades
        2 of spades queen of hearts 9 of hearts 5 of hearts
        queen of clubs 6 of clubs 4 of clubs 8 of diamonds
        6 of diamonds )
    )
```

15.14-15.17

[We have not shown associations or declarations involving Collection or its descendents, since the question did not ask for them. They would of course be part of the declaration of Box and Link. We have also simplified the problem somewhat from the description set forth in Exercise 8.5. In particular, the cut operation simply deletes the things that are cut and does not store them in a buffer. Otherwise the things cut must be stored in the buffer, but the previous contents of the buffer must be deleted.]

We assume that the association between Box and Link is traversed in both ways, but that links are created with two boxes, so the association need not be updated from the Link end. Furthermore, the association is implemented in one way from Link to Line_segment and from Line_segment to Point. When a box is cut or removed from a Link, then the Link must be deleted, including all its segments and points. To save space we have omitted the associations with Collection. These associations are implemented in a similar manner to the ones shown. Some supporting methods are not shown.

The program is implemented in C++. The interfaces of imported classes are:

```cpp
typedef int boolean;
class Object;
class String;

class Aggregate {
    public:
        virtual void add (Object &) = 0;
        virtual void remove (Object &) = 0;
};

class OrderedCltn : public Aggregate {
    public:
        void add (Object &);
        void remove (Object &);
        void reverse ();
};

class Set : public Aggregate {
    public:
        void add (Object &);
        void remove (Object &);
        int occurrencesOf (Object &);
};

class Iterator {
    public:
        Iterator (const Aggregate &); // make an iterator
        boolean operator++ (); // advance to next element
        Object & operator() (); // return current value
};
```

The code for the program:

```cpp
class Point : public Object {
        int x, y;
};

class Selection
{
    public:
        Set & boxes ();
};
```

```
class Sheet
{
    public:
        Set & boxes ();
};

class Link;

class Box: public Object {
    private:
        Set theLinks;
        String _text;
        int _left, _top, _width, _height;
        boolean _update_in_progress;
    public:
    // association methods
        void addLink (Link&);
        void removeLink (Link&);
        const Set & links () {return theLinks;}
    // interesting methods
        void cut ();
};

class Link: public Object {
    private:
        Box * _box1;
        Box * _box2;
        OrderedCltn theSegments;
        boolean _update_in_progress;
    public:
        Link (Box& box1, Box& box2,
            OrderedCltn& points);
        ~Link ();
        Box & box1 () {return * _box1;}
        Box & box2 () {return * _box2;}
        const OrderedCltn & segments () { return theSegments; }
    // association methods
        void removeBox (Box&);
};

class LineSegment: public Object {
    private:
        Point _point1;
        Point _point2;
    public:
        LineSegment (const Point& p1,const Point& p2);
        Point point1 () { return _point1; }
        Point point2 () { return _point2; }
};
```

```
// methods

void Box::addLink (Link& aLink)
{
    if(_update_in_progress) return;
// update this end of association
    _update_in_progress = 1;
    theLinks.add (aLink);
// links are created complete, so no need to add box to link
    _update_in_progress = 0;
}

void Box::removeLink (Link& aLink)
{
    if (_update_in_progress) return;
    _update_in_progress = 1;
    theLinks.remove(aLink);
    aLink.removeBox (*this);
    _update_in_progress = 0;
}

// Answer to Exercise 15.15.
void Box::cut ()
{
    Iterator it (theLinks);
// remove this box from all of its blinks
    while (it++) {
        Link link = (Link&)(it());
        link.removeBox (*this);
    }
    delete this;
}

// Answer to Exercise 15.16.
Link::Link(Box& box1, Box& box2, OrderedCltn& points)
{
    _box1 = &box1;
    _box2 = &box2;
    _update_in_progress = 1;
    Iterator it(points);
    int first=1;
    Point lastPoint;
    while (it++) {
        Point p = (Point &) it ();
        if (first) first=0;
        else {
            theSegments.add(*new LineSegment (p, lastPoint));
        }
        lastPoint = p;
    }
    _update_in_progress = 0;
}
```

```
Link::~Link ()
{
    // remove link from box1 and box2
    _update_in_progress = 1;
    _box1->removeLink (*this);
    _box2->removeLink (*this);
    // delete line segments
    Iterator it(theSegments);
    while (it++) {
        LineSegment * s = & (LineSegment &) it ();
        delete s;
    }
}

void Link::removeBox (Box& aBox)
{
    if (_update_in_progress) return;
    _update_in_progress = 1;
// remove links from both boxes
    if (&aBox == _box1 || &aBox == _box2) {
        _box1->removeLink (*this);
        _box2->removeLink (*this);
    }
    _update_in_progress = 0;
    delete this;
}

LineSegment::LineSegment (const Point& p1,const Point& p2)
{
    _point1 = p1;  _point2 = p2;
}

// 15.17a) Given a box, determine all other boxes directly
// linked to it
Set allDirectBoxes (Box& aBox)
{
    Set SetofAllBoxes;
    // ask it for its links
    const Set & aSetofLinks = aBox.links ();
    // get each box of the link
    Iterator it(aSetofLinks);
    while (it++) {
        Link& link = (Link &) it ();

        SetofAllBoxes.add (link.box1 ());
        SetofAllBoxes.add (link.box2 ());
    }
    // the box itself should not be in the set
    SetofAllBoxes.remove (aBox);
    return SetofAllBoxes;
}
```

```
// 15.17b) Given a box determine all boxes directly or
// indirectly connected
void _allBoxes (Box &aBox, Set& SetofAllBoxes);

Set allBoxes (Box& aBox)
{
    Set SetofAllBoxes;
    // recursively add new boxes
    _allBoxes (aBox, SetofAllBoxes);
    return SetofAllBoxes;
}

void _allBoxes (Box& aBox, Set& setofAllBoxes)
{
    int count = 0;
    // get all boxes of aBox and add them to set if they are
    // not there
    Set allDirect = allDirectBoxes (aBox);
    Iterator it (allDirect);
    while (it++) {
        Box & b = (Box &) it ();
        if (setofAllBoxes.occurrencesOf (b) == 0) {
            setofAllBoxes.add (b);
            _allBoxes (b, setofAllBoxes);
        }
    }
}

// 15.17c) Determine if a link involves a box
boolean link_involves_box (Link& aLink, Box& aBox)
{
    return ((& aLink.box1 () == &aBox) ||
        (& aLink.box2 () == &aBox));
}

// 15.17d) Given a box and a link, find the other box logically
// connected to the given box through the other end of the link

Box * other_box_of_link (Link& aLink, Box& aBox)
{
    if (link_involves_box (aLink, aBox))
        return (& aLink.box1 () == &aBox ? &aLink.box2() :
            &aLink.box1 ());
    else return 0;
}

// 15.17e) Given two boxes, determine all links between them
Set links_between_boxes (Box& box1, Box& box2)
{
    Set allLinks;

    Iterator it(box1.links ());
    while (it++) {
```

```
        Link& link = (Link &) it ();
        if (link_involves_box (link, box2)) {
            allLinks.add (link);
        }
    }
    return (allLinks);
}

// 15.17f) Given a selection and a sheet, determine which links
//   connect a selected box to a deselected box
Set select_deselect_links (Selection& aSelection,
    Sheet& aSheet)
{
    Set selectedLinks;
    Set & selectedBoxes = aSelection.boxes ();

    // for each box on the sheet
    Iterator it (aSheet.boxes ());
    while (it++) {
        Box& testBox = (Box &) it ();

        // ignore selected boxes
        if (selectedBoxes.occurrencesOf (testBox)) continue;
        // get links between each selected box and test box
        Iterator ib (selectedBoxes);
        while (ib++) {
            Box& box = (Box &) ib ();
            Iterator il (links_between_boxes (box, testBox));
            while (il++) {
                Link& link = (Link &) il ();
                selectedLinks.add (link);
            }
        }
    }
    return (selectedLinks);
}

// 15.17g) Given two boxes and a link, produce an
// ordered set of points.
OrderedCltn points_between_boxes (Box& box1, Box& box2,
    Link& link)
{
    OrderedCltn points;
    int rev;// direction reversed (box2 to box1 link)
    if (&link.box1() == &box1 && &link.box2() == &box2) rev=0;
    else if (&link.box1()== &box2 && &link.box2() == &box1)
rev=1;
    else return points; // link does not connect the boxes
    Iterator it(link.segments ());
    int first=1;
    while (it++) {
        LineSegment & s = (LineSegment &) it ();
```

```
        if (first) {
            points.add (s.point1());
            first = 0;
        }
        points.add (s.point2());
    }
    if (rev) points.reverse();
    return points;
}
```

15.18 [Project]

16

Non-Object-Oriented Languages

16.1a. The answers that we provide for this problem are in Ada. The classes that are requested are all container classes, which means that we will have to combine the implementation techniques discussed in this chapter with Ada's capability of defining a generic package. This is because the strong type-checking of Ada requires that we declare the type of the items within the container object. Since we wish to be able to use the container classes to hold objects of any type (unknown in advance), we use a generic formal parameter as a place-holder for the item type. When the client of the container class wishes to use the package for a specific type, the generic package will be *instantiated*, and the generic type parameter will be replaced by the specific type chosen by the client. (It should be noted that Ada's generic *instantiation* is done at compile-time, while the object-oriented *instantiation* of a class to create a new instance is performed at run-time.)

The dictionary package below requires the client to specify a type for both the key and the value fields in each key-value pair. For added flexibility, the client must also provide a function that will compare two keys to determine if they are equal. This is done so that more complex structured types can be used as dictionary keys. For example, if strings are used as dictionary keys, we will want to compare them by matching their character contents, not just by comparing two string pointers.

The package specification declares a dictionary type and shows the signature of each operation on a dictionary, but does not reveal the implementation of a dictionary. We have documented the semantics of each operation in comments.

```
generic
    type dictionary_key is private;
    type dictionary_value is private;
```

```
      with function equal( left, right : dictionary_key )
                  return boolean is <>;

  package dictionary_pkg is
     type dictionary is private;

     procedure add( self: in out dictionary;
                  key: in dictionary_key;
                  value: in dictionary_value );
     -- Add the key-value pair to the dictionary.
     -- If "key" already exists within the dictionary, its
     -- associated value will be updated.

     procedure delete( self: in out dictionary;
                  key: in dictionary_key );
     -- Delete key-value pair associated with "key" from
     -- dictionary. Raise "not_found" if the key is not found.

     function test( self: in dictionary;
                  key: in dictionary_key ) return boolean;
     -- Return True iff item is a member of the dictionary.

     function get_value(self: dictionary;
                key: dictionary_key ) return dictionary_value ;
     -- Return the value associated with "key" in the dictionary.
     -- Raise "not_found" if the key is not found.
     -- "Test" may be called before get_value to avoid raising
     -- the exception.

     procedure free( self: in out dictionary );
     -- Free all storage used by the dictionary.

     not_found : exception;

  private

     type dictionary_record;
     type dictionary is access dictionary_record;

  end dictionary_pkg;
```

The following code fragments show how the dictionary package would be used to define a dictionary of numbers and strings.

```
  declare
     type string_name is access string;
     package my_dictionary_pkg is new dictionary_pkg(
        dictionary_key => integer,
        dictionary_value => string_name,
        equal => "=" );
     use my_dictionary_pkg;
     my_dictionary: dictionary;
     function sn( s: string ) return string_name is ...
```

```
    -- omitted
begin
    add( my_dictionary, 1066, sn("Battle of Hastings");
    put( get_value( my_dictionary, 1066 ) );
end;
```

The body of this generic package provides the implementation, showing both the structure of a dictionary object, and the procedural code for each operation. We have chosen a very simple structure, implementing a dictionary as a singly-linked list of key-value pairs. This is not the fastest implementation; a hash table would have provided a faster lookup operation. The dictionary type itself is an access data type (more commonly known as a pointer).

```
with unchecked_deallocation;
package body dictionary_pkg is
    -- A Dictionary is a pointer to a linked list of nodes
    -- containing key-value pairs.

    type dictionary_record is record
        key: dictionary_key;
        value: dictionary_value;
        next: dictionary;
    end record;

    -- The following are set by the "test" function
    previous_node: dictionary:= null; -- dictionary last tested
    found_node: dictionary := null;-- node found by "test"

    procedure free_node is
        new unchecked_deallocation( dictionary_record,
            dictionary);

    -- Implementations of external operations:

    procedure add( self: in out dictionary;
                   key: in dictionary_key;
                   value: in dictionary_value ) is
        new_node: dictionary;
    begin
        if test( self, key ) then
            found_node.value := value;
        else
            new_node := new dictionary_record;
            new_node.key := key;
            new_node.value := value;
            new_node.next := self;
            self := new_node;
        end if;
    end add;
    procedure delete( self: in out dictionary;
        key: in dictionary_key ) is
    begin
        if test( self, key ) then-- key is in dictionary
```

```
            if previous_node = null then
                self := found_node.next;
            else
                previous_node.next := found_node.next;
                -- point beyond key
            end if;
            free_node( found_node );
        else
            raise not_found;
        end if;
    end delete;

    function test( self: in dictionary;
                   key: in dictionary_key ) return boolean is
        this_node: dictionary;
    begin
        previous_node := null;
        found_node := null;
        this_node := self;
        while this_node /= null loop
            if equal( this_node.key, key ) then
                found_node := this_node;
                return true;
            end if;
            previous_node := this_node;
            this_node := this_node.next;
        end loop;
        return false;
    end test;

    function get_value(self: dictionary;
            key: dictionary_key ) return dictionary_value is
    begin
        if test( self, key ) then-- key is in dictionary
            return found_node.value;
        else        -- not found
            raise not_found;
        end if;
    end get_value;

    procedure free( self: in out dictionary ) is
        next_node: dictionary;
        this_node: dictionary;
    begin
        next_node := self;
        while next_node /= null loop
            this_node:=next_node;
            next_node := this_node.next;
            free_node( this_node );
        end loop;
    end free;
end dictionary_pkg;
```

16.1b. The public interface of the set class is defined in Ada by its package specification, shown below. The client of this generic package must provide the type of item to be contained in the set, and a function to compare two items for equality.

```
generic
    type item_type is private;-- type of items in array
    with function equal( left, right : item_type )
        return boolean;

package set_pkg is
    type set is private;

    function create return set;
    -- Create a new set.

    procedure add( the_set: in out set; item: in item_type );
    -- Add "item" to "the_set".
    -- Return quietly if its already there.

    procedure delete( the_set: in out set; item: in item_type );
    -- Delete item from the_set, if it is a member.
    -- Return quietly if item is not a member of the_set.

    function test( the_set: in set;
                   item: in item_type ) return boolean;
    -- Return True iff item is a member of the_set.

    procedure free( the_set: in out set );
    -- Deallocate the_set.

private
    type set_record;
    type set is access set_record;
end set_pkg;
```

For the internal implementation of the *set* class, we again chose a single linked list. Contrasting our implementation of *set* with that for *dictionary*, you may detect a subtle design flaw in *dictionary*. If we have aliased references to a *dictionary* and then delete the first item from the *dictionary* using one of the references, the other references may become invalid. The designer of the *dictionary* class should either make *dictionary* a *limited private* type to prevent aliased references, or should implement *dictionary* with a header record (as we did with *set*) to allow aliasing while preserving encapsulation.

```
with unchecked_deallocation;
package body set_pkg is

    -- A Set is a pointer to a header that points to a linked
    -- list of nodes containing the items

    type node;
    type node_a is access node;
```

```
type set_record is record
   first: node_a := null;
   size: natural := 0;
end record;

type node is record
   contents: item_type;
   next: node_a;
end record;

-- The following are set by the "test" function
found_node: node_a := null;
   -- node found by the "test" function
previous_node: node_a := null;
   -- node preceding found_node in list

procedure free_node is
   new unchecked_deallocation( node, node_a );
procedure free_set is
   new unchecked_deallocation( set_record, set );

-- Implementations of external operations:

function create return set is
begin
   return new set_record;
end create;

procedure add( the_set: in out set; item: in item_type ) is
   new_node: node_a;
begin
   if not test( the_set, item ) then
      new_node := new node;
      new_node.contents := item;
      new_node.next := the_set.first;
      the_set.first := new_node;
      the_set.size := the_set.size + 1;
   end if;
end add;

procedure delete( the_set: in out set;
   item: in item_type ) is
begin
   if test( the_set, item ) then-- item is in set
      if previous_node = null then-- item is first
         the_set.first := found_node.next;
         -- point beyond item
      else
         previous_node.next := found_node.next;
         -- point beyond item
      end if;
      free_node( found_node );
      the_set.size := the_set.size - 1;
```

```
            end if;
        end delete;
        function test( the_set: in set; item: in item_type )
                    return boolean is
            this_node: node_a;
        begin
            previous_node := null;
            found_node := null;
            this_node := the_set.first;
            while this_node /= null loop
                if equal( this_node.contents, item ) then
                    found_node := this_node;
                    return true;
                end if;
                previous_node := this_node;
                this_node := this_node.next;
            end loop;
            return false;
        end test;

        procedure free( the_set: in out set ) is
            next_node: node_a;
            this_node: node_a;
        begin
            next_node := the_set.first;
            while next_node /= null loop
                this_node := next_node;
                next_node := this_node.next;
                free_node( this_node );
            end loop;
            free_set( the_set );
        end free;

    end set_pkg;
```

16.1c. The *dynamic_array* class is a little trickier to implement. Inherent in the notion of an array is the kind of tight packing and fast indexed access that comes from allocating a series of similar objects together in memory. In the following code, the objects in the array are indexed by the positive integers. The client must provide a special value to initialize the array contents so that the result of accessing an empty slot is defined. The client may also provide a *default_capacity*, which is a guess at the size of the array, either when the generic package is instantiated, or when a new instance of an array is created.

```
    generic
        type item_type is private;-- type of items in array
        default_capacity: Positive := 20;
            -- default initial capacity
        init_value: item_type;-- initial value of array items

    package dynamic_array_pkg is
        type dynamic_array is private;
        null_array : constant dynamic_array;
```

```
                    -- value of unallocated array

        function create( capacity: Positive := default_capacity )
                    return dynamic_array;
        -- Allocate a new array of the specified capacity.

        procedure free( self: in out dynamic_array );
        -- Deallocate storage for array (without deallocating items
        -- that may still be contained within it). Stores the
        -- "null_array" value in the array reference variable.

        function length( an_array: in dynamic_array )
            return Natural;
        -- Return highest index at which an item has been stored.
        -- Length is less than or equal to capacity.

        function index( an_array: in dynamic_array;
            index: in Positive ) return item_type;
        -- Return the value of the item stored at "index"
        -- without changing the state of the array.
        -- Raise length_error if index is beyond length.


        procedure replace( an_array: in out dynamic_array;
                    index: in Positive; item: in item_type );
        -- Replace value stored at "index" with new "item" value.
        -- Extend the array if necessary to accommodate "index".

        procedure insert( an_array: in out dynamic_array;
                    index: in Positive; item: in item_type );
        -- Insert "item" in "an_array" at "index", shifting the
        -- following items down by one position, incrementing the
        -- length. Reallocate the array if necessary.

        procedure delete( an_array: in out dynamic_array;
                    index: in Positive );
        -- Delete the value stored at "index", shifting the
        -- following values back by one position to take its place,
        -- and decrementing the length.

        length_error: exception;
        -- Exception indicating a requested index beyond the
        -- last item stored in the array.

private
    type dynamic_array_rec (capacity: Positive :=
        default_capacity);
    type dynamic_array is access dynamic_array_rec;
    null_array : constant dynamic_array := null;
end dynamic_array_pkg;
```

The actual implementation of dynamic arrays is hidden in the body of the package. When we have to expand the array, we must either point to a new "chunk" of memory with room for more objects, or simply reallocate a new piece large enough to contain the entire expanded array. In this simple implementation, we choose the latter strategy, which has the advantage of permitting very fast indexing, but will fail sooner when memory becomes fragmented.

Here we have decided to use an ordinary Ada array to implement a dynamic array. The array is created with a user-specified initial size, and the values of array-slots are initialized to the null_item. When a new value is added beyond the allocated bounds of the array, the array will be automatically reallocated at a larger size, and the array contents already set will be copied to the newly-allocated array. Because this reallocation could be costly, the allocated size is purposely over-estimated.

```ada
with unchecked_deallocation;
package body dynamic_array_pkg is

   type contents_array is array (Positive range <>)
      of item_type;

   type dynamic_array_rec (capacity: Positive :=
      default_capacity) is
   record
      contents: contents_array (1..capacity)
                 := (others => init_value);
      length: Natural := 0;
   end record;

   function create( capacity: Positive := default_capacity )
                 return dynamic_array is
   begin
      return new dynamic_array_rec( capacity );
   end create;

   procedure internal_free is
      new unchecked_deallocation( dynamic_array_rec,
         dynamic_array );

   procedure free( self: in out dynamic_array ) is
   begin
      if self /= null_array then
         internal_free( self );
      end if;
   end free;

   function max( i1, i2 : Integer ) return Integer is
   begin
      if i1 > i2 then
         return i1;
      else
         return i2;
```

```
      end if;
   end max;

   -- Reallocate: Reallocate array.contents with more storage.
   --           Copy old contents into newly-allocated contents.
   --           New capacity is at least twice the old capacity.
   procedure reallocate(an_array: in out dynamic_array;
                 index: in Positive) is
      old_capacity: constant Positive :=
         an_array.contents'last;
      new_capacity: Positive := max( index,
         max( 2*old_capacity, default_capacity ) );
      new_array: dynamic_array :=
         new dynamic_array_rec(new_capacity);
   begin
      for i in an_array.contents'range loop
         new_array.contents(i) := an_array.contents(i);
      end loop;
      new_array.length := an_array.length;
      free( an_array );
      an_array := new_array;
   end reallocate;

   function length( an_array: in dynamic_array )
      return Natural is
   begin
      return an_array.length;
   end length;

   function index( an_array: in dynamic_array;
      index: in Positive ) return item_type is
   begin
      if index > an_array.length then
         raise length_error;
      end if;
      return an_array.contents(index);
   end index;

   procedure replace( an_array: in out dynamic_array;
      index: in Positive; item: in item_type ) is
      capacity: constant Positive := an_array.contents'last;
   begin
      if index > capacity then
         reallocate( an_array, index );
      end if;
      an_array.contents(index) := item;
      if index > an_array.length then
         an_array.length := index;
      end if;
   end replace;
```

```
            procedure insert( an_array: in out dynamic_array;
                index: in Positive; item: in item_type ) is
                capacity: constant Positive := an_array.contents'last;
                old_length: Natural := an_array.length;
            begin
                if index > capacity or old_length = capacity then
                    reallocate( an_array, max(index,old_length+1) );
                end if;
                for i in index .. old_length loop
                    an_array.contents(old_length+index-i+1) :=
                            an_array.contents(old_length+index-i);
                end loop;
                an_array.contents(index) := item;
                an_array.length := max(index,old_length+1);
            end insert;

            procedure delete( an_array: in out dynamic_array;
                index: in Positive ) is
            begin
                if index > an_array.length then
                    raise length_error;
                end if;
                for i in index .. an_array.length loop
                    an_array.contents(i) := an_array.contents(i+1);
                end loop;
                an_array.length := an_array.length - 1;
            end delete;
        end dynamic_array_pkg;
```

16.2a. We have implemented the various kinds of associations requested, in Ada, by defining new classes whose instances are the associations. This approach was discussed in Section 10.7.3 (see Figure 10.11 in the book). The association objects thus implemented are essentially container objects whose contents are ordered pairs of object-ids.

We have used Ada overloading to permit the use of the same operation name (such as *get*) to operate on either end of the association, depending on the type of the argument. This is a cute trick that unfortunately fails if both ends of the association have the same type. In that case, the operations must be explicitly distinguished by direction, by using role names, for example.

The one-to-one association requested in Part a is shown below.

```
    generic
        type type_a is private;
        type type_b is private;

    package association_1_1_pkg is
        -- One-to-One Association Package
        -- This package provides associations between objects of 2
        -- arbitrary types.
        -- The associations can be traversed in either direction.
```

```
    type association_1_1 is private;

    function create return association_1_1;

    procedure add( self: association_1_1; aaa: type_a;
       bbb: type_b );

    procedure remove( self: association_1_1; aaa: type_a );
    procedure remove( self: association_1_1; bbb: type_b );

    function get( self: association_1_1; aaa: type_a )
       return type_b;
    function get( self: association_1_1; bbb: type_b )
       return type_a;

    not_found: exception;

private

    type assoc_record;
    type association_1_1 is access assoc_record;

end association_1_1_pkg;

with unchecked_deallocation;
package body association_1_1_pkg is

    type assoc_pair;
    type pair_access is access assoc_pair;

    type assoc_record is record
       pairs: pair_access := null;
    end record;

    type assoc_pair is record
       aaa: type_a;
       bbb: type_b;
       next: pair_access := null;
    end record;

    -- Variables set by the find procedure
    previous_pair: pair_access := null;-- node found by "find"
    found_pair: pair_access := null;
       -- node preceding found_node

    procedure free_pair is
       new unchecked_deallocation( assoc_pair, pair_access );

    function create return association_1_1 is
    begin
```

```
            return new assoc_record;
end;

procedure add( self: association_1_1; aaa: type_a;
    bbb: type_b ) is
    this_pair: pair_access;
    new_pair: pair_access;
begin
    new_pair := new assoc_pair;
    new_pair.aaa := aaa;
    new_pair.bbb := bbb;
    new_pair.next := self.pairs;
    self.pairs := new_pair;
end add;

function find( self: association_1_1; aaa: type_a )
            return boolean is
    this_pair: pair_access := self.pairs;
begin
    found_pair := null;
    previous_pair := null;
    while this_pair /= null loop
       if this_pair.aaa = aaa then
           found_pair := this_pair;
           return true;
       end if;
       previous_pair := this_pair;
       this_pair := this_pair.next;
    end loop;
    return false;
end find;

function find( self: association_1_1; bbb: type_b )
            return boolean is
    this_pair: pair_access := self.pairs;
begin
    found_pair := null;
    previous_pair := null;
    while this_pair /= null loop
       if this_pair.bbb = bbb then
           found_pair := this_pair;
           return true;
       end if;
       previous_pair := this_pair;
       this_pair := this_pair.next;
    end loop;
    return false;
end find;

procedure remove( self: association_1_1; aaa: type_a ) is
begin
```

```
        if find( self, aaa ) then
            if previous_pair /= null then
                previous_pair.next := found_pair.next;
            else
                self.pairs := found_pair.next;
            end if;
            free_pair( found_pair );
        else
            raise not_found;
        end if;
    end remove;

    procedure remove( self: association_1_1; bbb: type_b ) is
    begin
        if find( self, bbb ) then
            if previous_pair /= null then
                previous_pair.next := found_pair.next;
            else
                self.pairs := found_pair.next;
            end if;
            free_pair( found_pair );
        else
            raise not_found;
        end if;
    end remove;

    function get( self: association_1_1; aaa: type_a )
        return type_b is
    begin
        if not find( self, aaa ) then
            raise not_found;
        end if;
        return found_pair.bbb;
    end get;

    function get( self: association_1_1; bbb: type_b )
        return type_a is
    begin
        if not find( self, bbb ) then
            raise not_found;
        end if;
        return found_pair.aaa;
    end get;
end association_1_1_pkg;
```

16.2b. The answers to both Part b and Part c are the same except that Part c requires ordering in the direction of one-to-many. To solve both parts, we have implemented an ordered one-to-many association, which may be used without considering the ordering if desired. There is no performance penalty or space inefficiency for keeping the associated objects in order.

16.2c. The ordered one-to-many association class shown below keeps the "many" objects ordered according to their order of insertion. A more flexible arrangement would allow the user to add new pairs with the object on the "many" side going into a specified location relative to other objects.

```
generic
    type type_a is private;
    type type_b is private;
    type b_array is private;
    with function create( capacity: Positive := 20 )
        return b_array;
    with procedure insert( the_array: in out b_array;
        index: in Positive; item: in type_b );

package association_1_m_pkg is

    -- One-to-Many Association Package
    -- This package provides associations between two arbitrary
    -- types. The associations can be traversed in the direction
    -- from one to many.
    -- The ordering of "many" elements is preserved.

    type association_1_m is private;

    function create return association_1_m;

    procedure add( self: association_1_m; aaa: type_a;
        bbb: type_b );
    -- Add link (ordered pair) (aaa, bbb) to association

    -- ALL OF THE FOLLOWING raise not_found if index isn't
    -- found...

    procedure remove( self: association_1_m;
                aaa: type_a; bbb: type_b );
    -- Remove the link (aaa, bbb) from the association

    procedure remove( self: association_1_m; aaa: type_a );
    -- Remove all links to aaa from association; i.e. (aaa, *)

    procedure remove( self: association_1_m; bbb: type_b );
    -- Remove all links to bbb from association; i.e. (*, bbb)

    function get( self: association_1_m; aaa: type_a )
        return b_array;
    -- Return array of all type_b objects associated with aaa .
    -- Objects in array are ordered in order of insertion.

    not_found: exception;

    private
```

```ada
    type assoc_record;
    type association_1_m is access assoc_record;

end association_1_m_pkg;

with unchecked_deallocation;
package body association_1_m_pkg is

    -- Associations are implemented herein as
    -- linked lists of ordered pairs.

    type assoc_pair;
    type pair_access is access assoc_pair;

    type assoc_record is record
        pairs: pair_access := null;
        -- points to first pair in the list
        last_pair: pair_access := null;
        -- points to last pair in the list
    end record;

    type assoc_pair is record
        aaa: type_a;
        bbb: type_b;
        next: pair_access := null;
        -- points to next pair in the list
    end record;

    -- Variables set by the find procedure
    previous_pair: pair_access := null;
    -- node found by the "find" function
    found_pair: pair_access := null;
    -- node preceding found_node in list


    procedure free_pair is
        new unchecked_deallocation( assoc_pair, pair_access );

    function create return association_1_m is
    begin
        return new assoc_record;
    end;

    function find( start: pair_access; aaa: type_a )
        return boolean is
        this_pair: pair_access := start;
    begin
        while this_pair /= null loop
            if this_pair.aaa = aaa then
                found_pair := this_pair;
                return true;
            end if;
```

```
            previous_pair := this_pair;
            this_pair := this_pair.next;
        end loop;
        return false;
    end find;

    function find( start: pair_access; bbb: type_b )
        return boolean is
        this_pair: pair_access := start;
    begin
        while this_pair /= null loop
            if this_pair.bbb = bbb then
                found_pair := this_pair;
                return true;
            end if;
            previous_pair := this_pair;
            this_pair := this_pair.next;
        end loop;
        return false;
    end find;

    procedure add( self: association_1_m; aaa: type_a;
        bbb: type_b ) is
        this_pair: pair_access;
        new_pair: pair_access;
    begin
        if find( self.pairs, aaa ) then
            -- enforce 1-many multiplicity
            found_pair.bbb := bbb;-- update existing pair
        else
            new_pair := new assoc_pair;
            new_pair.aaa := aaa;
            new_pair.bbb := bbb;
            if self.pairs = null then
                self.pairs := new_pair;
            else
                self.last_pair.next := new_pair;
            end if;
            self.last_pair := new_pair;
        end if;
    end add;

    procedure unsplice( self: association_1_m ) is
    begin
        if previous_pair /= null then
            previous_pair.next := found_pair.next;
        else
            self.pairs := found_pair.next;
        end if;
        free_pair( found_pair );
    end unsplice;
```

```
procedure remove( self: association_1_m;
              aaa: type_a; bbb: type_b ) is
   this_pair: pair_access := self.pairs;
   found: boolean := false;
begin
   previous_pair := null;
   while find( this_pair, aaa ) loop
      if found_pair.bbb = bbb then
         unsplice(self);
         found := true;
         exit;
      end if;
      this_pair := found_pair.next;
   end loop;
   if not found then
      raise not_found;
   end if;
end remove;

procedure remove( self: association_1_m; aaa: type_a ) is
   this_pair: pair_access := self.pairs;
   found: boolean := false;
begin
   previous_pair := null;
   while find( this_pair, aaa ) loop
      this_pair := found_pair.next;
      unsplice(self);
      found := true;
   end loop;
   if not found then
      raise not_found;
   end if;
end remove;

procedure remove( self: association_1_m; bbb: type_b ) is
   this_pair: pair_access := self.pairs;
   found: boolean := false;
begin
   previous_pair := null;
   while find( this_pair, bbb ) loop
      this_pair := found_pair.next;
      unsplice(self);
      found := true;
   end loop;
   if not found then
      raise not_found;
   end if;
end remove;

function get( self: association_1_m; aaa: type_a )
            return b_array is
   this_pair: pair_access := self.pairs;
```

```
            the_array: b_array := create;
            index: Positive := 1;
            found: boolean := false;
        begin
            while find( this_pair, aaa ) loop
                insert( the_array, index, found_pair.bbb );
                index := index + 1;
                found := true;
                this_pair := found_pair.next;
            end loop;
            if not found then
                raise not_found;
            end if;
            return the_array;
        end get;
    end association_1_m_pkg;
```

16.2d. The implementation of a many-to-many association with traversal in both directions is straightforward, based on the previous chosen approach of implementing an association as a set of ordered pairs. Because the answer is so similar to the previous answer, we show only the parts that are different.

```
    generic
        type type_a is private;
        type type_b is private;
        type a_array is private;
        with function create( capacity: Positive := 20 )
            return a_array;
        with procedure insert( the_array: in out a_array;
            index: in Positive; item: in type_a );
        type b_array is private;
        with function create( capacity: Positive := 20 )
            return b_array;
        with procedure insert( the_array: in out b_array;
            index: in Positive; item: in type_b );

    package association_m_m_pkg is

        type association_m_m is private;

        ... code removed: see answer to Part c.

        function get( self: association_m_m; bbb: type_b )
            return a_array;
        -- Return array of all type_a objects associated with bbb .

        ... code removed: see answer to Part c.

    end association_m_m_pkg;

    with unchecked_deallocation;
    package body association_m_m_pkg is
```

```
      ... code removed: see answer to Part c.

      procedure add( self: association_m_m; aaa:
         type_a; bbb: type_b ) is
         this_pair: pair_access;
         new_pair: pair_access;
      begin
         if find( self.pairs, aaa )
            and then found_pair.bbb = bbb then
            null; -- the pair is already associated
         else
            ... code removed: see answer to Part c.
         end if;
      end add;

      ... code removed: see answer to Part c.

      function get( self: association_m_m; bbb: type_b )
                  return a_array is
      ... This function is analogous to get function in Part c.
      end get;
   end association_m_m_pkg;
```

16.3 Many programming languages provide memory allocation and deallocation functions as
      part of their run time libraries. For this example, we implement *allocate* and *deallocate*
      in Fortran, a language that does not have these functions.

      We give a simple answer for this exercise. *Memory* is an array of integers from which
      blocks are allocated and deallocated. Arrays *allocatedlist* and *allocatedsize* are collocat-
      ed arrays which contain the starting index and size for each block. Arrays *freelist* and
      freesize are collocated arrays which contain the starting index and size for each chunk
      of free space. There are many ways in which our simple implementation could be im-
      proved.

      • More carefully consolidate contiguous chunks of free memory than shown in subrou-
         tine *mem_return*.

      • Merge free and allocated lists together.

      • Define allocate and deallocate to return an index into the *allocate* table. Then objects
         could be moved about in memory to coalesce fragmented free space.

file mem.h
```
      parameter (NALLOCATED = 100000)
      parameter (MAXLIST = 100)
      parameter (MAXLISTM1 = 99)
      common /memory_/memory (NALLOCATED)
      common /memory_mgr_/ freelist (MAXLIST),
    1    freesize (MAXLIST),
    1    allocatedlist (MAXLIST),
    1    allocatedsize (MAXLIST)
      integer memory, freelist, freesize,
```

```
      1      allocatedlist, allocatedsize
          integer allocate
```

file memblk.f

```
          block data
          include 'mem.h'
          data freelist(1) /1/
          data (freelist(i),i=2,MAXLIST) / MAXLISTM1 * 0/
          data freesize(1) /NALLOCATED/
          data (freesize(i), i=2, MAXLIST) /MAXLISTM1 * 0/
          data allocatedlist /MAXLIST * 0/
          data allocatedsize /MAXLIST * 0/
          end
```

file mem.f

```
c         allocate n word of memory
c         return offset within "memory"
c
          integer function allocate (n)
          include 'mem.h'
          integer n, ptr

c         walk free list and find block of n or more
          do i = 1, MAXLIST
             if (freesize (i) .eq. 0) go to 100
             if (freesize (i) .gt. n) then
                ptr = freelist (i)
                freelist (i) = freelist (i) + n
                freesize (i) = freesize (i) - n
                call mem_update (ptr, n)
                go to 200
             endif
  100     enddo
c         error: put code here to handle out-of-memory exception
          allocate = 0
          return
c         success
  200     allocate = ptr
          return
          end
c
c         deallocate memory at "ptr"
c
          subroutine deallocate (ptr)
          include 'mem.h'
          integer ptr

c         find allocated ptr and return it to free list
          do i = 1, MAXLIST
             if (allocatedlist(i) .eq. ptr) then
                call mem_return (allocatedlist(i),
                   allocatedsize(i))
                allocatedlist(i) = 0
```

```
            allocatedsize(i) = 0
            go to 100
         endif
      enddo
100   return
      end


c***************
c     some internal routines
c***************
c     return allocated memory to free list
c
      subroutine mem_return (ptr, n)
      include 'mem.h'
      integer ptr, n

c  find a free slot. first look for addition to existing block
      do i = 1, MAXLIST
         if ((ptr + n) .eq. freelist(i)) then
            freelist(i) = ptr
            freesize(i) = freesize(i) + n
            go to 100
         endif
      enddo
c     now put it back anywhere
      do i = 1, MAXLIST
         if (freelist(i) .eq. 0) then
            freelist(i) = ptr
            freesize (i) = n
            go to 100
         endif
      enddo
c     warning:  normal loop exit means no more free list
c               entries. Waste memory and continue execution.
100   return
      end
c
c     update the allocated list
c
      subroutine mem_update (ptr, n)
      include 'mem.h'
      integer ptr, n
c     find empty allocated cell
      do i = 1, MAXLIST
         if (allocatedlist(i) .eq. 0) then
            allocatedlist(i) = ptr
            allocatedsize(i) = n
            go to 100
         endif
      enddo
c     put error code here to handle allocate list overflow
100   return
```

```
                end
```

Files *memblk.f*, *mem.f*, and *testex163.f* were compiled and linked to test our code.

file testex163.f

```
        c       test memory manager
        c
                include 'mem.h'
                dimension ivalues (1)
                equivalence (ivalues(1), memory(1))

                id1 = allocate (100)
                print *, id1
                id2 = allocate (10)
                print *, id2
                id3 = allocate (1000)
                print *, id3
                id4 = allocate (1)
                print *, id4
                id5 = allocate (100)
                print *, id5

                print *, 'deallocate in reverse order'

                call deallocate (id5)
                call deallocate (id4)
                call deallocate (id3)
                call deallocate (id2)
                call deallocate (id1)

                id1 = allocate (100)
                print *, id1
                id2 = allocate (10)
                print *, id2
                id3 = allocate (1000)
                print *, id3
                id4 = allocate (1)
                print *, id4
                id5 = allocate (100)
                print *, id5

                end
```

16.4 We implement the ordered aggregation in C using an array of pointers to cards in each collection and a pointer to the collection in each card. We assume that other files define the enumerated types *Visibility, Coordinate, Suit,* and *Rank* and the class structures.

```
#define DECKSIZE 52
struct Collection_of_cards
{
    struct Collection_of_cardsClass * class;
    Visibility visibility;
    Coordinate location_x;
```

```
        Coordinate location_y;
        struct Card * cards[DECKSIZE];
    };
```

The definitions of *Deck, Discard_pile,* and *Draw_pile* are exactly the same as *Collection_of_cards*. The definition of *Hand* is:

```
    struct Hand
    {
        struct Collection_of_cardsClass * class;
        Visibility visibility;
        Coordinate location_x;
        Coordinate location_y;
        struct Card * cards[DECKSIZE];
        int initial_size;
    };
```

The definition of *Card* is:

```
    struct Card
    {
        struct CardClass * class;
        Suit suit;
        Rank rank;
        struct Collection_of_cards * collection;
    };
```

The code for inserting a card into a collection in a given slot is:

```
    void collection_insert_card(collection, card, slot)
        struct Collection_of_cards * collection;
        struct Card * card; int slot;
    {
        int i;
        if(slot>=0 && slot<DECKSIZE)
        {
            for(i = DECKSIZE-1; i>slot; i--)
                collection->cards[i] = collection->cards[i-1];
            collection->cards[slot] = card;
            card->collection = collection;
        }
    }
```

The code for deleting a card from a collection is:

```
    void collection_delete_card(collection, card)
        struct Collection_of_cards * collection;
        struct Card * card;
    {
        int i; int slot;
        int collection_card_find_slot();
        slot = collection_card_find_slot(collection, card);
        if(slot<DECKSIZE)
        {
            card->collection = 0;
            for(i=slot; i<DECKSIZE-2; i++) collection->cards[i] =
```

```
                          collection->cards[i+1];
            collection->cards[DECKSIZE-1] = 0;
      }
}
int collection_card_find_slot(collection, card)
    struct Collection_of_cards * collection;
    struct Card * card;
{
    int slot;
    for(slot=0; slot<DECKSIZE; slot++)
    {
        if( card == collection->cards[slot] ) return slot;
    }
    return slot;
}
```

Functions are not needed for traversal because each card contains a pointer to its collection and each collection contains an array of cards.

16.5-16.8. These exercises parallel 15.14-15.17. Note how C++ concepts map into C. In this problem, inheritance is not used, so the C code can implement the algorithm directly without tricks. The implementation of the Collection subclasses, which is not shown, would require the implementation of generalization using one of the techniques described in the chapter.

The following code includes the answers for Parts 16.5 through 16.8. The answers also assume the existence of *Set* and *Ordered Collection* classes implemented as structures. These classes must support the methods Set_add, Set_remove, OrderedCltn_add, and OrderedCltn_remove. We also assume the existence of an *Iterator* class which supports iteration over the elements of a set or ordered collection. It supports the methods Iterator_init (from a set or ordered collection), Iterator_next (which increments the iterator to the next element and returns whether an element exists), and Iterator_value (which returns the element value).

The relevant parts of Sheet and Selection are shown, but the rest is omitted. Other classes and methods peripheral to the question have also been omitted.

In this code, we do not attempt to hide the attributes, since C cannot protect them from tampering anyway. There is some point to accessing attributes through methods even in C, but such encapsulation increases the size of the code. The C user desiring such features should seriously consider switching to C++. Compare this style of implementation with answer 16.11, which shows a C implementation that emulates many OO language features.

```
struct Box {
    struct Set * Links;
    struct String text;
    int left, top, width, height;
    boolean _update_in_progress;
};
```

```c
struct Link {
    struct Box * box1;
    struct Box * box2;
    struct OrderedCltn * Segments;
    boolean _update_in_progress;
};

struct Point {
    int x, y;
};

struct LineSegment {
    struct Point point1;
    struct Point point2;
};

struct Selection
{
    struct Set * boxes;
};

struct Sheet
{
    struct Set * boxes;
};

/* functions */

char * malloc ();
void Iterator__init ();
boolean Iterator__next ();
void* Iterator__value ();
struct LineSegment * LineSegment__create ();
struct Set * Set__create ();
struct OrderedCltn * OrderedCltn__create ();

/* methods */

void Box__addLink (this, aLink)
    struct Box * this; struct Link * aLink;
{
    if(this->_update_in_progress) return;
/* update this end of association */
    this->_update_in_progress = 1;
    Set__add (this->Links, aLink);
/* links are created complete, so no need to add box to link */
    this->_update_in_progress = 0;
}

void Box__removeLink (this, aLink)
    struct Box * this; struct Link * aLink;
{
```

```
    if (this->_update_in_progress) return;
    this->_update_in_progress = 1;
    Set__remove (this->Links, aLink);
    Link__removeBox (aLink, this);
    this->_update_in_progress = 0;
}

/* Answer to Exercise 16.6. */
void Box__cut (this)
    struct Box * this;
{
    Iterator it;
    struct Link * link;
    Iterator__init (&it, this->Links);
/* remove this box from all of its blinks */
    while (Iterator__next (&it)) {
        link = (struct Link *) Iterator__value (&it);
        Link__removeBox (link, this);
    }
    Box__destroy (this);
}

/* Answer to Exercise 16.7. */
struct Link * Link__create (box1, box2, points)
    struct Box * box1, * box2;
    struct OrderedCltn * points;
{
    struct Link * this = (struct Link *) malloc (
            sizeof (struct Link));
    Iterator it;
    int first=1;
    struct Point lastPoint;
    struct Point p;
    this->box1 = box1;
    this->box2 = box2;
    this->_update_in_progress = 0;
    Iterator__init (&it, points);
    while (Iterator__next (&it)) {
        p = * (struct Point *) Iterator__value (&it);
        if (first) first=0;
        else {
            OrderedCltn__add (this->Segments,
                    LineSegment__create (p, lastPoint));
        }
        lastPoint = p;
    }
    return this;
}

Link__destroy (this)
    struct Link * this;
{
```

```
    Iterator it;
    struct LineSegment* s;
    /* remove link from box1 and box2 */
    Box__removeLink (this->box1, this);
    Box__removeLink (this->box2, this);
    /* delete line segments */
    Iterator__init (&it, this->Segments);
    while (Iterator__next (&it)) {
        s = (struct LineSegment *) Iterator__value (&it);
        LineSegment__destroy (s);
    }
    free (this);
}

Link__removeBox (this, aBox)
    struct Link * this; struct Box * aBox;
{
    if (this->_update_in_progress) return;
    this->_update_in_progress = 1;
/* remove links from both boxes */
    if (aBox == this->box1 || aBox == this->box2) {
        Box__removeLink (this->box1,this);
        Box__removeLink (this->box2, this);
    }
    this->_update_in_progress = 0;
    Link__destroy (this);
}

struct LineSegment * LineSegment__create (p1, p2)
    struct Point p1, p2;
{
    struct LineSegment * this;
    this = (struct LineSegment *) malloc (
        sizeof (struct LineSegment));
    this->point1 = p1; this->point2 = p2;
    return this;
}

/* 16.8a) Given a box, determine all other boxes directly */
/* linked to it */
struct Set *allDirectBoxes (aBox)
    struct Box * aBox;
{
    Iterator it;
    struct Link * link;
    struct Set *SetofAllBoxes = Set__create ();
    struct Set *aSetofLinks;
/* ask it for its links */
    aSetofLinks = aBox->Links;
/* get each box of the link */
    Iterator__init (&it, aSetofLinks);
    while (Iterator__next (&it)) {
```

```
        link = (struct Link *) Iterator__value (&it);
        Set__add (SetofAllBoxes, link->box1);
        Set__add (SetofAllBoxes, link->box2);
    }
/* the box itself should not be in the set */
    Set__remove (SetofAllBoxes, aBox);
    return (SetofAllBoxes);
}


/* 16.8b) Given a box determine all boxes directly or */
/* indirectly connected */
struct Set * allBoxes (aBox)
    struct Box * aBox;
{
    struct Set * SetofAllBoxes = Set__create ();
/* recursively add new boxes */
    _allBoxes (aBox, SetofAllBoxes);
    return (SetofAllBoxes);
}


_allBoxes (aBox, SetofAllBoxes)
    struct Box * aBox; struct Set * SetofAllBoxes;
{
    struct Set * allDirect;
    Iterator it;
    struct Box * b;
    /* get all boxes of aBox and add them to set if they are
       not there */
    allDirect = allDirectBoxes (aBox);
    Iterator__init (&it, allDirect);
    while (Iterator__next (&it)) {
        b = (struct Box*) Iterator__value (&it);
        if (Set__occurrencesOf (allDirect, b) == 0) {
            Set__add (SetofAllBoxes, b);
            _allBoxes (b, SetofAllBoxes);
        }
    }
    Set__destroy (allDirect);
}

/* 16.8c) Determine if a link involves a box */
boolean link_involves_box ( aLink, aBox)
    struct Link * aLink; struct Box * aBox;
{
    return ((aLink->box1 == aBox) ||
        (aLink->box2 == aBox));
}


/* 16.8d) Given a box and a link, find the other box logically
connected to the given box through the other end of the link */
```

```c
struct Box *other_box_of_link (aLink, aBox)
    struct Link * aLink; struct Box * aBox;
{
    if (aLink->box1 == aBox) return aLink->box2;
    else if (aLink->box2 == aBox) return aLink->box1;
    else return 0;
}

/* 16.8e) Given two boxes, determine all links between them */
struct Set *links_between_boxes (box1, box2)
    struct Box * box1, * box2;
{
    struct Set * allLinks = Set__create ();
    Iterator it;
    struct Link * link;
    Iterator__init (&it, box1->Links);
    while (Iterator__next (&it)) {
        link = (struct Link *) Iterator__value (&it);
        if (link_involves_box (link, box2)) {
            Set__add (allLinks, link);
        }
    }
    return (allLinks);
}

/* 16.8f) Given a selection and a sheet, determine which links
    connect a selected box to a deselected box */
struct Set * select_deselect_links (aSelection, aSheet)
    struct Selection * aSelection;
    struct Sheet * aSheet;
{
    struct Set * selectedLinks = Set__create ();
    struct Set * selectedBoxes = aSelection->boxes;
    Iterator it, ib, il;
    struct Box * testBox, * box;
    struct Link * link;
    struct Set * dlinks;

    /* for each box on the sheet */
    Iterator__init (&it, aSheet->boxes);
    while (Iterator__next (&it)) {
        testBox = (struct Box *) Iterator__value (&it);

        /* ignore selected boxes */
        if (Set__occurrencesOf (selectedBoxes, testBox) > 0)
            continue;
        /* get links between each selected box and test box */
        Iterator__init (&ib, selectedBoxes);
        while (Iterator__next (&ib)) {
            box = (struct Box *) Iterator__value (&ib);
            dlinks = links_between_boxes (box, testBox);
            Iterator__init (&il, dlinks);
```

```
                    while (Iterator__next (&il)) {
                        link = (struct Link *) Iterator__value (&il);
                        Set__add (selectedLinks, link);
                    }
                    Set__destroy (dlinks);
                }
            }
        return (selectedLinks);
    }

    /* 16.8g) Given two boxes and a link, produce an */
    /* ordered set of points. */
    struct OrderedCltn * points_between_boxes (box1, box2, link)
        struct Box * box1, * box2;
        struct Link * link;
    {
        struct OrderedCltn * points = OrderedCltn__create ();
        int rev;/* direction reversed (box2 to box1 link) */
        int first=1;
        Iterator it;
        struct LineSegment * s;
        if (link->box1 == box1 && link->box2 == box2) rev=0;
        else if (link->box1 == box2 && link->box2 == box1) rev=1;
        else return 0; /* link does not connect the boxes */
        Iterator__init (&it, link->Segments);
        while (Iterator__next (&it)) {
            s = (struct LineSegment *) Iterator__value (&it);
            if (first) {
                OrderedCltn__add (points, s->point1);
                first = 0;
            }
            OrderedCltn__add (points, s->point2);
        }
        if (rev) OrderedCltn__reverse (points);
        return points;
    }
```

16.9 We solved this problem in Ada to show how the use of a *variant record* to emulate single inheritance can be extended to include multiple inheritance. Any of the workarounds for multiple inheritance described in Section 4.4.3 of the book could be applied to this problem. We chose the technique called "delegation using aggregation of roles" because neither the *AC* nor the *DC* superclass dominates. We view these abstract classes as *mixins* which are inherited in various combinations by the concrete subclasses.

The class hierarchy in the original problem statement (Exercise 15.1) shows no attributes contributed by the *DC* class, so we have added an attribute called *amps* to demonstrate how data from both the *AC* and *DC* mixins is inherited by the *Universal_Motor* class. We also added a simple operation, *get_amps*, to show how method resolution can be handled for multiple inheritance, using the technique described in Section 16.6.2. The package specification for this problem is very similar to the examples in Chapter 16 except that the subtypes *AC_Class* and *DC_Class* are non-disjoint.

```
package Electrical_Machine_pkg is
    type Electrical_Machine is private;
    subtype AC is Electrical_Machine;
    subtype DC is Electrical_Machine;
    subtype Synchronous is Electrical_Machine;
    subtype Induction is Electrical_Machine;
    subtype Universal_Motor is Electrical_Machine;
    subtype Permanent_Magnet is Electrical_Machine;

    improper_operation: exception;

    function get_amps( self: Electrical_Machine )
        return integer;

private
    type El_class is ( Synchronous_Class, Induction_Class,
        Universal_Motor_Class, Permanent_Magnet_Class );
    subtype AC_Class is El_Class
        range Synchronous_Class .. Universal_motor_Class;
    subtype DC_Class is El_Class
        range Universal_motor_Class .. Permanent_Magnet_Class;

    type Electrical_Machine_record( class: El_Class );
    type Electrical_Machine is access
        Electrical_Machine_record;

end Electrical_Machine_pkg;
```

In the package body, we first define two record types that will represent the abstract superclasses *AC* and *DC*. These are then used as *mixins* to define the concrete subclasses of the *Electrical_Machine* class in the form of a record with variant parts containing the data specific to each particular type of machine.

```
package body Electrical_Machine_pkg is

    type AC_mixin (class: AC_Class) is record
        frequency: float;
        case class is
            when Synchronous_Class =>
                rated_field_voltage: float;
                synchronous_speed: float;
            when Induction_Class =>
                rated_speed: float;
            when others =>
                null;
        end case;
    end record;

    type DC_mixin (class: DC_Class) is record
```

```
            amps: integer;
            case class is
               when Permanent_Magnet_Class =>
                  null;
               when others =>
                  null;
            end case;
         end record;

         type Electrical_Machine_record ( class: EL_Class )
            is record
            case class is
               when Synchronous_Class | Induction_Class =>
                  AC_body: AC_mixin(class);
               when Universal_Motor_Class =>
                  AC_aspect: AC_mixin(class);
                  DC_aspect: DC_mixin(class);
               when Permanent_Magnet_Class =>
                  DC_body: DC_mixin(class);
            end case;
         end record;

         function get_amps( self: Electrical_Machine )
            return integer is
         begin
            case self.class is
               when Universal_Motor_Class =>
                  return self.DC_aspect.amps;
               when Permanent_Magnet_Class=>
                  return self.DC_body.amps;
               when others=> raise improper_operation;
            end case;
         end get_amps;
      end Electrical_Machine_pkg;
```

16.10 The same implementation strategies suggested in the answers for 15.4 will work equally well in a non-object-oriented language. None of the suggested implementations depend on inheritance or dynamic binding, so the programmer would not even need to use the techniques described in Chapter 16 (implementing inheritance and method resolution in non-OO languages). However, you are unlikely to have a container class library in a non-OO language, so you will have to make up the data structures you need. The *Sorted_dictionary* and the *Polygon* implementations require the use of an *Array* object (answer to Exercise 16.1c). To implement the *Index*, use the *Sorted_dictionary* as a data structure (answer to Exercise 16.1a).

16.11 This exercise parallels Exercise 15.8 which was answered using Smalltalk. Here we use the same algorithms but implemented in C. This implementation performs dynamic method lookup using a pointer in each object to a class object that contains a function pointers to each method. Furthermore, the attributes and methods of each class are declared using macros so that they can be easily included in subclasses. Although the macros are somewhat unwieldy, they permit future changes to be automatically inherited by all subclasses. Contrast this "pure OO" style of implementation with the more conventional C implementation shown in problem 16-5-16.8. Each style represents a different trade-off among clarity, power, and maintainability.

Two classes are implemented in the answer: *Object* and *BinaryTree*. The *compare* operation must be provided by any object we wish to store in the binary tree. We provide three sample test classes: *Integer*, *String* and *Complex*.

We have omitted include files from the following C code:

file Object.h

```
typedef int Boolean;
#define OBJECT_OPERATIONS(class) \
    char* name; \
    struct class *(*Create) (); \
    int (*compare) ()

struct Object *Object__Create ();
int Object__compare ();

#define OBJECT_METHODS \
    Object__compare

#define OBJECT_INIT(class) \
    struct class *this;\
    this = (struct class *) malloc (sizeof (struct class));\

struct ObjectClass {
    OBJECT_OPERATIONS(Object);
};

struct Object {
    struct ObjectClass *class;
};
```

file Object.c

```
struct ObjectClass ObjectClass = {
    "Object",
    Object__Create,
    OBJECT_METHODS
};

struct Object *Object__Create ()
{
    OBJECT_INIT(Object);
}

int Object__compare (this, anObject)
    struct Object *this; struct Object *anObject;
{
    /* error -- must be overridden by subclass */
```

```
      }
```
file BinaryTree.h
```
      struct BinaryTree *BinaryTree__Create ();
      struct BinaryTree *BinaryTree__delete ();
      void BinaryTree__insert ();
      Boolean BinaryTree__test ();
      Boolean BinaryTree__isEmpty ();
      struct Object *BinaryTree__findMaxValue ();

      #define BINARY_TREE_OPERATIONS(class) \
         OBJECT_OPERATIONS(class);\
         struct BinaryTree *(*delete) ();\
         void (*insert) ();\
         Boolean (*test) (); \
         Boolean (*isEmpty) (); \
         struct Object *(*findMaxValue) ()

      #define BINARY_TREE_METHODS \
         OBJECT_METHODS,\
         BinaryTree__delete, \
         BinaryTree__insert, \
         BinaryTree__test, \
         BinaryTree__isEmpty, \
         BinaryTree__findMaxValue

      #define BINARY_TREE_ATTRIBUTES \
         struct BinaryTree *left; \
         struct BinaryTree *right; \
         struct Object *node_contents

      #define BINARY_TREE_INIT(class) \
         OBJECT_INIT(class); \
         this->node_contents = NULL; \
         this->left = NULL; \
         this->right = NULL

      struct BinaryTreeClass {
         BINARY_TREE_OPERATIONS(BinaryTree);
      };

      struct BinaryTree {
         struct BinaryTreeClass *class;
         BINARY_TREE_ATTRIBUTES;
      };
```
file BinaryTree.c
```
      struct BinaryTreeClass BinaryTreeClass = {
         "BinaryTree",
         BinaryTree__Create,
         BINARY_TREE_METHODS
       };
```

```c
struct BinaryTree *BinaryTree__Create (anObject)
   struct Object * anObject;
{
   BINARY_TREE_INIT(BinaryTree);
   this->node_contents = anObject;
   return (this);
}

struct BinaryTree *BinaryTree__delete (this, anObject)
   struct BinaryTree *this; struct Object *anObject;
{
/* Delete one occurrence of anObject from the receiver.
   Return the new root node of the tree */
  struct BinaryTree * temp;
  int comparison = (*this->node_contents->class->compare)
                         (this->node_contents, anObject);
  if (comparison == 0) {
   if (this->left == NULL) {
      temp = this->right;
      free (this);
      return temp;
   }
   else if (this->right == NULL) {
      temp = this->left;
      free (this);
      return temp;
   }
   /* both subtrees exist, pull up maximum value on left */
   this->node_contents =
      (*(this->left->class->findMaxValue)) (this->left);
   this->left = (*(this->left->class->delete))
      (this->left, this->node_contents);
  }
  else if (comparison < 0) {
   if (this->left != NULL)
      this->left = (*(this->left->class->delete))
         (this->left, anObject);
  }
  else /* comparison > 0 */ {
   if (this->right != NULL)
      this->right = (*(this->right->class->delete))
         (this->right, anObject);
  }
  return (this);
}

struct Object *BinaryTree__findMaxValue (this)
   struct BinaryTree *this;
{
   if (this->right == NULL)
      return (this->node_contents);
   else
```

```
            return (*this->right->class->findMaxValue)
                    (this->right);
    }

    void BinaryTree__insert (this, anObject)
        struct BinaryTree *this; struct Object *anObject;
    {
    /* Insert an object that supports magnitude comparison
        into this, an ordered binary tree. */

        if ((*anObject->class->compare)
                    (anObject, this->node_contents) < 0) {
            if (this->left == NULL) {
                this->left = (*this->class->Create) (anObject);
            }
            else {
                (*this->left->class->insert)(this->left, anObject);
            }
        }
        else {
            if (this->right == NULL) {
                this->right = (*(this->class->Create)) (anObject);
            }
            else {
                (*this->right->class->insert)
                        (this->right,anObject);
            }
        }
    }

    Boolean BinaryTree__test (this, anObject)
        struct BinaryTree *this; struct Object *anObject;
    {
    /* Return TRUE iff anObject is contained in this. */
        int comparison = (*this->node_contents->class->compare)
                    (this->node_contents, anObject);
        if (comparison == 0) return (TRUE);
        if (comparison < 0) {
            if (this->left) return (*this->left->class->test)
                        (this->left, anObject);
            else return FALSE;
        }
        /* else comparison > 0 */
        if (this->right)
            return (*this->right->class->test)
                        (this->right,anObject);
        else return FALSE;
    }
```

file String.h
```
    struct String *String__Create ();
    int String__compare ();
```

```
#define STRING_OPERATIONS(class) \
    OBJECT_OPERATIONS(class)

#define STRING_METHODS \
    OBJECT_METHODS

#define STRING_ATTRIBUTES \
    char *value

#define STRING_INIT(class) \
    OBJECT_INIT(class); \
    this->value = malloc (strlen (value) + 1);\
    strcpy (this->value, value)

struct StringClass {
    STRING_OPERATIONS(String);
};

struct String {
    struct StringClass *class;
    STRING_ATTRIBUTES;
};
```

file String.c

```
struct StringClass StringClass = {
    "String",
    String__Create,
    STRING_METHODS
 };

struct String *String__Create (value)
    char *value;
{
    STRING_INIT(String);
    /* replace Object's compare method */
    this->class->compare = String__compare;
    return (this);
}

int String__compare (this, aString)
    struct String *this;
    struct String *aString;
{
    /* Compare one string with another */

    return (strcmp (this->value, aString->value));
}
```

file Integer.h

```
struct Integer *Integer__Create ();
int Integer__compare ();
```

```
#define INTEGER_OPERATIONS(class) \
    OBJECT_OPERATIONS(class)

#define INTEGER_METHODS \
    OBJECT_METHODS

#define INTEGER_ATTRIBUTES \
    int value

#define INTEGER_INIT(class) \
    OBJECT_INIT(class); \
    this->value = value

struct IntegerClass {
    INTEGER_OPERATIONS(Integer);
};

struct Integer {
    struct IntegerClass *class;
    INTEGER_ATTRIBUTES;
};
```

file Integer.c

```
struct IntegerClass IntegerClass = {
    "Integer",
    Integer__Create,
    INTEGER_METHODS
};

struct Integer *Integer__Create (value)
    int value;
{
    INTEGER_INIT(Integer);
    /* replace Object's compare method */
    this->class->compare = Integer__compare;
    return (this);
}

int Integer__compare (this, anInteger)
    struct Integer *this;
    struct Integer *anInteger;
{
    if (this->value > anInteger->value) return (1);
    else if (this->value < anInteger->value) return (-1);
    else return (0);
}
```

file Complex.h

```
struct Complex *Complex__Create ();
int Complex__compare ();

#define COMPLEX_OPERATIONS(class) \
    OBJECT_OPERATIONS(class)
```

```
#define COMPLEX_METHODS \
    OBJECT_METHODS

#define COMPLEX_ATTRIBUTES \
    double real, imaginary

#define COMPLEX_INIT(class) \
    OBJECT_INIT(class); \
    this->real = real; this->imaginary = imaginary

struct ComplexClass {
    COMPLEX_OPERATIONS(Complex);
};

struct Complex {
    struct ComplexClass *class;
    COMPLEX_ATTRIBUTES;
};
```

file Complex.c

```
struct ComplexClass ComplexClass = {
    "Complex",
    Complex__Create,
    COMPLEX_METHODS
 };

struct Complex *Complex__Create (real, imaginary)
    double real; double imaginary;
{
    COMPLEX_INIT(Complex);
    /* replace Object's compare method */
    this->class->compare = Complex__compare;
    return (this);
}

int Complex__compare (this, aComplex)
    struct Complex *this; struct Complex *aComplex;
{
/* Compare one complex with another based on real part,
    then imaginary */
    if (this->real < aComplex->real) return -1;
    if (this->real > aComplex->real) return 1;
    if (this->imaginary < aComplex->imaginary) return -1;
    if (this->imaginary > aComplex->imaginary) return 1;
    return 0;
}
```

16.12 (Project)

17

Relational Databases

17.1 All in all, we consider Figures E17.3 and E17.4 most desirable. Figures E17.1 and E17.2 are poor models. Some observations are:

- Figure E17.1 fails to properly indicate that each *from-to* vertex pair may be associated with many edges.

- Figure E17.1 may make it difficult to answer queries that specify an edge name. Figure E17.2 may make it difficult to answer queries that specify a vertex name.

- The symmetry in Figure E17.2 can be confusing. Some implementations of Figure E17.2 may require that instances be entered twice or that an edge be searched through both qualifiers in order to find all pertinent instances.

- Figure E17.2 cannot represent the case where only one edge connects to a vertex.

- Figures E17.3 and E17.4 are better than the first two figures because they give vertex and edge equal stature. Vertices and edges seem equally important in the construction of directed graphs so they both should be recognized as object classes.

- Figures E17.3 and E17.4 can be extended to permit dangling edges and/or vertices by changing the "1" multiplicity to "0,1" multiplicity. This distinction can be important for software that must support partially completed diagrams.

- Figures E17.3 and E17.4 capture more multiplicity constraints than the first two figures. Each edge has exactly one *from* vertex and one *to* vertex.

- An implementation of Figure E17.4 must assign the *end* qualifier an enumeration data type with values: *from* and *to*. Enforcing the enumeration may be awkward for some databases and languages.

- Figure E17.4 can most easily find all edges connected to a given vertex.

17.2 We arbitrarily choose not to use ID's for this problem (see Section 17.3.2).

Table model for Figure E17.1. The object diagram is incorrect with respect to the candidate key for the *To-from-association* table. The combination of *to-vertex-name* and *from-vertex-name* is not a candidate key since a given pair of vertices may correspond to multiple edges.

Vertex table

Attribute name	Nulls?	Domain
vertex-name	N	name

Candidate key: (vertex-name)
Primary key: (vertex-name)
Frequently accessed: (vertex-name)

To-from-association table

Attribute name	Nulls?	Domain
to-vertex-name	N	name
from-vertex-name	N	name
edge-name	N	name

Candidate key: (edge-name)
Primary key: (edge-name)
Frequently accessed: (to-vertex-name) (from-vertex-name) (edge-name)

Figure A17.1 Table model for Figure E17.1

Table model for Figure E17.2. The *Vertex-association* table is awkward to query on edge. The underlying object diagram is a poor model.

Edge table

Attribute name	Nulls?	Domain
edge-name	N	name

Candidate key: (edge-name)
Primary key: (edge-name)
Frequently accessed: (edge-name)

Vertex-association table

Attribute name	Nulls?	Domain
edge1-name	N	name
end1	N	end-enum
edge2-name	N	name
end2	N	end-enum
vertex-name	N	name

Candidate key: (edge1-name, end1, edge2-name, end2)
Primary key: (edge1-name, end1, edge2-name, end2)
Frequently accessed: (edge1-name) (edge2-name) (vertex-name)

Figure A17.2 Table model for Figure E17.2

Table model for Figure E17.3. We could have split the buried *from-vertex-name* and *to-vertex-name* links in the *Edge* table into separate association tables.

Edge
table

Attribute name	Nulls?	Domain
edge-name	N	name
from-vertex-name	N	name
to-vertex-name	N	name

Candidate key: (edge-name)
Primary key: (edge-name)
Frequently accessed: (edge-name) (from-vertex-name) (to-vertex-name)

Vertex
table

Attribute name	Nulls?	Domain
vertex-name	N	name

Candidate key: (vertex-name)
Primary key: (vertex-name)
Frequently accessed: (vertex-name)

Figure A17.3 Table model for Figure E17.3

Table model for Figure E17.4. *Edge-name + vertex-name* is not a candidate key for the association table because an edge may connect a vertex with itself.

Edge
table

Attribute name	Nulls?	Domain
edge-name	N	name

Candidate key: (edge-name)
Primary key: (edge-name)
Frequently accessed: (edge-name)

Vertex table is the same as that in Figure A17.3 ...

Edge-vertex-
association
table

Attribute name	Nulls?	Domain
edge-name	N	name
end	N	end-enum
vertex-name	N	name

Candidate key: (edge-name, end)
Primary key: (edge-name, end)
Frequently accessed: (edge-name) (vertex-name)

Figure A17.4 Table model for Figure E17.4

17.3a. SQL commands to create database tables and indexes for Figure E17.3.

```
CREATE TABLE Vertex
    ( vertex-name        char(30)      not null ,
    PRIMARY KEY (vertex-name));


CREATE TABLE Edge
    ( edge-name          char(30)      not null ,
      from-vertex-name   char(30)      not null ,
      to-vertex-name     char(30)      not null ,
    PRIMARY KEY (edge-name),
    FOREIGN KEY (from-vertex-name) REFERENCES Vertex,
    FOREIGN KEY (to-vertex-name) REFERENCES Vertex);


CREATE SECONDARY INDEX Edge-i01
    ON Edge (from-vertex-name);


CREATE SECONDARY INDEX Edge-i02
    ON Edge (to-vertex-name);
```

b. SQL commands to create database tables and indexes for Figure E17.4.

```
CREATE TABLE Edge
    ( edge-name          char(30)      not null ,
    PRIMARY KEY (edge-name));


CREATE TABLE Vertex
    ( vertex-name        char(30)      not null ,
    PRIMARY KEY (vertex-name));


CREATE TABLE Edge-vertex-association
    ( edge-name          char(30)      not null ,
      end                char(4)       not null ,
      vertex-name        char(30)      not null ,
    PRIMARY KEY (edge-name, end),
    FOREIGN KEY (edge-name) REFERENCES Edge,
    FOREIGN KEY (vertex-name) REFERENCES Vertex);


CREATE SECONDARY INDEX Edge-vertex-association-i01
    ON Edge-vertex-association (edge-name);


CREATE SECONDARY INDEX Edge-vertex-association-i02
    ON Edge-vertex-association (vertex-name);
```

17.4 Populated database tables for the directed graph in Figure E17.5.
Populated database tables for model in Figure E17.3.

Edge table

edge-name	from-vertex-name	to-vertex-name
e1	v5	v4
e2	v3	v4
e3	v2	v3
e4	v2	v1
e5	v1	v5
e6	v5	v2

Vertex table

vertex-name
v1
v2
v3
v4
v5

Figure A17.5 Populated database tables for Figure E17.3

Populated database tables for model in Figure E17.4.

Edge table

edge-name
e1
e2
e3
e4
e5
e6

Vertex table

vertex-name
v1
v2
v3
v4
v5

Edge-vertex-association table

edge-name	end	vertex-name
e1	from	v5
e1	to	v4
e2	from	v3
e2	to	v4
e3	from	v2
e3	to	v3
e4	from	v2
e4	to	v1
e5	from	v1
e5	to	v5
e6	from	v5
e6	to	v2

Figure A17.6 Populated database tables for Figure E17.4

17.5a. Given the name of an edge, determine the two vertices that it connects.

```
SELECT edge-name, end, vertex-name
FROM Edge-vertex-association
WHERE edge-name = :given-edge;
```

b. Given the name of a vertex, determine all edges connected to or from it.

```
SELECT edge-name, end, vertex-name
FROM Edge-vertex-association
WHERE vertex-name = :given-vertex;
```

c. Given a pair of vertices, determine the edge.

```
SELECT A1.edge-name
FROM Edge-vertex-association A1,
     Edge-vertex-association A2
WHERE ((A1.end = "from" AND A2.end = "to") OR
      (A1.end = "to" AND A2.end = "from")) AND
      A1.edge-name = A2.edge-name AND
      A1.vertex-name = :given-vertex-1 AND
      A2.vertex-name = :given-vertex-2;
```

d. Given a vertex, determine vertices connected through transitive closure. So much code is required because SQL provides no intrinsic support for transitive closure.

```
Vertex-Transitive-Closure (vertex-name):
    SET OF vertex-name;
    visited-vertices := {};
        /* set visited-vertices to the empty set */
    Find-Next-Vertex (vertex-name, visited-vertices);
    RETURN (visited-vertices);
END OF Vertex-Transitive-Closure



Find-Next-Vertex (vertex-name, visited-vertices);
    /* The following code shows a SQL query returning a */
    /* set. Most SQL programming language interfaces do */
    /* not permit return of a set and would require     */
    /* looping through a cursor to accumulate the       */
    /* answer in a set.                                 */
    SELECT A2.vertex-name INTO :temp-set
    FROM Edge-vertex-association A1,
        Edge-vertex-association A2
    WHERE A1.vertex-name = :vertex-name  AND
        A1.edge-name = A2.edge-name  AND
        A1.end = "from"  AND  A2.end = "to";

    /* do not revisit a vertex */
    FOR EACH element IN temp-set DO
        IF element IS IN visited-vertices THEN
            temp-set := temp-set - element;
        ENDIF
    END FOR EACH
    /* add remaining vertices to visited set */
    FOR EACH element IN temp-set DO
        visited-vertices := visited-vertices + element;
    END FOR EACH

    /* recurse for newly discovered vertices */
    FOR EACH element IN temp-set DO
        Find-Next-Vertex (element, visited-vertices);
    END FOR EACH
END OF Find-Next-Vertex
```

17.6 We chose to use ID's for this problem because otherwise it is difficult to reference entities. We arbitrarily chose to bury the one-to-many aggregations. Given the recursion in
the object model it is best to have distinct superclass and subclass tables. It would be
awkward to try to optimize and further reduce the number of tables. We added a discrim-
inator so that we can navigate from the superclass table to the subclass tables.

Term
table

Attribute name	Nulls?	Domain
term-ID	N	ID
term-type	N	enum

Candidate key: (term-ID)
Primary key: (term-ID)
Frequently accessed: (term-ID)

Expression
table

Attribute name	Nulls?	Domain
term-ID	N	ID
binary-operator	N	string
first-operand-ID	N	ID
second-operand-ID	N	ID

Candidate key: (term-ID)
Primary key: (term-ID)
Frequently accessed: (term-ID) (first-operand-ID) (second-operand-ID)

Variable
table

Attribute name	Nulls?	Domain
term-ID	N	ID
name	N	name

Candidate key: (term-ID)
Primary key: (term-ID)
Frequently accessed: (term-ID) (name)

Constant
table

Attribute name	Nulls?	Domain
term-ID	N	ID
value	N	string

Candidate key: (term-ID)
Primary key: (term-ID)
Frequently accessed: (term-ID)

Figure A17.7 Table model for Figure E17.6

17.7 SQL commands for Figure E17.6.

```
CREATE TABLE Term
    ( term-ID            ID        not null ,
      term-type          char(10)  not null ,
    PRIMARY KEY (term-ID));


CREATE TABLE Expression
    ( term-ID            ID        not null ,
      binary-operator    char(10)  not null ,
      first-operand-ID   ID        not null ,
      second-operand-ID  ID        not null ,
    PRIMARY KEY (term-ID),
    FOREIGN KEY (term-ID) REFERENCES Term,
    FOREIGN KEY (first-operand-ID) REFERENCES Term,
    FOREIGN KEY (second-operand-ID) REFERENCES Term);


CREATE SECONDARY INDEX Expression-i01
    ON Expression (first-operand-ID);


CREATE SECONDARY INDEX Expression-i02
    ON Expression (second-operand-ID);


CREATE TABLE Variable
    ( term-ID            ID        not null ,
      name               char(30)  not null ,
    PRIMARY KEY (term-ID),
    FOREIGN KEY (term-ID) REFERENCES Term);


CREATE TABLE Constant
    ( term-ID            ID        not null ,
      value              char(30)  not null ,
    PRIMARY KEY (term-ID),
    FOREIGN KEY (term-ID) REFERENCES Term);
```

17.8   Populated database tables for Figure E17.6

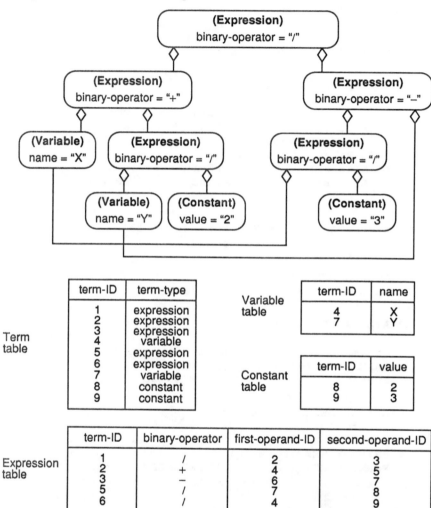

Figure A17.8 Populated database tables for Figure E17.6

17.9 We use IDs in our solution to this problem, as no other possibility for primary keys is specified for all the object classes. We assume a real coordinate system in assigning domains. We arbitrarily choose to fold associations into related object class tables where possible. Note that *Polyline* and *Group of objects* tables are not needed. A real problem would contain more attributes than shown in the exercise. In general, most of these additional attributes would further describe classes and would be permitted to be null.

Note that we show separate tables for *Ellipse* and *Rectangle* even though they have the same attributes in Figure E17.7. We chose to separate these tables because an ellipse and rectangle are really two different things. The object model would most likely have attributes added to it in the future which would distinguish *Ellipse* and *Rectangle*.

We show (*document-ID*, *page-number*) as a candidate key for the page table. This constraint is based on our understanding of the problem domain, that is desktop publishing, and cannot be deduced from the object model alone.

	Attribute name	Nulls?	Domain
Document table	document-ID	N	ID
	page-width	N	real
	page-height	N	real
	left-margin	N	real
	right-margin	N	real

Candidate key: (document-ID)
Primary key: (document-ID)
Frequently accessed: (document-ID)

	Attribute name	Nulls?	Domain
Page table	page-ID	N	ID
	page-number	N	integer
	document-ID	N	ID

Candidate key: (page-ID) (document-ID, page-number)
Primary key: (page-ID)
Frequently accessed: (page-ID) (document-ID, page-number)

	Attribute name	Nulls?	Domain
Drawing-object table	drawing-object-ID	N	ID
	drawing-object-type	N	char(20)
	line-thickness	N	integer
	page-ID	N	ID
	group-ID	Y	ID

Candidate key: (drawing-object-ID)
Primary key: (drawing-object-ID)
Frequently accessed: (drawing-object-ID) (page-ID) (group-ID)

Figure A17.9 Table model for Figure E17.7

Ellipse
table

Attribute name	Nulls?	Domain
drawing-object-ID	N	ID
bounding-box-ID	N	ID

Candidate key: (drawing-object-ID) (bounding-box-ID)
Primary key: (drawing-object-ID)
Frequently accessed: (drawing-object-ID) (bounding-box-ID)

Rectangle
table

Attribute name	Nulls?	Domain
drawing-object-ID	N	ID
bounding-box-ID	N	ID

Candidate key: (drawing-object-ID) (bounding-box-ID)
Primary key: (drawing-object-ID)
Frequently accessed: (drawing-object-ID) (bounding-box-ID)

Polyline-point-
association
table

Attribute name	Nulls?	Domain
drawing-object-ID	N	ID
point-ID	N	ID

Candidate key: (point-ID)
Primary key: (point-ID)
Frequently accessed: (drawing-object-ID) (point-ID)

Point
table

Attribute name	Nulls?	Domain
point-ID	N	ID
x	N	real
y	N	real

Candidate key: (point-ID)
Primary key: (point-ID)
Frequently accessed: (point-ID)

Figure A17.10 Table model for Figure E17.7 — continued

Textline
table

Attribute name	Nulls?	Domain
drawing-object-ID	N	ID
alignment	Y	char(10)
text	N	char(200)
point-ID	N	ID
font-ID	N	ID

Candidate key: (drawing-object-ID) (point-ID)
Primary key: (drawing-object-ID)
Frequently accessed: (drawing-object-ID) (point-ID) (font-ID)

Font
table

Attribute name	Nulls?	Domain
font-ID	N	ID
font size	N	integer
font-family	N	enum-font-family
is-bold	N	enum-yes-no
is-italic	N	enum-yes-no
is-underlined	N	enum-yes-no

Candidate key: (font-ID)
Primary key: (font-ID)
Frequently accessed: (font-ID)

Bounding-box
table

Attribute name	Nulls?	Domain
bounding-box-ID	N	ID
left-edge	N	real
top-edge	N	real
width	N	real
height	N	real

Candidate key: (bounding-box-ID)
Primary key: (bounding-box-ID)
Frequently accessed: (bounding-box-ID)

Figure A17.11 Table model for Figure E17.7 — continued

17.10 The answer to this exercise is the same as that to Exercise 17.9 except for the following changes.

Polyline-point-
association
table

Attribute name	Nulls?	Domain
drawing-object-ID	N	ID
point-sequence-number	N	integer
point-ID	N	ID

Candidate key: (drawing-object-ID, point-sequence-number) (point-ID)
Primary key: (point-ID)
Frequently accessed: (drawing-object-ID) (point-ID)

Figure A17.12 Changes to table model for Exercise 17.10

Note that a relational DBMS stores the rows of a table in an arbitrary order, and not necessarily in the order specified by *point-sequence-number*. To retrieve points in the proper order an *ORDER BY* clause must be included in the SQL query, such as:

```
SELECT point-sequence-number, point-ID
FROM Polyline-point-association
WHERE drawing-object-ID = :given-drawing-object
ORDER BY point-sequence-number;
```

17.11 The table model for this exercise is exactly the same as that for Exercise 17.9 except for the following differences.

- The *Point* table has an additional attribute *point-type* which cannot be null and has domain *enum-point-type*.

- In order to stay consistent with our naming protocol we would rename the table *Polyline-point-association* to *Polyline-polyline-point-association*.

This type of revision to an object model adds a structural constraint. Instead of just stating that a point may or may not associate with a textline, a point may or may not associate with a polyline, we can be more specific. We can state that each point associates with exactly one polyline or textline. However such a change adds clutter to the object diagram. The decision on whether to include the revision depends on the importance of the constraint.

Unfortunately current RDBMS provide no support for generalization. Thus it is difficult to enforce the exclusive 'or' nature of a generalization relationship in RDBMS tables. There are basically two alternatives.

- Forget about trying to enforce the generalization constraint. (Disadvantage: loses the constraint.)

- Enforce the generalization constraint with application code. (Disadvantage: error prone, may be omitted due to oversight, time consuming.)

17.12 SQL commands to create database tables and indexes for Figure E17.7. Note that the SQL code does not enforce the exclusive 'or' aspect of generalization. Also we have defined 'unique' secondary indexes where possible to enforce candidate keys.

```
CREATE TABLE Document
    ( document-ID          ID          not null ,
      page-width           real        not null ,
      page-height          real        not null ,
      left-margin          real        not null ,
      right-margin         real        not null ,
    PRIMARY KEY (document-ID));
CREATE TABLE Page
    ( page-ID              ID          not null ,
      page-number          integer     not null ,
      document-ID          ID          not null ,
    PRIMARY KEY (page-ID),
    FOREIGN KEY (document-ID) REFERENCES Document);

CREATE UNIQUE SECONDARY INDEX Page-i01
    ON Page (document-ID, page-number);

CREATE TABLE Drawing-object
    ( drawing-object-ID    ID          not null ,
      drawing-object-type  char(20)    not null ,
      line-thickness       integer     not null ,
      page-ID              ID          not null ,
      group-ID             ID                    ,
    PRIMARY KEY (drawing-object-ID),
    FOREIGN KEY (page-ID) REFERENCES Page,
    FOREIGN KEY (group-ID) REFERENCES Drawing-object);

CREATE SECONDARY INDEX Drawing-object-i01
    ON Drawing-object (page-ID);

CREATE SECONDARY INDEX Drawing-object-i02
    ON Drawing-object (group-ID);

CREATE TABLE Ellipse
    ( drawing-object-ID    ID          not null ,
      bounding-box-ID      ID          not null ,
    PRIMARY KEY (drawing-object-ID),
    FOREIGN KEY (drawing-object-ID)
      REFERENCES Drawing-object,
    FOREIGN KEY (bounding-box-ID)
      REFERENCES Bounding-box);
```

```
CREATE UNIQUE SECONDARY INDEX Ellipse-i01
   ON Ellipse (bounding-box-ID);


CREATE TABLE Rectangle
   ( drawing-object-ID     ID          not null ,
     bounding-box-ID       ID          not null ,
   PRIMARY KEY (drawing-object-ID),
   FOREIGN KEY (drawing-object-ID)
     REFERENCES Drawing-object,
   FOREIGN KEY (bounding-box-ID)
     REFERENCES Bounding-box);
CREATE UNIQUE SECONDARY INDEX Rectangle-i01
   ON Rectangle (bounding-box-ID);


CREATE TABLE Polyline-point-association
   ( drawing-object-ID     ID          not null ,
     point-ID              ID          not null ,
   PRIMARY KEY (point-ID),
   FOREIGN KEY (drawing-object-ID)
     REFERENCES Drawing-object,
   FOREIGN KEY (point-ID) REFERENCES Point);


CREATE SECONDARY INDEX Polyline-point-association-i01
   ON Polyline-point-association (drawing-object-ID);


CREATE TABLE Point
   ( point-ID              ID          not null ,
     x                     real        not null ,
     y                     real        not null ,
   PRIMARY KEY (point-ID));


CREATE TABLE Textline
   ( drawing-object-ID     ID          not null ,
     alignment             char(10)             ,
     text                  char(200)   not null ,
     point-ID              ID          not null ,
     font-ID               ID          not null ,
   PRIMARY KEY (drawing-object-ID),
   FOREIGN KEY (drawing-object-ID)
     REFERENCES Drawing-object,
   FOREIGN KEY (point-ID) REFERENCES Point,
   FOREIGN KEY (font-ID) REFERENCES Font);


CREATE UNIQUE SECONDARY INDEX Textline-i01
   ON Textline (point-ID);
```

```
CREATE SECONDARY INDEX Textline-i02
   ON Textline (font-ID);


CREATE TABLE Font
   ( font-ID               ID        not null ,
     font-size             integer   not null ,
     font-family           char(10)  not null ,
     is-bold               char(3)   not null ,
     is-italic             char(3)   not null ,
     is-underlined         char(3)   not null ,
   PRIMARY KEY (font-ID));
CREATE TABLE Bounding-box
   ( bounding-box-ID       ID        not null ,
     left-edge             real      not null ,
     top-edge              real      not null ,
     width                 real      not null ,
     height                real      not null ,
   PRIMARY KEY (bounding-box-ID));
```

17.13 Some design trade-offs are as follows:

- We could have made the *Document—Page* association an explicit table. The explicit table has the advantage that a given page can belong to many documents. (This may be useful if multiple views of the same document are desired in a future enhancement.) The explicit table has the disadvantage that it creates another table; the explicit table also makes it more difficult to enforce the constraint that every page is associated with a document.

- Similarly, we could have made the *Page—Drawing-object* association an explicit table.

- The *Ellipse* and *Rectangle* tables could be eliminated by adding a field to *Bounding-box* to indicate the corresponding ellipse or rectangle. (The problem statement indicates that each bounding box is associated with exactly one ellipse or rectangle. Generalization could have been used here in the object model, similar to that shown in Figure E17.8.) This change reduces the number of tables. However optimization causes the tables to deviate from the object model. Then there is a less direct correspondence between the object model and application code, the user interface, and so forth. Eliminating the ellipse and rectangle tables makes it more difficult to enforce the constraint that bounding box only applies for drawing objects which are ellipses or rectangles.

- The *Font* table could be collapsed into the *Textline* table, but this violates third normal form. (Font attributes only indirectly depend on *textline-ID*.) Also this makes it more difficult to extend the system by naming and reusing fonts.

- *Polyline* and *Group-of-objects* could be explicit tables. However, there is no need to do so for now, since they have no attributes.

- It is impractical to eliminate the *Drawing-object* superclass because of the recursion introduced by *Group-of-objects*.

- We could fold the subclasses into the superclass, but this violates third normal form. It also makes the database structure more difficult to extend and understand.

17.14 This exercise is similar to the edge-vertex problem from Exercise 17.1. *City* is analogous to *Vertex* and *Route* is analogous to *Edge*. Note that the object models in Figure E17.3 and Figure E17.4 would also correctly model the relationship between *City* and *Route*.

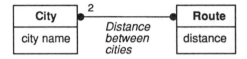

Figure A17.13 Object diagram for Figure E17.9

17.15 SQL code to determine distance between two cities for Figure E17.9 is listed below. This code is similar to that for Exercise 17.5c that determines the edge for a pair of vertices.

```
SELECT distance
FROM Route, City C1, City C2,
     Distance-between-cities D1,
     Distance-between-cities D2
WHERE D1.route-ID = D2.route-ID   AND
      D1.route-ID = Route.route-ID   AND
      D1.city-ID = C1.city-ID   AND
      D2.city-ID = C2.city-ID   AND
      C1.city-name = :given-name1   AND
      C2.city-name = :given-name2;
```

17.16 The object diagram in Figure A17.14 corresponds to the SQL code in Figure E17.10. Note that this object diagram is similar to Figure E17.1. Figure A17.14 is a better model that Figure E17.1; each pair of cities has a single value of distance as Figure A17.14 correctly states; however each pair of vertices corresponds to many edges and not one edge as shown in Figure E17.1.

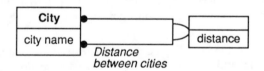

Figure A17.14 Object diagram for Figure E17.10

17.17 SQL code to determine distance between two cities for Figure E17.10.

```
SELECT distance
FROM City C1, City C2, Distance-between-cities D
WHERE D.city1-ID = C1.city-ID  AND
      D.city2-ID = C2.city-ID  AND
      C1.city-name = :given-name1  AND
      C2.city-name = :given-name2;
```

17.18 We make the following observations about Figure A17.13 and Figure A17.14.

- Figure A17.14 is awkward because of the symmetry between city1 and city2. Either data must be stored twice with waste of storage, update time, and possible integrity problems, or special application logic must enforce an arbitrary constraint.

- Figure A17.13 has an additional table.

All in all, Figure A17.13 is a much better approach. With a self association it is frequently helpful to promote the association to a class in order to break the symmetry.

17.19 For both the edge-vertex and city-route problems we have discouraged use of symmetrical models because they are confusing, lead to possible redundancy, and complicate search and update code. The general conclusion is, where possible, try to avoid self associations.

In the edge-vertex problem there are two classes that arise from the problem domain, *Edge* and *Vertex*. Thus most persons would tend to avoid the symmetrical model without giving it much thought. In the city-route problem there is only one obvious class, *City*. The *Route* class is contrived in order to simplify modeling of the problem.

A given pair of cities has only a single value of distance. In contrast, two vertices may have any number of edges between them. Thus the object model for Exercise 17.16 with a self association on city is correct. The object model in Figure E17.1 with a self association on vertex is wrong.

The city-route problem is more like undirected graphs. Two cities relate to a route and there is no natural way to distinguish the cities. In a directed graph there is a *from* vertex and a *to* vertex.

17.20 Once again, there are multiple correct answers for this problem, depending on the mapping rules that you choose to use. Ideal table models for Figure E17.11, Figure E17.12, and Figure E17.13 are as follows.

For the 1:1 association, the two classes and association can all be collapsed into a single table. In general, it may, or may not, be a good idea to merge the objects into a single table. For instance, merging the objects into a single table damages their sense of identity: two distinct entities are mixed together. This would be more apparent if both country and capital each had many attributes. Nevertheless, merging is always an option for a 1:1 association and may improve performance. For a 1:1 association, each object cannot exist without the other. Thus every country must have a capital; each capital must correspond to a country. In general, you should scrutinize 1:1 associations and reconsider the existence dependency. For a 1:1 association, neither object class identifier can be null; either identifier can serve as the primary key.

Country-capital table	Attribute name	Nulls?	Domain
	country-name	N	name
	capital-name	N	name

Candidate key: (country-name) (capital-name)
Primary key: (country-name)
Frequently accessed: (country-name)

Figure A17.15 Table model for 1:1 association

For a 1:0,1 association, the two classes can still be merged into a table. However, the identifier for the optional class may be null. Since it may be null, the optional class cannot uniquely identify all records, and cannot be a candidate or primary key.

Person-passport table	Attribute name	Nulls?	Domain
	person-name	N	name
	passport-number	Y	passp-num

Candidate key: (person-name)
Primary key: (person-name)
Frequently accessed: (person-name) (passport-number)

Figure A17.16 Table model for 1:0,1 association

For a 0,1:0,1 association, the two classes should not be merged into a single table since they are independent classes and do not require each other's existence. (Of course, they could be merged anyhow, but then the resulting table would lack a primary key and violate second normal form.)

Icon
table

Attribute name	Nulls?	Domain
icon-name	N	name

Candidate key: (icon-name)
Primary key: (icon-name)
Frequently accessed: (icon-name)

Equipment
table

Attribute name	Nulls?	Domain
equipment-name	N	name

Candidate key: (equipment-name)
Primary key: (equipment-name)
Frequently accessed: (equipment-name)

Icon-
equipment
table

Attribute name	Nulls?	Domain
icon-name	N	name
equipment-name	N	name

Candidate key: (icon-name) (equipment-name)
Primary key: (equipment-name)
Frequently accessed: (icon-name) (equipment-name)

Figure A17.17 Table model for 0,1:0,1 association

17.21 Figure A17.18 is the same object diagram that we used in our answer in Chapter 3.

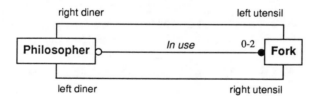

right diner   left utensil

Philosopher — In use — 0-2 — Fork

left diner   right utensil

Figure A17.18 Object model for dining philosopher's problem

If we apply mapping rules and bury links where possible, we get the table model shown in Figure A17.19.

	Attribute name	Nulls?	Domain
Philosopher table	philosopher-ID left-fork-ID right-fork-ID	N N N	ID ID ID

Candidate key: (philosopher-ID, left-fork-ID, right-fork-ID)
Primary key: (philosopher-ID)
Frequently accessed: (philosopher-ID, left-fork-ID, right-fork-ID)

	Attribute name	Nulls?	Domain
Fork table	fork-ID philosopher-using-fork	N Y	ID ID

Candidate key: (fork-ID)
Primary key: (fork-ID)
Frequently accessed: (fork-ID)

Figure A17.19 Table model for dining philosopher's problem

SQL commands are as follows:

```
CREATE TABLE Philosopher
    ( philosopher-ID      ID           not null ,
      left-fork-ID        ID           not null ,
      right-fork-ID       ID           not null ,
    PRIMARY KEY (philosopher-ID));


CREATE UNIQUE SECONDARY INDEX Philosopher-i01
    ON Philosopher (left-fork-ID);


CREATE UNIQUE SECONDARY INDEX Philosopher-i02
    ON Philosopher (right-fork-ID);


CREATE TABLE Fork
    ( fork-ID             ID           not null ,
      philosopher-using-fork  ID                 ,
    PRIMARY KEY (fork-ID));
```

The contents of the populated database table are shown in Figure A17.20 for the case where each philosopher has the left fork.

Philosopher
table

philosopher-ID	left-fork-ID	right-fork-ID
1	15	11
2	11	12
3	12	13
4	13	14
5	14	15

Fork
table

fork-ID	philosopher using fork
11	2
12	3
13	4
14	5
15	1

Figure A17.20 Populated database table for dining philosopher's problem

17.22 We arbitrarily chose to bury links where possible. There are additional correct answers for this problem.

Meet
table

Attribute name	Nulls?	Domain
meet-ID	N	ID
date	Y	date
location	Y	place

Candidate key: (meet-ID)
Primary key: (meet-ID)
Frequently accessed: (meet-ID)

Station
table

Attribute name	Nulls?	Domain
station-ID	N	ID
location	Y	place
meet-ID	N	ID

Candidate key: (station-ID)
Primary key: (station-ID)
Frequently accessed: (station-ID) (meet-ID)

Event
table

Attribute name	Nulls?	Domain
event-ID	N	ID
starting-time	Y	time
meet-ID	N	ID
station-ID	N	ID

Candidate key: (event-ID)
Primary key: (event-ID)
Frequently accessed: (event-ID) (meet-ID) (station-ID)

Judge
table

Attribute name	Nulls?	Domain
judge-ID	N	ID
name	Y	name

Candidate key: (judge-ID)
Primary key: (judge-ID)
Frequently accessed: (judge-ID)

Figure A17.21 Table model for scoring system problem

Station-judge-association table

Attribute name	Nulls?	Domain
station-ID	N	ID
judge-ID	N	ID

Candidate key: (station-ID, judge-ID)
Primary key: (station-ID, judge-ID)
Frequently accessed: (station-ID) (judge-ID)

Trial table

Attribute name	Nulls?	Domain
trial-ID	N	ID
net-score	Y	score
event-ID	N	ID
competitor-ID	N	ID

Candidate key: (trial-ID)
Primary key: (trial-ID)
Frequently accessed: (trial-ID) (event-ID) (competitor-ID)

Raw-score table

Attribute name	Nulls?	Domain
raw-score-ID	N	ID
value	Y	score
trial-ID	N	ID
judge-ID	N	ID

Candidate key: (raw-score-ID)
Primary key: (raw-score-ID)
Frequently accessed: (raw-score-ID) (trial-ID) (judge-ID)

Competitor table

Attribute name	Nulls?	Domain
competitor-ID	N	ID
name	N	name
age	N	age
address	Y	address
telephone-number	Y	phone-num

Candidate key: (competitor-ID)
Primary key: (competitor-ID)
Frequently accessed: (competitor-ID)

Figure A17.22 Table model for scoring system problem — continued

SQL commands to create database tables and indexes for Figure A17.21 and Figure A17.22.

```
CREATE TABLE Meet
     ( meet-ID            ID          not null ,
       date               date                 ,
       location           char(30)             ,
     PRIMARY KEY (meet-ID));


CREATE TABLE Station
     ( station-ID         ID          not null ,
       location           char(30)             ,
       meet-ID            ID          not null ,
     PRIMARY KEY (station-ID),
     FOREIGN KEY (meet-ID) REFERENCES Meet);


CREATE SECONDARY INDEX Station-i01 ON Station (meet-ID);


CREATE TABLE Event
     ( event-ID           ID          not null ,
       starting-time      time                 ,
       meet-ID            ID          not null ,
       station-ID         ID          not null ,
     PRIMARY KEY (event-ID),
     FOREIGN KEY (meet-ID) REFERENCES Meet,
     FOREIGN KEY (station-ID) REFERENCES Station);


CREATE SECONDARY INDEX Event-i01 ON Event (meet-ID);


CREATE SECONDARY INDEX Event-i02 ON Event (station-ID);


CREATE TABLE Judge
     ( judge-ID           ID          not null ,
       name               char(30)             ,
     PRIMARY KEY (judge-ID));


CREATE TABLE Station-judge-association
     ( station-ID         ID          not null ,
       judge-ID           ID          not null ,
     PRIMARY KEY (station-ID, judge-ID),
     FOREIGN KEY (station-ID) REFERENCES Station,
     FOREIGN KEY (judge-ID) REFERENCES Judge);


CREATE SECONDARY INDEX Station-judge-association-i01
     ON Station-judge-association (station-ID);
```

```
CREATE SECONDARY INDEX Station-judge-association-i02
    ON Station-judge-association (judge-ID);


CREATE TABLE Trial
    ( trial-ID          ID              not null ,
      net-score         integer                  ,
      event-ID          ID              not null ,
      competitor-ID     ID              not null ,
    PRIMARY KEY (trial-ID),
    FOREIGN KEY (event-ID) REFERENCES Event,
    FOREIGN KEY (competitor-ID) REFERENCES Competitor);


CREATE SECONDARY INDEX Trial-i01 ON Trial (event-ID);


CREATE SECONDARY INDEX Trial-i02 ON Trial (competitor-
ID);


CREATE TABLE Raw-score
    ( raw-score-ID      ID              not null ,
      value             integer                  ,
      trial-ID          ID              not null ,
      judge-ID          ID              not null ,
    PRIMARY KEY (raw-score-ID),
    FOREIGN KEY (trial-ID) REFERENCES Trial,
    FOREIGN KEY (judge-ID) REFERENCES Judge);


CREATE SECONDARY INDEX Raw-score-i01
    ON Raw-score (trial-ID);


CREATE SECONDARY INDEX Raw-score-i02
    ON Raw-score (judge-ID);


CREATE TABLE Competitor
    ( competitor-ID     ID              not null ,
      name              char(30)        not null ,
      age               integer         not null ,
      address           char(100)                ,
      telephone-number  char(15)                 ,
    PRIMARY KEY (competitor-ID));
```

17.23 As stated in the text, SQL lacks many features and has many flaws. The following features would improve SQL support for object-oriented concepts.

- Faster navigation between objects along links. Joins are much too slow. Improved navigational performance is a major motivation behind OO-DBMS research.

- Provide richer data types, operations, and special access paths.

- Fully support primary and foreign keys. The SQL standard is addressing this topic, but commercial implementations are lagging behind.

- Enforce the partitioning among subclasses implied by single inheritance and disjoint multiple inheritance. Each entry in the superclass table must appear in exactly one subclass table. Current SQL cannot enforce this constraint and the application must do so.

- Support identity. Maybe SQL should provide a built-in function to assign the next ID upon request.

- Fully support views for reading and writing (where writing is logically appropriate). This would improve our ability to use the three schema architecture for object models.

18

Object Diagram Compiler

18.1 The meta model given in the exercise supports object classes, object attributes, and binary associations. An argument could be made that it also supports ternary associations. However, there is no way to store candidate keys in the given meta model. For binary associations, candidate keys can be derived from role multiplicity. Although not mentioned in the exercise, class names are also supported.

The given meta model has the interesting property that only the constructs that it supports were used in drawing it. Therefore an object diagram compiler based on the meta model could compile the meta model.

18.2 The completed instance diagram is shown in Figure A18.1.

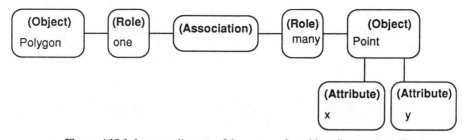

Figure A18.1 Instance diagram of the output of an object diagram compiler corresponding to the polygon-points object diagram

18.3 The completed instance diagram of the output of the object diagram compiler with the meta model as input is shown in Figure A18.2.

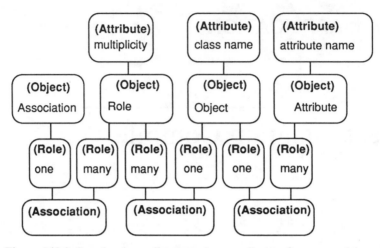

Figure A18.2 Completed compiler output instance diagram for meta model

18.4   There are several possible correct answers. One possible meta model that satisfies the conditions given in the exercise is shown in Figure A18.3. Another possibility is shown in Figure A18.4. The meta model in Figure A18.4 is simpler than the one in Figure A18.3, but it requires a multiplicity of zero-one in several places.

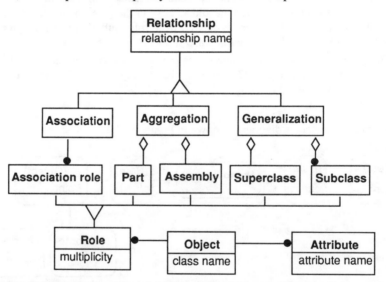

Figure A18.3 Self-descriptive meta model for an object diagram compiler that supports association, aggregation, and generalization relationships

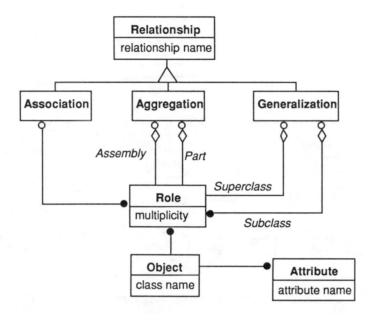

Figure A18.4 Another self-descriptive meta model for an object diagram compiler that supports association, aggregation, and generalization relationships

18.5 This exercise is more work than it might seem at first glance. In fact, we recommend that you ask the students to simply count the number of instances of each class in the compiler output. For example, the instance diagram for Figure A18.3 contains 3 associations, 4 aggregations, 2 generalizations, 6 association roles, 4 part roles, 4 assembly roles, 2 superclass roles, 8 subclass roles, 12 objects, and 4 attributes for a total of 49 instances. The instance diagram for Figure A18.4 contains 3 associations, 4 aggregations, 1 generalization, 18 roles, 7 objects, and 4 attributes for a total of 37 instances. The instance diagram corresponding to Figure A18.4 is shown in Figure A18.5.

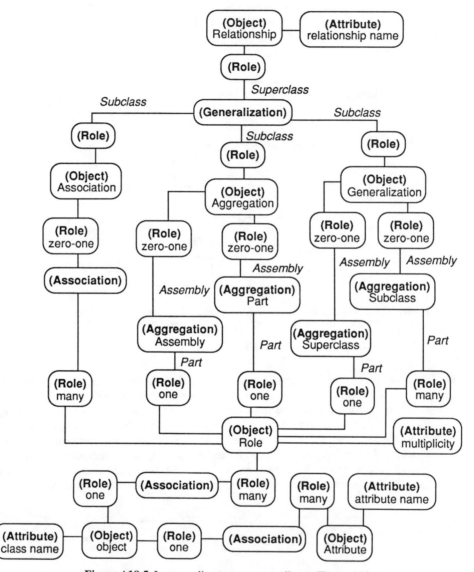

Figure A18.5 Instance diagram corresponding to Figure A18.4

19

Computer Animation

19.1a. We would not recommend extending *OSCAR* to colorizing movies. Although it might be feasible to add classes and relationships to the object model to represent frames, there are several major changes that would be needed. First, the approach of modeling in three dimensions and rendering in two dimensions is not adequate for typical movie scenes. Besides the problem of inferring three dimensional information from two dimensional scenes, the state of the art of geometric modeling is not adequate for the detail found in movie scenes. Consider the difficulty of modeling a river, a crashing car, or an explosion, for example. For colorizing, a two dimensional approach is needed. The most important part of the system is the colorizing algorithm, which must track the identity of arbitrarily bounded two dimensional areas from one frame to the next.

    We also observe that the system design of *OSCAR* is not really suited for colorizing. There is no need for an interactive script generator, a director, a renderer, or a windowing system. Primary emphasis is on the frame editor and the user interface.

    b. *OSCAR* is very well suited to provide the display from the cockpit for a flight simulator for training pilots. The level of detail that *OSCAR* can furnish is just about right. The camera in the animation system can be used to simulate the pilot's point of view. The landscape is built from geometric models in a database. These models can be placed by changing the actor attributes for the model. Motion is controlled using cues. Simulation is started and run by scene. There is no need to extend the object model. All that is needed is an interface between *OSCAR* and the simulation of the plane.

    c. *OSCAR* is very well suited to provide the display for a video games system. Moving objects are represented by models of different characters. Models are associated with actors. Changing the actors' position and orientation moves the models on the game. Some sort of a game master must be added to the system to oversee the action. The game master must determine who has hit who (if this is a combat game) or tally successes and failures (if this is a sports game) or keep track of where treasures and villains are (if this is an adventure game). Different classes of game masters can control different types of games. An object to receive input from joy sticks or other input devices must be created. These interface objects can control moving objects by sending them messages using Oscar messaging facilities.

19.2a. Each atom and bond is an actor. A molecule is a collection of atoms and bonds. The model for an atom is a sphere. The color and radius of an atom are set using the actor's scale and color attributes. Several types of bonds may exist including single and double. These are represented by either lines or elliptical cylinders.

b. Many types of actors are used. For example, we have seen letters, hammers, fireworks, arches, grids, balls, disks, and loops. Expect your students to turn in a wide variety of answers. Objects move, change shape, blink, etc. Simulation of lighting is particularly well done, with objects shining and sparkling. However, actors are usually limited in complexity and it is easy to tell that the scene is not "real". For example, lifelike rivers, crashing cars, people, or trees are not likely to be seen.

c. Actors include gears, cams, pistons, levers, pumps, bearings, belts, cranks, pins, springs, and spheres, to name a few.

19.3 The approach is similar to that described in the answer to Exercise 19.1b. Use the object-oriented simulator described in the answer to Exercise 12.2 to compute the motion of the glider. Prepare an interface between *OSCAR* and the simulator. *OSCAR* must supply control parameters to the simulator. The simulator in turn must provide *OSCAR* with the position and orientation of the glider. The position and orientation of the camera can be computed from the position and orientation of the glider and the mounting position and orientation of the camera with respect to the glider. This computation can be done either as part of the simulation or within *OSCAR*.

19.4 *OSCAR* has a dynamic simulation architecture. The object diagram compiler has a batch transformation architecture. *OSCAR* takes full advantage of object-oriented techniques by using object-oriented design and implementation. The object diagram compiler uses object-oriented techniques to design data structures followed by a conventional procedural implementation. *OSCAR* uses inheritance heavily, while inheritance was not used at all in the object diagram compiler. The scope of operation for *OSCAR* is local, while for the object diagram compiler all operations are global in scope. Objects in *OSCAR* are active. Objects in the object diagram compiler are passive data structures.

19.5 [The exercise was not specific about the motion of the ball. A good bowler spins the ball as it is thrown. The ball starts out sliding down the alley. Frictional forces accelerate the ball and change the angular momentum of its spin. The net effect is a complicated motion in which the ball curves accross the alley. Our answer treats the problem as an exercise in animation rather than in simulation. We have ignored the actual dynamics of a bowling ball by making several simplifying assumptions. We have greatly simplified the motion of the ball as it is being thrown. After the ball is thrown, we assume the ball is rolling about the x axis and translating in the x-y plane. Since we do not constrain the ball's rotation to match its translation, it may be sliding.]

[Also note that we have omitted finger holes, and placed the bug on the surface of the ball, where it will no doubt be crushed.]

Model pins, alley, and ball. Since all pins are alike, use one model with multiple actors to control the positions and orientations of pins. The ball can initially be modeled with a sphere. Later, a more detailed model with finger holes can be substituted. Model the bug with a camera. Have it move along with the ball and rotate it about its position (yaw, pitch, and or roll). Cues describe all motion. Each cue controls one main motion such as rolling, approach, hitting pins, etc. The scene acts as the main bowling loop.

```
-- set up some actors for the alley and pins

actor new: alley;
actor new: ball modeller=sphere;
actor new: pin1 modeller=pin;
actor new: pin2 modeller=pin;
   .
   .
   .
actor new: pin10 modeller=pin;
collection new: pins members=(pin1,pin2,...,pin10);

scalar new: ball_radius = .5; -- offset for bug

-- a cue to set the pins
cue new: set_pins
   resolution=1 duration=1
   tick_actions="pin1 position=(0,3);
       pin2 position=(-1,2);
       pin3 position=(1,2);
       pin4 position=(-2,1);
       pin5 position=(0,1);
       pin6 position=(2,1);
       pin7 position=(-3,0);
       pin8 position=(-1,0);
       pin9 position=(1,0);
       pin10 position=(3,0);
       pins orientation=(0,0,0);"
```

```
ball position = (30,0,5);

camera new: bug -- start bug out looking at pin1
    position=[ball position?]
-- move position along line of sight to compensate
-- for ball radius. This puts camera (bug) on the surface
-- of the ball.
    distance- ball_radius
    focal_point=[pin1 position?];

cue new: approach
    tick_actions="ball position+(delta_x, delta_y, 0);";

cue new: drop
    tick_actions="ball position+(0, 0, -5);";

cue new: roll -- a simple rotation about x
    tick_actions="ball rotate_x: angle
        position+(delta_x, delta_y);";
cue new: follow
    tick_actions="bug position=[ball position?]
            pitch: angle
            distance- ball_radius;"; -- put bug on surface

phigs new: aRenderer
    actors=([actor instances?]
    camera=bug;

-- set up times for cues
approach start=0 duration=5;
drop start=[approach end?] duration=1;
roll start=[drop end?] duration=15;
hit start=[roll end?] duration=.5;
follow start=[approach start?] end=[hit end?];

scene new: Bowl
    cues=(approach, drop, roll, hit, return, follow)
    renderers=aRenderer;

Bowl start!;
```

20

Electrical Distribution Design System

20.1 A state diagram is a template for describing the behavior of instances and thus describes behavior for each database record in the system described in this exercise. The completed state diagram is shown in Figure A20.1. This exercise is based on a technique for building an object-oriented database on top of a relational database that is described in "An Object-Oriented Relational Database" by WJ Premerlani, et al, *Communications of the ACM*, *33*, 11 (November 1990). The reference to this article at the end of Chapter 20 is incorrect. The following is a description of the actions:

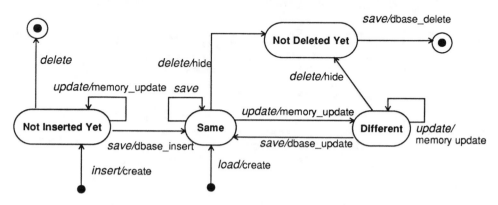

Figure A20.1 State diagram for a system to buffer database operations by shadowing records with object instances

Memory_update updates the data in memory. *Dbase_insert* inserts data into the database. *Dbase_update* updates the corresponding data in the database. *Dbase_delete* deletes the corresponding data from the database. *Hide* simply makes the data invisible to queries. *Create* creates a new object.

20.2   [The answers for this exercise are longer than we expected. We recommend assigning only one or two parts. Note that some functions that we have defined are used in more than one operation.]

[We suggest that you ask for answers in the form of pseudo code. The intended format of the answer was a short narrative explanation of how to carry out the given operations. However, we found that answers in this format were vague.]

[There is more than one way to carry out the requested operations. The point is for the student to think in object-oriented terms.]

Figure E20.2 models the situation in which networks must connect to symbols at predefined locations. Several networks may connect to a given port. Figure E20.3 models the situation in which networks connect to symbols anywhere at the edges of the symbol. Figure E20.4 does not accurately model graphical diagrams in which a network is connected more than once to the same symbol.

20.2a. [This part of the exercise is flawed and we recommend you do not assign it unless you change it. As stated the operation is more complicated than we intended.] It is too difficult to determine the set of networks that connect only to unselected symbols using the given inputs. More reasonable inputs are a set of all networks and a set of symbols that have been selected. In that case an algorithm that will determine bridging networks using Figure E20.2 is:

```
partition_networks( all_networks , selected_symbols )
/* returns partitioning through these global sets:
   selected_networks - connected to selected symbols
   unselected_networks - connected to unselected symbols
   bridging_networks - bridging */
{
   initialize selected_networks to empty;
   initialize unselected_networks to empty;
   initialize bridging_networks to empty;
   for each Network in all_networks
       classify ( Network , selected_symbols );
   end each Network
}

classify ( Network , selected_symbols )
/* classifies Network depending on whether the
   Network connects only selected symbols, only
   unselected symbols, or a mixture */
{
   connected_symbols = find_symbols( Network );
   selected_connected_symbols =
       connected_symbols INTERSECT selected_symbols;
```

```
        if( selected_connected_symbols == connected_symbols )
           add Network to selected_networks;
        else
           if( selected_connected_symbols == NULL )
              add Network to unselected_networks;
           else
              add Network to bridging_networks
           endif
        endif
   }

   find_symbols( Network ) returns set of symbols
   /* finds all symbols connected to Network */
   /* this function is defined in Part c of this exercise */
```

The algorithm for finding all symbols connected to a network is given in Part c of this exercise and is the only part of the operation that is not the same for the three object diagrams given in the exercise. Although Figure E20.4 is not an accurate representation, it can be used to satisfy the query.

20.2b. An algorithm for finding networks that form more than one connection with a symbol using Figure E20.2 is:

```
   find_multiply_connected_networks ( given_symbol )
      returns set of multiply_connected_networks
   {
      initialize set of multiply_connected_networks to empty;
      for each Symbol_port associated with given_symbol
         treat the Symbol_port as a Port;
         get the Connection associated with Port;
         for each Port associated with Connection
            if Port is a Network_port
               get the Network associated with Network port;
               if check_multiply ( Network, given_symbol )
                  add Network to multiply_connected_networks
               endif
            endif
         end each Port
      end each Symbol_port
      return multiply_connected_networks;
   }

   check_multiply ( Network, given symbol ) returns true/false
   {
      initialize count to 0;
      for each Network_port associated with Network
         treat Network_port as a Port;
         get the Connection associated with Port;
         for each Port associated with Connection
            if Port is a Symbol_port
               get Symbol associated with Symbol_port;
```

```
                if Symbol == given_symbol
                    count = count + 1;
                endif
            endif
        end for each Port
    end for each Network port
    if count >= 2 return true
    else return false
    endif
}
```

The algorithm using Figure E20.3 is simpler:

```
find_multiply_connected_networks ( given_symbol )
    returns set of multiply_connected_networks
{
    initialize set of multiply connected networks to empty;
    for each Connection associated with given_symbol
        get the Network associated with Connection
        if check_multiply ( Network, given_symbol )
            add Network to multiply_connected_networks
        endif
    end each Connection
    return multiply_connected_networks;
}

check_multiply ( Network, given symbol )
    returns true/false
{
    initialize count to 0;
    for each Connection associated with Network
        get the Symbol associated with Connection;
        if Symbol == given_symbol
            count = count + 1;
        endif
    end for each Connection
    if count >= 2 return true
    else return false
    endif
}
```

Since Figure E20.4 does not support networks which connect more than once to the same symbol, it cannot be used for the query.

20.2c. An algorithm for finding symbols connected to a network using Figure E20.2 is:

```
find_symbols( Network ) returns set of symbols
/* returns a set of symbols connected to Network */
{
    initialize set of connected_symbols to empty;
    for each Network_port associated with Network
```

```
        treat Network_port as a Port;
        get the Connection associated with Port;
        for each Port associated with Connection
            if Port is a Symbol_port
                add Symbol to set of connected_symbols
            endif
        end for each Port
    end for each Network_port
    return connected_symbols;
}
```

An algorithm for finding symbols connected to a network using Figure E20.3 is:

```
find_symbols( Network ) returns set of symbols
/* returns a set of symbols connected to Network */
{
    initialize set of connected_symbols to empty;
    for each Connection associated with the given Network
        get the Symbol associated with Connection
        add Symbol to set of connected_symbols
    end for each Connection
}
```

Aside from the fact Figure E20.4 is not an accurate representation, the association between *Symbol* and *Network* can be used directly to obtain the set of symbols connected to a network.

20.2d. [Although not explicitly stated in the problem, it was our intent that the operations make copies of association links, connections, and ports so as to copy the structure of the selected networks. Also, it will simplify the operation if self associations are added to some of the classes to navigate from copy to original. We assume that the set of all networks is available.]

It is convenient to extend the object diagram given in Figure E20.2 to that shown in Figure A20.2.

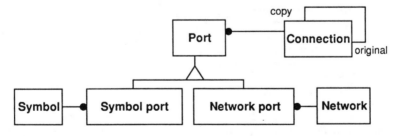

Figure A20.2 Connectivity object diagram extended to simplify copy operations

The requested copy operation proceeds as follows:

```
network_copy( all_networks , selected_symbols )
    returns copy_of_selected_symbols
    /* copy_of_selected_symbols is a set */
{
    initialize copy_of_selected_symbols to empty;
    /* copy symbols */
    for each Symbol in selected_symbols
        Symbol_copy = copy of Symbol;
        add Symbol_copy to copy_of_selected_symbols;
        for each Symbol_port associated with Symbol
            Symbol_port_copy = copy of Symbol_port;
            associate Symbol_copy with Symbol_port_copy;
            treat Symbol_port as Port;
            treat Symbol_port_copy as Port_copy;
            get Connection associated with Port;
            Connection_copy = copy associated with Connection;
            if Connection_copy does not exist
                Connection_copy = copy of Connection;
                associate Connection_copy with Connection;
            endif
            associate Port_copy with Connection_copy;
        end for each Symbol_port
    end for each Symbol
    /* determine nets that need to be copied */
    partition_networks( all_networks, selected_symbols);
    /* copy selected networks */
    for each Network in selected_networks
        Network_copy = copy of Network;
        for each Network_port associated with Network
            Network_port_copy = copy of Network_port;
            associate Network_copy with Network_port_copy;
            treat Network_port as Port;
            treat Network_port_copy as Port_copy;
            get Connection associated with Port;
            Connection_copy = copy associated with Connection;
            if Connection_copy does not exist
                Connection_copy = copy of Connection;
                associate Connection_copy with Connection;
            endif
            associate Port_copy with Connection_copy;
        end for each Network_port
    end for each Network
}
```

The function *partition_networks* is defined in Part a. The algorithm for Figure E20.3 is:

```
network_copy( all_networks , selected_symbols )
   returns the set, copy_of_selected_symbols
{
   initialize copy_of_selected_symbols to empty;
   /* copy symbols */
   for each Symbol in selected_symbols
      Symbol_copy = copy of Symbol;
      add Symbol_copy to copy_of_selected_symbols;
      for each Connection associated with Symbol
         Connection_copy = copy associated with Connection;
         if Connection_copy does not exist
            Connection_copy = copy of Connection;
            associate Connection_copy with Connection;
         endif
         associate Symbol_copy with Connection_copy;
      end for each Connection
   end for each Symbol
   /* determine nets that need to be copied */
   partition_networks( all_networks, selected_symbols);
   /* copy selected networks */
   for each Network in selected_networks
      Network_copy = copy of Network;
      for each Connection associated with Network
         Connection_copy = copy associated with Connection;
         if Connection_copy does not exist
            Connection_copy = copy of Connection;
            associate Connection_copy with Connection;
         endif
         associate Network_copy with Connection_copy;
      end for each Connection
   end for each Network
}
```

A self association on the class *Connection* in Figure E20.2 and Figure E20.3 was used to facilitate the copy operation. In Figure E20.4 the class *Connection* has been eliminated. A self association on the class *Symbol* can be used to aid the operation. An algorithm for the copy operation is:

```
network_copy( all_networks , selected_symbols )
   returns the set, copy_of_selected_symbols
{
   initialize copy_of_selected_symbols to empty;
   /* copy symbols */
   for each Symbol in selected_symbols
      Symbol_copy = copy of Symbol;
      associate Symbol_copy with Symbol;
      add Symbol_copy to copy_of_selected_symbols;
   end for each Symbol
   /* determine nets that need to be copied */
   partition_networks( all_networks, selected_symbols);
   /* copy selected networks and connections */
```

```
    for each Network in selected_networks
        Network_copy = copy of Network;
        for each Symbol associated with Network
            Symbol_copy = copy associated with Symbol;
            associate Network_copy with Symbol_copy;
        end for each Symbol
    end for each Network
}
```

20.2 e. The algorithm for computing the transitive closure using Figure E20.2 is:

```
transitive_closure ( set_of_symbols )
{
/* returns the transitive closure in the global variable
   visited_symbols by doing a depth first traversal */
/* set_of_symbols is a set of given Symbols */
/* initialize recursion for computation of
   transitive closure */
    initialize visited_symbols to empty;
    for each Symbol in set_of_symbols
        recursive_transitive_close ( Symbol );
    end for each Symbol
}

recursive_transitive_close ( Symbol )
{
/* performs a depth first transitive closure on Symbol */
/* for efficiency, a symbol is visited only once */
    if Symbol is not in visited_symbols set
        add Symbol to visited_symbols;
        for each Symbol_port associated with Symbol
            treat the Symbol_port as a Port;
            get the Connection associated with Port;
            for each Network_port associated with Connection
                get Network associated with Network_port;
                for each Network_port associated with Network
                    treat Network_port as Port;
                    get Connection associated with Port;
                    for each Symbol_port linked to Connection
                    get Symbol linked to Symbol_port;
                    recursive_transitive_close( Symbol );
                    end for each Symbol_port
                end for each Network_port
            end for each Network_port
        end for each Symbol
    endif
}
```

The algorithm for computing the transitive closure using Figure E20.3 is:

```
transitive_closure ( set_of_symbols )
{
/* returns the transitive closure in the global variable
   visited_symbols by doing a depth first traversal */
/* set_of_symbols is a set of given Symbols */
/* initialize recursion for computing transitive closure */
   initialize visited_symbols to empty;
   for each Symbol in set_of_symbols
      recursive_transitive_close ( Symbol );
   end for each Symbol
}
recursive_transitive_close ( Symbol )
{
/* performs a depth first transitive closure on Symbol */
/* for efficiency, a symbol is visited only once */
   if Symbol is not in visited_symbols set
      add Symbol to visited_symbols;
      for each Connection associated with Symbol
         get the Network associated with Connection;
         for each Connection associated with Network
            get Symbol associated with Connection;
            recursive_transitive_close ( Symbol );
         end for each Connection
      end for each Connection
   endif
}
```

The algorithm for computing the transitive closure using Figure E20.4 is:

```
transitive_closure ( set_of_symbols )
{
/* returns the transitive closure in the global variable
   visited_symbols by doing a depth first traversal */
/* set_of_symbols is a set of given Symbols */
/* initialize recursion for computation of
   transitive closure */
   initialize visited_symbols to empty;
   for each Symbol in set_of_symbols
      recursive_transitive_close ( Symbol );
   end for each Symbol
}

recursive_transitive_close ( Symbol )
{
/* performs a depth first transitive closure on Symbol */
/* for efficiency, a symbol is visited only once */
   if Symbol is not in visited_symbols set
      add Symbol to visited_symbols;
      for each Network associated with Symbol
         for each Symbol associated with Network
            recursive_transitive_close ( Symbol );
```

```
            end for each Symbol
        end for each Network
    endif
}
```

20.3 Shallow copy methods use less space than deep copy methods. Subsequent changes to the original are automatically inherited by a shallow copy. A deep copy is independent of the original.

    a. For library objects a shallow copy has the advantage of saving a great deal of space since it is likely there will be many copies of the original. We assume there are two types of applications that will access library objects. A librarian will have read and write access to the original. All other applications will have read only access. With a shallow copy a change in the original is automatically reflected in the copies. This may be desirable in some applications and undesirable in others. A danger of the shallow copy is that a mistake while using the librarian program could have disastrous results.

    b. Because changes in the new sheet should not affect the old sheet a deep copy must be used.

    c. Either a shallow copy or a deep copy is suitable for copying selected items from one place on a sheet to another, depending on the desired behavior. Use a shallow copy if the copies should inherit changes made to the original. Use a deep copy if it is desired to change the copies independently.

20.4 The revised diagrams are shown in Figure A20.3 and Figure A20.4. The subtree for layout operations has been moved from the main state tree to the auxiliary state tree.

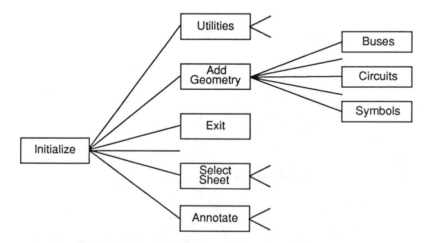

Figure A20.3 Revised main state tree for a one-line diagram editor

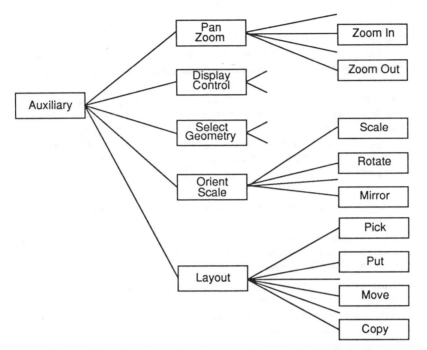

Figure A20.4 Revised auxiliary state tree for a one-line diagram editor

20.5 The point of this exercise is to make the student realize how ubiquitous diagrams are. Students' answers will depend on their background. Diagrams that we are familiar with include object diagrams, state diagrams, data flow diagrams, electrical schematics, one-line diagrams, decision trees, BNF diagrams, functional flow diagrams, process flow diagrams, piping and instrumentation diagrams, block diagrams, stick diagrams (for integrated circuits), higraphs, and road maps. We will discuss a few here.

- Schematic diagrams are used to represent electrical circuits. Schematic diagrams are composed of symbols and networks. A symbol represents an electrical component or subsystem which can itself be represented by a schematic diagram. Several different standardized symbols are used to represent common components such as a transistor, transformer, switch, diode, or capacitor. A network is a collection of interconnected straight lines, usually horizontal or vertical, representing interconnections. Networks connect several symbols. Edges are undirected. Connections of networks to symbols are allowed only at predefined locations. For example, a transistor has base, emitter and collector connections. There are no limitations to how networks are connected, although it is customary to keep them as simple as possible without dangling lines. Any number of networks could be connected to a symbol at a connection point, although in practice a limit of four is observed. Location of symbols in the diagram has no physical significance. Although schematic diagrams can be enhanced with color, they do not lose any meaning in a black and white representation.

- Stick diagrams are used in the design and fabrication of very large scale integrated circuits to represent chip layout. They are a compromise between a schematic diagram and geometrical layout. A schematic diagram is easy to read, but contains no information about physical layout. Although a physical layout diagram is a complete two dimensional specification of the chip fabrication, it is nearly impossible to look at it and understand how the chip works. A stick diagram contains both types of information. Narrow vertical or horizontal straight lines represent the approximate locations of the active areas of the chip, eliminating the visual clutter that is in the complete layout. A chip can be quickly designed using stick diagrams. The stick diagram can then be compiled into physical layout and the chip can be automatically fabricated.

  Several types of networks are drawn in color, with a different color for each physical layer of the chip. Networks of the same color which cross are connected electrically. Certain pairs of other types of networks are assumed to interact where they cross. Other pairs do not interact at all unless they are connected by a dot (representing a via) where they cross.

  In the case of stick diagrams, networks are n-ary. Edges are undirected. Except for the connection dot, there are no symbols. There are different types of networks. Networks can be connected to other networks and/or together. Most of the ends of networks dangle. Exactly two networks connect or interact at a point.

- BNF diagrams are used to describe a grammar using networks and symbols. Networks are n-ary. Very simple symbols are used, usually circles and lozenges. Edges, which are constructed from straight lines and/or arcs, are directed. Connections are allowed anywhere on symbols, although connections to lozenges are usually made at the ends. The location of a connection to a symbol does not convey any special meaning. Except for the starting and ending points, ends of networks may not be unconnected. There are no restrictions on how many networks connect at the same point.

20.6 These are problems that we actually encountered in implementing *OLIE*. Some problems are easy to solve if you are free to change the subsystems, otherwise they are difficult. The exercise points out pitfalls that can arise when a system is built on top of subsystems that have not been carefully thought out.

   For some problems the solution may be more painful than the problem. Other problems represent roadblocks that must be overcome at all costs.

   a. You must resolve this problem somehow, or you will not be able to proceed. Since the subsystems are not under your control, you cannot fix the problem by changing names. If the problem is caused by the same function being included in several library modules that must be loaded, you can ignore the linker warnings. If the same name is used to represent completely different functions in different modules, you may have to resort to more drastic steps such as linking the subsystems as separate processes and using interprocess communications to interface them.

b. You must solve this problem. In many cases preprocessor incompatibilities can be resolved by splitting a source file that uses several preprocessors into several files in such a way that each file contains only compatible preprocessor constructs. Function calls can be used for integration.

Another solution than can be used in some cases is to edit the output of the preprocessor. This solution is not convenient if the source is going to be updated frequently.

c. This problem is annoying, but can be tolerated in some applications. Memory fault errors may not be tolerable for some applications. However, the solution may be more difficult than the problem. If you know the routines that the subsystems are calling you may decide to rewrite them.

d. The problem that we encountered could be tolerated at the expense of a clumsy user interface. The problem was that the way the subsystems were implemented, an asynchronous subsystem was linked with a synchronous one in a single program. As a result, the synchronous process could block the I/O intended for the asynchronous process. One solution is to use interprocess communications to decouple the subsystems.

20.7 These problems vanish if you do it right the first time:

a. Change the offending names.

b. Consolidate the preprocessor syntaxes into a unified language or reorganize into orthogonal languages.

c. Use the same memory allocation scheme in all subsystems. The scheme should handle an out of memory condition gracefully.

d. Use a single, integrated, asynchronous user interface that is shared by all subsystems.